The Chief Rabbi's
HAGGADAH

HEBREW AND ENGLISH TEXT WITH
NEW ESSAYS AND COMMENTARY BY

Jonathan Sacks

HarperCollins*Publishers*

HarperCollins*Publishers*
77–85 Fulham Palace Road, London W6 8JB
www.**fire**and**water**.com

First published in Great Britain in 2003 by HarperCollins*Publishers*

1 3 5 7 9 10 8 6 4 2

Commentary and essays copyright © 2003 Jonathan Sacks.
English Haggadah translation © Rabbi Shlomo Riskin. Used by permission.

Jonathan Sacks asserts the moral right to be identified
as the author of the commentary and essays in this work.

A catalogue record for this book is available from the British Library.

ISBN 0 00 714825 9

Designed by Michael Marks at The Custard Design Partnership

Printed in Great Britain by Creative Print & Design (Wales), Ebbw Vale, Gwent

Note on the text

The Chief Rabbi's Essays on Passover begin on page 1.

The Haggadah reads from right to left in the normal
Hebrew fashion, and along with its English translation,
and the accompanying commentary, is to be found at the
other end of the book.

Essays on Passover

The Story of Stories

Remember the days of old,
Consider the generations long ago;
Ask your father to recount it,
And your elders to tell you the tale.

Deuteronomy 32:7

The seder service on Pesach is the oldest surviving ritual in the Western world, dating back some 3,300 years to the night, possibly in the reign of Ramses II, when the Israelites ate their last meal in Egypt, preparing for their journey to freedom. Certain features still remain from biblical times: the *matzah* and *maror*, the reminder of the paschal offering (a mere reminder until the rebuilding of the Temple), the questions asked by a child, and the explanations given by an adult. In some, especially oriental, communities it is still the custom to dress as the Israelites did then, 'your loins girded, your shoes on your feet and your staff in your hand.'

The seder is, of course, more than a ritual. It is an act of remembering, the telling of a story – the Haggadah – and none has been more lovingly sustained. Each age has added something of its own. In the course of a single night, as well as biblical passages, we encounter Hillel in the days of the Second Temple, the second century sages at their seder in Bnei Brak, the teachings of the Amoraim of the third and later centuries, poems by Yannai and Kalir from the post-talmudic period, an addition from Ashkenaz provoked by the terrible sufferings of the First Crusade, and children's songs from medieval Germany. Every word we say has a history. Even the *mah nishtanah*, the questions asked by a child, go back some two thousand years. The weaving together of these many contributions into a single narrative is the achievement of no ordinary author. It is the collective voice of the Jewish people through centuries and continents as it has encountered and responded to the word of God.

Through the Haggadah more than a hundred generations of Jews have handed on their story to their children. The word *haggadah* means 'to relate, to tell, to expound'. But it comes from a Hebrew root that also means 'to bind, to join, to connect'. By reciting the Haggadah, Jews give their children a sense of connectedness to Jews throughout the world and to the Jewish people through time. It joins them to a past and future, a history and destiny, and makes them characters in its drama. Every other people known to mankind have been united because they lived in the same place, spoke the same language, were part of the same culture. Jews alone, dispersed across continents, speaking different languages and participating in different cultures, have been bound together by a narrative, the Pesach narrative, which they told in the same way on the same night. More than the Haggadah was the story of a people, Jews were the people of a story.

During Israel's early history – the biblical era – the Exodus narrative embodied their collective memory as a nation, forged in slavery and led miraculously to freedom. Not only was it the record of their past; it was their template of ideals for the future, their aspiration to create a society dedicated to liberty under the sovereignty of God. But its influence did not end with the collapse of Jewish sovereignty in Israel. If anything, during the long centuries when Jews were scattered throughout the world, its effect was more remarkable still. It sustained Jewish identity, linking one generation to the next through the bonds of shared memory. In times of suffering – and there were many – it kept hope alive, the hope expressed at the very beginning of the Haggadah that though 'this year we are slaves, next year we will be free; this year we are here, next year we will be in the land of Israel.' In ages of prosperity, it became a tutorial in mutual responsibility. It taught the great lesson of human solidarity, that we cannot enjoy the food of affluence while others eat the bread of affliction. We are not fully free if others are oppressed.

Nor was its influence confined to Jews alone. Through a long and circuitous route, the story of the exodus eventually came to influence not only Jews but Western civilization as a whole. In the seventeenth and eighteenth centuries, through such figures as John Locke and Thomas Jefferson, it gave rise to a new vision of freedom. It told of how a people might liberate themselves from oppressive governments and construct a society in which 'all men are created equal,' possessing inalienable dignity and collective freedom. It set forth a narrative, never surpassed, of the human drama as the long journey to redemption, not in heaven but on earth in the structures of our common life. No story has had greater influence in inspiring revolution or evolution toward a just and humane society. It is the West's great meta-narrative of liberty.

More remarkably still, in the nineteenth century it inspired a series of figures, some religious, others secular but moved none the less by the power of the ancient narrative, to set in motion a new exodus and homecoming of the Jewish people. It began with a new Egypt – the rise of racial antisemitism, followed by the Russian pogroms, then the anti-Jewish programme of the Nazis which moved inexorably to the Final Solution, the worst recorded crime of man against man. It culminated in a redemption more astonishing than any other in post-biblical history: the only time a people dispersed for two thousand years has returned to its land to begin its history again as a sovereign power. Speaking in the United Nations in 1947, David Ben Gurion argued the case for the creation of the state of Israel and did so by referring to Pesach and the Haggadah:

> Three hundred years ago a ship called the Mayflower set sail to the New World. This was a great event in the history of England. Yet I wonder if there is one Englishman who knows at what time the ship set sail? Do the English know how many people embarked on this voyage? What quality of bread did they eat? Yet more than three thousand three hundred years ago, before the Mayflower set sail, the Jews left Egypt. Every Jew in the world, even in America or Soviet Russia, knows on exactly what date they left – the fifteenth of the month of Nisan. Everyone knows what kind of bread they ate. Even today the Jews worldwide eat matzah on the fifteenth of Nisan. They retell the story of the Exodus and all the troubles Jews have endured since being exiled. They conclude this evening with two statements: *This year, slaves. Next year, free men. This year here. Next year in Jerusalem, in Zion, in Eretz Yisrael.* That is the nature of the Jews.

Thus history repeated itself, and a new chapter was written in the Jewish story of exile and homecoming more than three thousand years after the first. The story of the modern state of Israel, with its restoration of Jewish sovereignty, the ingathering of exiles from 103 countries, speaking 82 languages, the rebirth of Hebrew, the language of the Bible, and the rebuilding of Jerusalem, Israel's ancient capital, exemplifies one of Judaism's most hope-creating truths: that a vision can shape the destiny of a people. Ideas, if we live them, have the power to change the world.

The great message of Pesach is that history is not what Joseph Heller once called it: 'a trashbag of random coincidences blown open by the wind'. It is, or can become, a journey toward a place where people are valued not for the wealth they own or the power they wield, but for who they are – a trace of God in a world that so often seems to deny His presence. In ways that remain obscure yet still majestic, a whole series of individuals – beginning with Abraham, reaching a culmination in Moses, and continuing through an almost unending sequence of prophets, visionaries, sages, saints, philosophers, poets, jurists and commentators – was inspired by a vision of society in which simple acts, relationships and lives could become vehicles of the Divine presence.

As we sit around the seder table on Pesach, rehearsing the journey from the bread of affliction to the wine of freedom, we commit ourselves to a momentous proposition: that history has meaning. We are not condemned endlessly to repeat the tragedies of the past. Not everywhere is an Egypt; not all politics are the exploitation of the many by the few; life is potentially something other and more gracious than the pursuit of power. Though we have not yet constructed the perfect social order and despite the fact that the messianic age with its reign of peace remains over the horizon, we are not wrong to travel in that direction, however long it may take before we reach our destination. In his *A History of the Jews*, Paul Johnson expressed as well as anyone has the nature of the Jewish journey:

> No people has ever insisted more firmly than the Jews that history has a purpose and humanity a destiny. At a very early stage of their collective existence they believed they had detected a divine scheme for the human race, of which their own society was to be a pilot. They worked out their role in immense detail. They clung to it with heroic persistence in the face of savage suffering... The Jewish vision became the prototype for many similar grand designs for humanity, both divine and man-made. The Jews, therefore, stand right at the centre of the perennial attempt to give human life the dignity of a purpose.

'The dignity of a purpose': that remains, even today, a radical hope. Throughout history there has been no shortage of those who claim that ideals are illusions and hope a form of hubris destined to end in failure. Today that view is as likely to come from science (specifically 'scientism', the belief that science is all there is) as anywhere else. We are, on this view, a mere concatenation of chemicals, cosmic dust on the surface of infinity, living out lives that are no more than infinitesimal disturbances in a blind and purposeless universe that came into being for no reason, and for no reason will, billions of years from now, cease to be.

Judaism is now, as it has been since its earliest days, a protest against such despair in the name of humanity and of God whose breath we breathe and whose voice, if we listen, we can still hear through the echoes of time. The universe is not blind to our hopes, deaf to our prayers. Somewhere at the core of being is a personal presence, a transcendental Thou, who created the world in love, brought us into being as a parent does a child, who spoke to Abraham and Sarah, asking them and their descendants to undertake a long and momentous journey, and who is with us on the way. Pesach is the festival of faith, the faith of our ancestors, who followed that voice across the wilderness of space and time, in search of a freedom that honours the presence of God in the affairs of mankind.

Few texts have received more attention than the Haggadah. There are thousands of commentaries, and more are published each year. Anyone who contemplates adding to this number must ask not 'Why is this night different?' but 'Why is this edition different?' My answer is that I wrote this commentary because, amongst all the many I have read, I could not find one that explained in their full richness and scope the fundamental themes of the Pesach story: the Jewish concept of a free society, the role of memory in shaping Jewish identity, and the unique connection that exists in Judaism between spirituality and society, giving rise to what I have called elsewhere 'the politics of hope'. Nor could I find a Haggadah that told me in detail about the role of Pesach in shaping Jewish identity through the millennia, or its influence on Western thought as a whole.

Traditional commentaries are usually close readings of individual words and phrases rather than reflections on the meaning of the whole. That is a classic Jewish response, and I have not hesitated (in the latter essays, and the commentary to the text) to do likewise. In some of the essays ('The Sages at Bnei Brak' is my personal favourite) I have tried to say things I have not heard said before. That is the imperative of *chiddush*, finding the new in the old. But it is the great themes, the overarching principles, that are often neglected or taken for granted, and it is worth saying why.

Pesach is an intensely political festival. It is about the central Jewish project: constructing a society radically unlike any that had existed before and most that have come into being since. It poses a fundamental question: can we make, on earth, a social order based not on transactions of power but on respect for the human person – each person – as 'the image of God'? Pesach, like Judaism generally, is not about *salvation*, a private drama of the soul, but about *redemption*, the life we share as fellow citizens under the sovereignty of God. It is about freedom, justice, equity, the ethics of the market place and the responsible use of power to secure the common good. Before Plato's *Republic*, Hobbes' *Leviathan* and Rousseau's *The Social Contract* the exodus story pioneered a path to a just and gracious society. I believe that it embodies not only a more religious, but also a more humane, vision than these other works. At its heart is a never-surpassed idea: that the free God seeks the free worship of free human beings, and invites those who heed His call to become His co-architects in creating what Rabbi Aharon Lichtenstein calls 'societal beatitude'.

Much of the Hebrew Bible, spanning a period of almost two thousand years, is about how the people of the covenant wrestled with this challenge, sometimes succeeding, often failing, but never losing sight of the task, the call, the dream. The challenge, however, presupposed that Jews had political power – a land, a nation, a state, within which they could construct a free society that honoured its members and served as an example and inspiration to others. That was never easy. Israel was a small country in a strategic location surrounded by great powers. It experienced many wars, internal tensions and eventually a fateful split into two nations. In the sixth century BCE the Babylonians conquered the remaining southern kingdom of Judah, destroyed the Temple and took many of the people into exile. A generation later, some returned, and eventually the Temple was rebuilt. But after two disastrous rebellions against the Romans, in 66 and 132 CE, the Temple was destroyed again, Jerusalem lay in ruins, and Jews faced their longest exile.

For eighteen centuries, between the destruction of the Second Temple and European emancipation, they were exiled, dispersed, and without political organization. Wherever they went, they ran their own communities, built impressive educational and welfare infrastructures, and adjudicated internal disputes, but they lacked sovereignty and civil rights. They had local autonomy, but as far as the politics of nations were concerned, they had neither vote nor voice. In neither Christian nor Islamic lands were they citizens. Until recently, therefore, the Pesach story was a memory and a hope: a memory of one journey to freedom in the distant past, and the hope that it would happen again. 'This year we are slaves, but next year...'

That prayer has begun to be answered. In Israel, Jews have recovered sovereignty and re-entered the mainstream of history. In the Diaspora, wherever they live in pluralist, liberal democracies, they have both a vote and a voice. Inescapably, after a lapse of eighteen centuries, Jews have re-entered the political arena. They can do so in two ways: by defending Jewish interests, or by articulating Judaic principle. With regard to the first, there is no essential difference between Jews and any other religious or ethnic group. Each fights for its rights and defends its space. With regard to the second, however, there is a very great difference. Jews have something distinctive to contribute to the public domain. They are the bearers of the oldest, and in many ways most remarkable, political vision in the West. In that sense, every Jew is heir to the ideals of Moses and the prophets. The Pesach story is no longer – as it was for so many centuries – primarily about a distant past and an equally distant future. It is about the present and the values by which we should strive to live.

It is fair to say that Jewish religious thought has not fully caught up with this development. That is hardly surprising. Modernity confronted Jews as a series of traumatic onslaughts – first, the assimilatory demands of European emancipation, then the rising tide of racial antisemitism, then the nightmare of the Holocaust, and finally the challenge of forging a new nation in Israel under pressures, internal and external, that might easily have defeated a less hardy people. Distress, said the sages and Maimonides, inhibits prophecy, because it makes people turn in on themselves, rather than outward to the world and to God. But we must now begin to study Torah, and the Pesach story in particular, in a new way, as shapers, rather than the victims, of history. That means going back to first principles and a fresh encounter with the biblical narrative.

For the past few years I have been trying to study, teach and write Torah in an old-new way. I call it *Torah ve-Chokhmah*, 'Torah and wisdom', in contradistinction to certain other approaches. In nineteenth century Germany the favoured phrase among disciples of Rabbi Samson Raphael Hirsch was *Torah im derekh eretz*, 'Torah and general culture'. In the United States, the preferred principle was *Torah u-Madda*, 'Torah and Science'. Neither of these rubrics is particularly helpful. *Torah im derekh eretz* is a quotation from the teachings of Rabban Gamliel III (third century CE) who used it to mean something else, 'Torah together with a worldly occupation'. *Torah u-Madda* is a modern coinage with no source in tradition. *Chokhmah*, by contrast, is a biblical category. One book, Proverbs, is devoted to it, and several others – notably Job and Ecclesiastes – belong to what is generally known as the 'wisdom literature'. *Chokhmah* is a concept with many shades of meaning, but its primary sense is human wisdom as such: the universals of mankind's intellectual quest.

Chokhmah is the truth we discover; Torah is the truth we inherit. *Chokhmah* is the shared heritage of mankind; Torah is the particular heritage of the Jewish people. *Chokhmah* is the world of 'is', of fact; Torah is the world of 'ought', of command. *Chokhmah* is where we encounter God through creation; Torah is how we hear God through revelation. The two are not equal in their significance to Jews – Torah is holy in a way *chokhmah* cannot be – yet both are significant, for if we are to apply Torah to the world, we must understand the world to which it applies. Because the God of creation is also the God of revelation, there is ultimate harmony between them, even though, given the imperfections in our understanding of both, it may not be evident at any given moment. There must, I believe, be an ongoing conversation between them, for otherwise Torah will remain a closed system with no grip, no purchase, no influence, on the world outside its walls. That was inevitable during the long centuries in which Jews and Judaism had no dialogue with the world outside, but it is neither inevitable nor desirable now. If we have re-entered the political arena, as a nation-state in Israel and as citizens of liberal democracies elsewhere, we need the confidence and the language to recover our voice in the conversation of mankind, bringing our own distinctive truths to the public domain. Once we do so, we discover new strata of meaning in Torah itself. We also discover that Torah – especially the exodus narrative – has played a larger role than we suspected in guiding the West to create its own versions of a free society.

The essays can be divided into three sections. The first is about the relationship between Pesach, Jewish identity and Jewish history – about the part the story has played in sustaining a people through the vicissitudes of time. The second is about Pesach and its place in the Western political imagination. Most histories of political thought begin with the great thinkers of ancient Greece. It is my argument, however, that ancient Israel was where the idea of freedom was born, and in many respects it remains a surer guide to liberty than the short-lived democracy of Athens. In the third section I offer some new interpretations of the ancient texts.

I begin, however, with a personal reminiscence of an occasion where I had an unusual opportunity to say what the story of Pesach meant to Jews and why it is, for me, the story of stories. It took place in Windsor Castle, home of Britain's kings and queens and the oldest continuously inhabited castle in the world. In 2000 I was invited to deliver the St. George's Lecture, an annual address in the presence of Prince Philip. As the first Jew to be accorded this honour, I thought hard about what to say. I thought of the history of Jews in Europe, driven for so many centuries from country to country without rights, power, or a home. I found myself thinking back across the centuries to an earlier and painful age in British history: the first blood libel in Norwich in 1144, the massacre in York in 1190, and the expulsion of the Jews by Edward I in 1290. Those events set a pattern that was to be followed in one European country after another during the following two hundred years. What would our ancestors, harried and afflicted, have said had they been able to foresee that one day one of their number would be invited back to the home of the king who had sent them into exile? I remembered a verse in the Book of Psalms (119:46), 'I will speak of your statutes before kings and not be ashamed,' and I was determined to be faithful to it.

I wanted to honour the memory of those Jews of an earlier age, to tell of their courage and tenacity and thus say something of what it meant and still means to be a

Jew. In the course of my remarks I said this: 'I try to imagine what it must be like to inherit a building like Windsor Castle. To live in such a place, so steeped in history, is to want to know that history – how this building came to be, and why. In the course of asking the question, I would learn about how it began, in the days of William the Conqueror, on the legendary site of King Arthur's Round Table. I would discover that it had been added to, rebuilt, extended and changed many times in the course of the ensuing centuries, by Henry II, Henry III and Edward III and their successors.

'Learning this history would be more than simply discovering facts. Because I had inherited the building it would be my history. I would not have chosen it. It would have chosen me. Inescapably, though, I would have entered into a set of obligations, a moral relationship with the past and future. I would be part of the story of the castle and its heirs. The very fact that it was still here, still dominating the landscape, part of the historic legacy of Britain, would tell me something of great significance to my life. I would slowly realize that generation after generation of the kings and queens of England had endeavoured to preserve the castle and hand it on intact to future generations. They had vested their hopes in those who would come after them, that they too would do the same. And now that it had come to me, I would know beyond doubt that I too was morally bound to protect it, and that if I failed to do so I would have betrayed the trust of those earlier generations, as well as failing to honour my responsibility to England as a whole. The result would be that when disaster struck – as it did in the great fire of 1992 – I would know that I had to restore the damaged buildings, not necessarily exactly as before, but at least in keeping with the whole. That is what it is to live in the context of history.

'Jews,' I said, 'will never own buildings like Windsor Castle. We are not that kind of people. But we own something that is, in its way, no less majestic and even more consecrated by time. The Jewish castle is built not of bricks or stone, but of words. But it too has been preserved across the centuries, handed on by one generation to the next, added to and enhanced in age after age, lovingly cherished and sustained. As a child I knew that one day I would inherit it from my parents, as they had inherited it from theirs. It is not a building but it is, nonetheless, a home, a place in which to live. More than it belongs to us, we belong to it; and it too is part of the heritage of mankind. What we have is not a physical construction but something else – a story.

'It was given to me by my parents when I was a child. I received it on the festival of Passover. It is an exceptionally moving story. It tells of how our ancestors were once slaves who, through a succession of wondrous events, were given their freedom. They then began a journey across the desert for forty years, and later through a wilderness of dispersion for two thousand years, in search of a home, a promised land, a place of grace and justice and freedom and dignity. Though at times the destination seemed to lie beyond the furthest horizon of hope, they did not give up. They never ceased to travel. And I am part of that journey. I did not choose to be, any more than the member of a royal family chooses to be born into royalty; but this is my legacy, my heritage. It defines who I am.

'I know, just as does the heir to a castle, that I am a link in the chain of generations, and that I owe a duty of loyalty to the past and to the future. That is what Edmund Burke had in mind when he called society a partnership 'not only between those who are living but between those who are living, those who are dead, and those who are to be born.' I am part of a story whose earlier chapters were written by my ancestors and whose next chapter I am now called on to write. And when the time comes, I must hand it on to my children, and they to theirs, so that the Jewish story, no less than Windsor Castle, can live on.'

That was the story I told that night, and it is the story each of us tells on the night of the seder. Its message, undiminished through the years, still has the capacity to inspire. It suggests that to be a Jew is to be part of a history touched, in a mysterious yet unmistakable way, by the hand of Providence. Jewry is not a mere secular people, an ethnic group, one of the myriad cultures in the anthropological lexicon of mankind. Had that been all there is to Jewish identity, there would be no Jews today. No culture or ethnicity has survived two thousand years of dispersion and minority status. Had the Israelites of ancient times not been moved by a religious vision, they would have assimilated among the Egyptians. Had they not carried the Torah with them into Israel, they may have won their independence but they would, today, be numbered along with the Canaanites, Jebusites, Perizites and the other peoples of the ancient Near East, now remembered, if at all, as exhibits in museums. We are who and what we are because of a momentous faith, the faith of which the Haggadah is a supreme expression. We are a people touched by the Divine presence.

Often, we are too little aware of the majesty and uniqueness of the Jewish heritage. Moses once said, in words of great wisdom, 'It is not up in heaven... Nor is it beyond the sea... The word is very close to you; it is in your mouth and in your heart, waiting to be done.' One of Judaism's great insights is that religious truth is not exotic. It does not need to be sought far away in an ashram in India, or in a private ecstasy of the soul. No faith has worshipped a more transcendental God, but no faith has brought God so close. The Shekhinah, the Divine presence, lives in the very texture of everyday acts and relationships if we train ourselves to hear their music and open our eyes to their radiance. It is there in the beauty of the Jewish home, the resonance of our rituals, the drama and sweep of Jewish history, the sheer persistence of our people and the determination of generation after generation of Jews to live their faith and hand it on to their children when they might so easily have done otherwise. And it began on Pesach, when a much-afflicted people began its long journey across space and time in response to a Divine call.

We are Jews to show ourselves and others what it is to bring the Divine presence into ordinary lives, human relationships, marriage, the family, homes and communities, and thus begin to build a society which honours the 'image of God' in mankind, a society free in the deepest and most generous sense of the word. On Pesach, as we trace our own route from the bread of affliction to the wine of freedom, we become part of that journey. Making it our own, we are drawn into a narrative at once intimate and vast, just like the seder service itself. This is our people and our story. Challenging then, it is no less challenging now.

2

A Tale of Two Civilisations

'I will make thy seed as the dust of the earth' (Genesis 13:16). As the dust of the earth is from one end to the other, so your children will be dispersed from one end of the world to the other. As dust is trodden by all, so your children will be trod upon by the peoples of the world. As dust outlives all vessels of metal and endures for ever, so other nations of the world will cease to be, while Israel endures for ever. Genesis Rabbah

Travel to Egypt today and you can still see the great temples built by Ramses II, assumed by most scholars to be the Pharaoh of the Exodus. Luxor, Karnak, Abu Simbel: they still stand, three thousand years later, in little less than their former glory, astonishing achievements that seem to defy time. Yet the civilisation that produced them is no more. The Egypt of the Pharaohs was one of the greatest and most long-lived of the empires of the ancient world, but already by the time of Ramses II it had reached its peak, and shortly thereafter began its long decline. By the time of Alexander the Great it was a shadow of its former glory, and it fell to the Greeks. Like other imperial powers, in its day it 'bestrode the narrow world like a colossus' and then faded into oblivion. The monuments remain, but the culture that brought them forth was all too mortal.

Among the builders of those monuments were a small migrant people known to the Egyptians as Hebrews, *Ivrim*, meaning nomads, people who wander from place to place without a fixed home. In the late nineteenth century great interest was aroused by the discovery, in an Egyptian village known as El-Amarna, of a cache of some 350 clay tablets dating back to the fifteenth century BCE. Written in Akkadian, they contained reference to a group known as *Habiru* who seemed to bear some similarity to the Israelites of that time. They too were a nomadic group who appeared from time to time, arousing fears on the part of other residents in the land of Canaan. There is even a record, in the form of two papyri from the reign of Ramses II, of Habiru workers being employed to transport materials for the pharaoh's construction projects.

Scholars today are less likely to identify the Habiru of the Amarna letters with the

Hebrews of the Bible. The word appears to be not the name of a specific people but a generic description for roaming groups of marauders. But the existence of such groups may help to explain why a powerful empire like Egypt regarded the Israelites as a threat. Some centuries before, it had suffered an invasion from the East, by a group known as the Hyksos, who seized hold of the country for 160 years, and the memory remained. Egypt was on its guard against outsiders.

The fact that Abraham and his descendants were known to others as *Ivrim* suggests that they too were seen as Habiru, a potential danger to the more settled peoples of the region. Abraham himself, despite his long residence in Canaan, was forced to describe himself as 'an alien and a temporary resident' when he came to buy land from the local Hittites as a burial place for his wife, Sarah. Nor did the Egyptians take readily to outsiders. A text of the time complained that 'strangers from outside have come into Egypt... Foreigners have become people everywhere.' So it is altogether likely that, faced with a growing population of semitic herdsmen from Canaan, the Egyptians would have sensed a potential threat.

We do not have independent confirmation of the events of the Exodus. But we have enough background information to understand the context in which a Pharaoh would say, 'Look, the Israelites have become much too numerous for us. Come, we must deal shrewdly with them or they will become even more numerous and, if war breaks out, will join our enemies, fight against us and leave the country' (Exodus 1:9–10). They make eminent sense, given the conditions of the time. With them a great drama began that was to leave its mark ever afterward on the life of the group whose descendants the Jews of today are.

The contrast between the two peoples could not have been greater. Egypt at that time was an indomitable power. It held sway over the whole ancient Near East. Ramses II conducted successful campaigns against the Hittites and the Libyans and launched punitive raids against Edom and Moab. He used the technical prowess and prosperity of Egypt to undertake a series of monumental building projects that have few rivals in the ancient world. He had colossal statues of himself erected throughout the country. The prefix Ra in his name tells us that he was seen as the sun god, a divine being whose rule was written in the heavens and whose word carried absolute command.

The Israelites, for their part, were a landless people, entirely at the mercy of the Egyptians. They had no power and, at first, no effective leadership. They were easily conscripted into forced labour. The Torah tells us that they were employed to build two of Ramses II's great projects, the cities of Pithom (Per-Atum) and Ramses (probably Per-Ramesses-Meri-Imen). No group seemed less likely to become the people of eternity.

Had anyone suggested at the time that it would not be the Egypt of the Pharaohs that would survive and change the moral landscape of the world, but instead a group of Hebrew slaves, it would have seemed an ultimate absurdity. The Egyptians believed that the Israelites were already on the verge of extinction. The earliest known reference to Israel outside the Bible is an inscription produced by Ramses' successor, Merneptah, in the thirteenth century BCE. The Merneptah stele, a giant slab of black granite which stands today in the Cairo Museum, contains these words: 'Israel is laid waste. His seed is no more.'

The clash between Moses and Ramses was no ordinary encounter. It deserves to be seen, in retrospect, as one of the defining confrontations of history. Between the most powerful empire of the ancient world and a powerless group of slave labourers, an immense question was being framed. What endures and what wanes? What survives and what is eclipsed? Ancient Egypt and ancient Israel were two nations that posed the great question of time: how, in a world of flux and change, do we create something that defeats mortality? The Egyptians gave one answer, a response that has long appealed to emperors and kings. We defeat time by building monuments that will outlive the winds and sands of time. Ancient Israel gave a different and altogether counter-intuitive reply. We can identify exactly the moment when it occurred. It is set out in the twelfth and thirteenth chapters of the Book of Exodus.

The Israelites were about to go free. Nine of the ten plagues had already taken place. The tenth, they knew, would be the last. According to the biblical account, Moses gathered the people and instructed them on the preparations they were to make. By any standards it was an epic moment. For 210 years the Israelites had been in exile. They had experienced suffering, slavery and attempted genocide. Now they were about to begin the journey known to history as the Exodus. What would Moses say? He might have spoken about freedom, or the promised destination, the 'land flowing with milk and honey'. He might have chosen to speak about the arduous journey that lay ahead, what Nelson Mandela called 'the long road to freedom'. Any of these would have been the great speech of a great leader.

Moses did none of these things. Instead he spoke about children, and the distant future, and the duty to pass on memory to generations yet unborn. Three times he turned to the theme:

> And when your children ask you, 'What do you mean by this rite?' you shall say... (Exodus 12:26–27)

> And you shall explain to your child on that day, 'It is because of what the Lord did for me when I went free from Egypt.' (Exodus 13:8)

> And when, in time to come, your child asks you, saying, 'What does this mean?' you shall say to him... (Exodus 13:14)

About to gain their freedom, the Israelites were told that they were to become a *nation of educators*. That is what made Moses not just a great leader but a unique one. Freedom – he was suggesting – is won not on the battlefield nor in the political arena but in the human imagination and will. As the American justice, Judge Learned Hand, put it: 'Liberty lies in the hearts of men and women; when it dies there, no constitution, no law, no court can save it; no constitution, no law, no court can even do much to help it.' *To defend a land you need an army, but to defend freedom you need education.* You need parents, families and homes and a constant conversation between the generations. Above all you need memory – the kind of memory that never forgets the bread of affliction and the bitter herbs of slavery.

Freedom is more than revolution. The pages of history are littered with peoples who won their freedom only to lose it again. The 'constitution of liberty' is one of the most vulnerable of all human achievements. Individual freedom is simple. Collective freedom – a society that honours the equal dignity of all – depends on constant vigilance, a sustained effort of education. If we forget where we came from, the battles our ancestors fought and the long journey they had to take, then in the end we lose it again.

So Moses led his people along the least likely path to eternity. The Israelites became builders, but what they constructed was not monuments of stone. Instead it was a way of life inspired by the twin ideals of justice and compassion. Its bricks were holy deeds; its mortar, study and the life of the mind. What Moses taught, and what the Jewish people came to discover, is that you achieve immortality not by building pyramids or statues – but by *engraving your values on the hearts of your children, and they on theirs, so that our ancestors live on in us and we in our children, and so on until the end of time.*

It was an astonishing insight, so unlike anything else in the ancient world that, contemplating it, it is hard not to feel oneself in the presence of transcendence, a totally unpredictable moment when one of the great truths of the human situation emerged for the first time. The people who survived and eventually became a nation of visionaries and prophets, scholars and sages, had little in their immediate past to suggest future greatness, except one thing: a voice heard intermittently since the days of the patriarchs, summoning them to a way of life quite different from their neighbours. It said that God is not the power that enslaves but the power that sets free. Instead of worshipping mighty rulers, it taught that God is to be served by protecting the dignity of the widow, the orphan, the stranger, the weak, the vulnerable and the neglected. Holiness is found not in monumental architecture but in words and teachings, above all in the instruction that takes place at home. 'Call them not your children but your builders,' said the sages, and it was an insight Jews did not forget. No civilisation, no faith has been as child-centred as Judaism. As a result, none has stayed so perennially young, so self-renewing through time. On Pesach, telling our story to our children, we relive the secret of Jewish renewal.

The men and women who built Ramses' temples lived through one of the great revelations of history. Because of it the Jewish people became a nation, a nation dedicated to bringing new generations into being and handing on to them the heritage of the past. The result was that Jewish identity, and with it the Jewish dream, never died. By telling the Israelites in Egypt to become a nation of educators, Moses turned a group of slaves into a people of eternity.

3

Pesach, Freud
and Jewish Identity

So they asked him, 'Tell us… what do you do? Where do you come from? What is your
country? From what people are you?'
He answered, 'I am a Hebrew and I worship the Lord, God of heaven, who made the
sea and the land.'   Jonah 1:8–9

Moses' **first question to God was** *mi anokhi*, 'Who am I?' That remains
the question of Jews throughout the ages. No people has puzzled longer
and harder about its own identity, and this was, perhaps, inevitable. For
much of history, Jews have been a minority in lands not their own.
Even as a sovereign nation, they were surrounded by great empires and indomitable
powers. Almost always, what was most conspicuous about them was that they were
different. They told a different story, heard a different music, lived a way of life that
was singular and counter-cultural, quite unlike that of their neighbours.

The word *kadosh*, holy, in the Bible means, among other things, 'distinctive', 'set
apart'. Understanding the word *ivri*, 'Hebrew', to mean 'a side', or more specifically,
'the opposite side', the sages interpreted the description of Abraham as *ha-ivri*, 'the
Hebrew' to mean that 'he was on one side while the rest of the world was on the other'.
Identity has never been something Jews could take for granted. It involved, among
other things, the courage to swim against the tide, to stand apart from the *Zeitgeist*, the
spirit of the times. Beneath the simple question of a child, 'Why is this night different?'
is another, deeper, query: 'Why is this people different?' or 'Who am I?' We answer by
telling a story – the story of our ancestors long ago, but also the story of which we are
a part. Pesach is the festival of Jewish identity. It is the night on which we tell our
children who they are.

On a superficial reading of the Bible, Moses was asking, 'Who am I to stand before
Pharaoh?' He was asking, not about identity, but about his personal worthiness for
such a mission. Moses, the Torah intimates, was not a man convinced of his place in
history. He did not seek leadership. On the contrary, he kept refusing it. 'They will not

believe me… I am slow of speech and tongue… Please send someone else.' He was, a later passage says, 'a very humble man, more so than anyone else on the face of the earth.' He accepted the divine call not because he held a high opinion of himself but because the task was real, the need great, the hour pressing, and the command inescapable. He had, in Shakespeare's phrase, 'greatness thrust upon him'.

There is, though, a deeper level at which Moses was indeed asking a question of identity. He faced a problem that has become acute wherever – in the Diaspora, even in the state of Israel itself – Jews have become part of a wider culture. A biographer, describing Moses at the point at which he first heard the call of God, would have had difficulty in knowing who he was and where his loyalties lay. This was a man rescued as a child by an Egyptian princess, adopted by her, raised in Pharaoh's palace, and brought up as an Egyptian prince. When he escaped to Midian and rescued Jethro's daughters at the well, they went back and told their father, 'An Egyptian rescued us.' In appearance, manner, dress and speech, Moses looked like an Egyptian, not an Israelite.

Moses' question, 'Who am I?' was therefore real and acute – an existential crisis. Who was he and where did his destiny lie? Was he an Egyptian or an Israelite, a prince or a slave, a member of the ruling family of the greatest empire of the time, or part of a people groaning under oppression? The mind reels at such a choice. Before him lay two alternative futures: on the one hand a life of quietude in Midian with his father-in-law's family, tending the flock in remote pastures, far from the noise of politics and power. On the other lay a life of struggle and an almost impossible challenge: to lead a people from slavery and teach them to be free – servants of no man, but of God alone.

What Moses discovered, alone with his flocks on the mountain, was that there are some choices from which we cannot hide. Almost the first words God says to him are, 'I am the God of your father, the God of Abraham, the God of Isaac and God of Jacob.' God is not, at this point, telling Moses who God is. That came later, in the famous and enigmatic words *Ehyeh asher Ehyeh*, 'I am who I am.' Instead God is telling Moses who he – Moses – is: the child of Abraham, Isaac and Jacob, three people who left the securities of land, birthplace and father's house, to begin a journey to an unknown destination, their only security the voice of God. Moses – God is saying – is not a prince of Egypt but the child of his ancestors and therefore the brother of those who, at that moment, were tasting the bitterness of slavery. Their plight was his responsibility. Their fate was his.

In his innermost heart, Moses knew this. There is a fascinating verse near the beginning of his story: 'One day, after Moses grew up, he went out to where his people were and he saw their hard labour.' Even then, Moses knew he was one of them. Seeing a Hebrew being beaten by an Egyptian taskmaster, he intervened. To be a Jew is to know that one cannot be indifferent when one's people are suffering. 'Israel,' said Rabbi Shimon bar Yochai, 'is like a single body with one soul. When one is injured, all feel the pain.'

A similar self-discovery affected several individuals who became, in the nineteenth century, protagonists of Zionism, among them Moses Hess and Theodor Herzl. Highly assimilated Jews, they none the less identified with the plight of their people as they witnessed antisemitism – during the Damascus Blood Libel (1840) in the case of Hess, the Dreyfus trial in France (1894–5) in the case of Herzl. In a moment of truth they knew that to be a Jew is to be part of a covenant of fate through which, in the rabbinic phrase, 'All Israel are responsible for one another.'

Jewish identity is a phenomenon of birth because ultimately we carry within us not only the genes but also the hopes, tears, commitments and dreams of our ancestors. Our God is the God of Abraham and Sarah and of the hundreds of generations of their descendants whose children we are. That is what a child discovers on Pesach, even though it may be many years before he or she can articulate it in these terms: we are part of a story that began long before our birth and will continue after we are no longer here. More than identity is something we choose, it is something that chooses us. To be a Jew is to hear a voice from the past, summoning us to an often tempestuous and never less than demanding future, and knowing inescapably that this is the narrative of which I am a part. That is what Moses discovered alone on the mountain, watching a bush that seemed to catch fire and burn without being consumed.

At the end of his life, Sigmund Freud wrote a strange work called *Moses and Monotheism*. Few works have been more closely studied as a key to Freud's identity. This may have been his intention, because it was the last book he wrote, and by the time it was published, in 1939, Freud was living as a refugee in London. In Vienna, where he previously lived and worked, Jews were being attacked in the streets. Austrians had welcomed their annexation into Hitler's Germany in March 1938, and almost immediately the Jews of Vienna, who made up one-sixth of the city's population, were stripped of all civic rights: to own property, to be employed, to exercise a profession and to enter restaurants or public parks. SS sentries took leading Jews, among them Vienna's Chief Rabbi, Dr Israel Taglicht, then a man of seventy-five, and forced them to wash the city's pavements in full view of passers-by, who watched with amusement and derision. Within a month, knowing that worse was to come, more than five hundred Austrian Jews had committed suicide. This was no passing madness. In 1897, Vienna had elected as its mayor the publicly anti-Jewish Karl Lueger and it was there, between 1908 and 1913, that the young Adolf Hitler received his first and most influential lessons in antisemitism.

Moses and Monotheism, Freud's last testament, is an extraordinary work. In it he tries to prove that Moses was an Egyptian who turned his attention to the Israelites after the failure of Amenhotep IV, later known as Ikhnaton, to introduce an early and primitive form of monotheism (actually, sun-worship) into Egypt. Many books have been written in an effort to understand what Freud was trying to achieve by this generally discredited speculation, and what he was communicating, consciously or otherwise, about his own identity as a Jew. That is not my concern here. Early on in the book, however, there is a curious detail whose significance has not been adequately commented on or understood. I call it Freud's greatest and most fascinating Freudian slip.

The context in which it occurs is a digression in which Freud notes that many legendary stories of heroes in antiquity share a common narrative structure. The hero's birth is fraught with danger. As a child, he is exposed to the elements in a way that would normally lead to his death. Instead, however, he is rescued and brought up by adoptive parents. Only much later does he discover his true identity. This, or something like it, is the tale told of the Babylonian hero Sargon, and among others, Cyrus, Oedipus, Romulus, Karna, Paris, Perseus, Heracles and Gilgamesh. It is also the story of Moses.

At this point, however, Freud notes that in one respect the Moses narrative is diametrically different from the others. In all the other stories the hero is a person of noble birth who is brought up by a family in humble circumstances and only later discovers that royal blood flows in his veins. In the case of Moses, the opposite is the case. He is brought up as a prince. His true identity is that he belongs to a nation of slaves.

Freud draws attention to this fact, but – assuming, as I cannot, that the biblical story is a human construct, a myth – immediately concludes that the Moses narrative is a fabrication designed to mask its original form. In this earlier version, Moses actually *is* an Egyptian prince, whose life was in danger because Pharaoh had been told in a prophetic dream that a child born within his own household would one day threaten his throne and kingdom. According to this version, it was Pharaoh who ordered the baby to be thrown into the Nile, and a Jewish couple – Amram and Jocheved – who rescued him and brought him up as their own. Freud is aware of the fact that the existence of such a story is utterly implausible. Who, after all, would have told it? Not the Egyptians, because it glorified a man who became their enemy. Not the Israelites, because it turned their own deliverer into a member of the very people who had afflicted them. That, says Freud, is why the tale was changed – leaving unexplained, indeed inexplicable, his own hypothesis, that it originally had a different form.

What Freud failed to see – despite the fact that the evidence was in front of him – was that the story of Moses is not a myth but an anti-myth, a protest against the social and spiritual assumptions of the mythic age. In myth, people are born to greatness. The universe is hierarchical. Some are born to rule, others – the vast majority – are born to be ruled. That view, common to all pagan cultures and still held by Plato and Aristotle, was what Judaism denied. Heroism is not a fact of birth. It is a matter of moral courage. It is not found only, or even primarily, among kings or princes. Abraham and Sarah, Isaac and Rebecca, Jacob, Rachel and Leah – these are simple people living ordinary lives, transfigured only by a vision, a call.

Saul, Israel's first king, looks the part. He is tall, 'head and shoulders' above his contemporaries. Yet he proves to lack the moral strength needed by a leader. David, Israel's greatest ruler, is the youngest of eight brothers, so insignificant that when Samuel, on God's instruction, visits the family, they forget about him until the prophet, having rejected the other siblings, asks if there is anyone else. True royalty, the Bible intimates, does not lie in physical strength, outward appearance or noble ancestry. Not accidentally does the life of Moses contradict the stories told of other heroes in antiquity. He is not a prince in disguise. His greatness lies in the fact that he is the child of slaves whose lives were touched and transformed by the word of God.

Freud had mixed feelings about his own identity. He admired Jews and never denied his Jewishness, but he was tone-deaf to the music of Judaism and of religion generally. Who knows whether, seeing the unleashing of those dark instinctual forces he believed to exist just below the surface of civilization as Nazism gripped Vienna, Freud tried to shift the blame for monotheism from Jews to a long-dead Egyptian, as if to say, 'We are not to blame for the repression of those instincts which are now returning with murderous fury.' Whatever his reason, there is no doubt that Freud missed one of the most powerful truths of the Bible, conveyed specifically in the detail of the Moses story that he noted and then misinterpreted. Those whom the world despises, God loves. A child of slaves can be nobler than a prince. God's standards are not power or privilege. As God tells Samuel just before he first sets eyes on David: 'The Lord does not see as a man sees; men judge by appearances but the Lord judges by the heart.' To have faith, as Judaism understands it, is to recognize God's image in the weak, the powerless, the afflicted, the suffering, and then to fight for their cause. Had he understood this, Freud might have sent a quite different message of courage to his people as they faced their darkest night. We, at least, can see what Freud did not: that in deciding that his destiny lay, not in an Egyptian palace, but with his people, Moses helped write one of the greatest narratives of hope in the literature of mankind.

4

Building a Society of Freedom

Rabbi Jochanan said: Wherever you find mentioned the greatness of the Holy One,
blessed be He, there you will find also mention of His humility... Thus it is written in
the Torah, 'For the Lord your God is God of gods and Lord of lords, the great, mighty
and awesome God, who shows no regard for persons and accepts no bribe'; and
immediately afterwards it says, 'He upholds the cause of the fatherless and the widow,
and loves the stranger, giving him food and clothing.'

Liturgy for the conclusion of the Sabbath

e do not know why it was in Israel, an otherwise small and undistinguished people, that a divine call was heard that was to change not only them but eventually the moral horizons of mankind. Little has survived from the archaeological records of those times that might shed light on this sequence of events. Little *could* survive, since by definition we speak not of great military victories recorded in triumphal inscriptions on monumental buildings, but of a revolution in consciousness. Nor should we believe that the religion of ancient Israel had, as it were, no historical context. There were systems of law before that of Moses, the Hammurabi code being only the most famous of the several that have survived from ancient times. Mesopotamian, Egyptian and Hittite documents attribute acts of justice and kindness to kings. The covenant – the single most important concept of the Hebrew Bible and of Jewish thought generally – is an ancient institution, part of the diplomatic vocabulary of the Near East in patriarchal times, specifically as a form of peace treaty between nations. Even monotheism itself, as we noted in the previous chapter, though it began in Israel, was at least prefigured in the failed religious reforms of Amenhotep IV, who sought to reduce the number of gods in the Egyptian pantheon. We do no justice to the originality of Israel's faith if we seek to remove it from history altogether, for it was precisely in and through history that Israel sensed the providence of God.

Yet there can be no doubt that the religion of ancient Israel was one of the most stunning transformations ever wrought in humanity's moral imagination, never more so than in the fact of the exodus itself. In antiquity the gods were on the side of the established power. They underwrote the reign of kings, emperors and princes – an idea revived in Europe in the Middle Ages in the form of the doctrine of the 'divine right of kings'. Rulers ruled because they were gods, or children of the gods, or prime intermediaries between the gods and mankind. They held sway on earth for the same reason as did the sun in the sky: there was an order on earth as in heaven, by which the strong ruled the weak, and power was the guarantor of order. That God, creator of heaven and earth, might intervene in history *to liberate slaves* was the ultimately unthinkable. Thus a paradox was born, which ever since has had the power to inspire men and women to break the chains of their oppression: that true power is distinguished by its concern for the powerless, that greatness is measured by the ability to hear the cry of the otherwise unheard – the weak, the vulnerable, 'the widow, the orphan and the stranger' – and that freedom is not worthy of its name unless it means freedom for all.

Again we owe to the historian Paul Johnson one of the finest descriptions of what Judaism contributed to the history of moral thought:

> All the great conceptual discoveries of the intellect seem obvious and inescapable once they have been revealed, but it requires a special genius to formulate them for the first time. The Jews had this gift. To them we owe the idea of equality before the law, both divine and human; of the sanctity of life and the dignity of the human person; of the individual conscience and so of personal redemption; of the collective conscience and so of social responsibility; of peace as an abstract ideal and love as the foundation of justice, and many other items which constitute the basic moral furniture of the human mind. Without the Jews it might have been a much emptier place.

We cannot be certain what it was about the first Hebrews that allowed them to hear a voice from heaven summoning them to a quite new conception of religious life. It cannot, however, be accidental that Jewish history begins with two momentous journeys, Abraham and Sarah's from Mesopotamia and Moses and the Israelites' from pharaonic Egypt. Mesopotamia and Egypt were the two greatest powers of their day, the first centres of civilization – whose technical prowess is still, in retrospect, awesome in its achievements. Yet what we sense between the lines of the Bible is that, despite their proficiency, they were ethically deficient. They were highly stratified societies in which great wealth and power were concentrated in relatively few hands, and in which the many lived lives of quiet desperation.

It is surely no coincidence that the patriarchs – and Moses himself at the time of his call – were shepherds who spent long stretches of time alone, tending their flocks in the silence of hills and fields. It was to them that God was revealed not as something seen but as a presence heard – a voice, a call. This was a God radically unlike the deities of myth, who were for the most part personified forces of nature: the sun, the sea, the rain, the storm. The God of Abraham and Moses created and thus *transcended* nature. He was therefore, in the purest sense, *free*, and summoned mankind to a similar freedom. No longer bound, as were the gods of myth, to a particular place, culture and social order, He taught those who heard His voice to realize, for the first time, that existing social structures were not written into the fabric of the universe. They were human creations; and could, under divine guidance, be replaced by a more just and equitable dispensation. Above all, the realization that God was singular and alone gave unprecedented dignity to the human person, singular and alone. For the first time it became possible to conceive that *every* human life has sanctity; that we all carry within us a fragment of the divine.

The religious passion of the ancient world was, above all, for order in the midst of an ever-threatening chaos, whether in the form of floods and droughts, foreign invasions, or damaging internal conflicts of power. The mindset of myth is profoundly conservative, seeking to canonize the status quo. An ancient Egyptian text attributed to Neferrohu expresses the horror felt at social disturbances that brought about change: 'I show thee a land in lamentation and distress. The man with a weak arm (now) has (a strong) arm... I show thee how the undermost is turned to uppermost.' Compare this with the exhilaration of Hannah's song of thanksgiving when she gives birth to a long-awaited son: 'The Lord sends poverty and wealth; He humbles and exalts. He raises the poor from the dust and lifts the needy from the ash-heap; he seats them with princes and has them inherit a throne of honour.' For the first time, God is associated with change, transformation, revolution. Nothing is fixed in the human landscape except the rules of ethics themselves – God's eternal word, calling for justice, equity and compassion, and constantly challenging, through a succession of prophets, the corruptions of power and the exploitation of the weak.

The exodus became a watershed in Israel's history. The Mosaic books constantly refer to it. The revelation and covenant at Mount Sinai begin with it: 'I am the Lord your God who brought you out of Egypt, out of the land of slavery.' It formed the framing logic of Israel's laws. Not only did it serve to explain why the people were bound in loyalty to the God who rescued them and gave them freedom. No less importantly, it was a standing reminder of what a society can become when people forget God and instead worship human constructs, such as power itself. Through reflection on the experience of their ancestors in Egypt, the Israelites would remember what it feels like to be on the receiving end of persecution, and thus develop a sense of solidarity with the poor. Their task in the promised land was to build a counter-Egypt, an antithesis of empire, an alternative society established on the principles of *tzedakah* and *mishpat*, distributive and retributive justice, and the covenantal virtues of *chessed* and *rachamim*, kindness and compassion. The God of freedom asks nothing less of His covenantal people than that they shape a social order of universal freedom, in which the basic requirements of human dignity are available to all.

The architectonics of biblical liberty are immensely detailed, but they can be summarized along three dimensions. The first is a humane concern for the poor – an insistence that they should never suffer hunger, nor be humiliated by their economic circumstances:

> When you make a loan of any kind to your neighbour, do not go into his house to get what he is offering as a pledge. Stay outside and let the man to whom you are making the loan bring the pledge out to you. If the man is poor, do not go to sleep with his pledge in your possession. Return his cloak to him by sunset so that he may sleep in it... Do not take advantage of a hired man who is poor and needy, whether he is a brother Israelite or an alien living in one of your towns. Pay him his wages each day before sunset, because he is poor and is counting on it... Do not deprive the alien or the fatherless of justice, or take the cloak of a widow as a pledge. Remember that you were slaves in Egypt and the Lord your God redeemed you from there. That is why I command you to do this thing.

> When you are harvesting in your field and you overlook a sheaf, do not go back and get it. Leave it for the alien, the fatherless and the widow, so that the Lord your God may bless you in all the work of your hands. When you beat the olives from your trees, do not go over the branches a second time. Leave what remains for the alien, the fatherless and the widow. When you harvest the grapes in your vineyard, do not go over the vines again. Leave what remains for the alien, the fatherless and the widow. Remember that you were slaves in Egypt. That is why I command you to do this. (Deuteronomy 24:10–22)

There is something extraordinarily humane about these ordinances, and although they speak to an agrarian order more than three thousand years ago, the principle they adumbrate remains true and compelling today. Freedom, as Nobel Prize-winning economist Amartya Sen reminds us, involves more than an absence of constraints. 'The bonded labourer born into semi-slavery, the subjugated girl child stifled by a repressive society, the helpless, landless labourer without substantial means of earning an income are all deprived not only in terms of well-being, but also in terms of the ability to lead responsible lives, which are contingent on having certain basic freedoms.' A society in which the few have wealth and many are on the verge of starvation is not free by the standards of the Hebrew Bible.

The second, equally radical, and essentially tied to Israel's experience of exile, is concern for the rights and welfare of *the stranger*. The Mosaic books never tire of this theme – the rabbis pointed out that whereas the Torah in one place commands love of the neighbour, in no less than thirty-six places it urges love of the stranger. 'Do not oppress a stranger, because *you yourselves know how it feels to be a stranger: you were* strangers in Egypt' (Exodus 23:9). For the ancient world generally, even for such as Plato and Aristotle, strangers were aliens, beyond the radius of concern, unentitled to civil rights or citizenship. Few things would have been less intelligible to them than the principle that 'The community is to have the same rules for you and for the stranger living among you... You and the stranger shall be the same before the Lord' (Numbers 15:16). This is the second revolution of the exodus, and part of Israel's moral struggle against tribalism and its modern successor, xenophobic nationalism. Strangers, too, have rights and make a legitimate claim on our humanity, for we are all strangers to someone else. This is something Israel is expected not merely to know abstractly but to feel in the deepest recesses of its collective memory. 'You yourselves were strangers in Egypt'.

The third and most compelling impact of Egypt was the enactment of freedom in time: the threefold sabbatical structure of the seventh day, the seventh year and the jubilee, the year that marked the completion of seven septennial cycles. Despite attempts of historians to trace a connection to the Babylonian calendar, the Sabbath was an unprecedented innovation. It meant that one day in seven all hierarchies of wealth and power were suspended. No one could be forced to work: not employees, or slaves, or even domestic animals. In the seventh year, debts were remitted and slaves sent free. In the Jubilee – when the shofar was sounded, proclaiming 'liberty throughout the land to all its inhabitants' (Leviticus 25:10) – all ancestral land was returned to its original owners. The logic of these laws is simple: 'For the Israelites belong to Me as servants; they are My servants whom I brought out of Egypt' (Leviticus 25:55). Those who are servants to God may not be slaves to man.

Biblical law did not end slavery. That did not happen in the West until the nineteenth century, and in the case of the United States, not without a civil war. It did however end it as a given of birth, an ontological fact. Under biblical law it became a temporary condition, something suspended every seventh day and ended after seven years. Shabbat, the sabbatical year and the Jubilee became Judaism's most original contribution to political life. In the history of the human mind there have been many utopias, imagined paradises. None has been realized. Indeed the word 'utopia' itself means 'no place'. Utopias never happen because they come without a realistic map of how to get from here to there. They are discontinuous with the present. They can only be brought about by revolution, and almost without exception, revolutions replace iniquities and inequities with injustices of their own. What is unique to Judaism is the sabbatical concept of *utopia now*, a rehearsal, every seventh day and seventh year, of an ideal social order in which rest is a part of the public domain, available equally to all. The Sabbath is the lived enactment of the messianic age, a world of peace in which striving and conflict are (temporarily) at an end and all creation sings a song of being to its Creator.

At the end of his long and detailed analysis of early Israel, Norman Gottwald comes – rightly, I believe – to the conclusion that its faith is 'the distinctive self-consciousness of a society of equals'. Israel, he says, '*thought* it was different because it *was* different: it constituted an egalitarian social system in the midst of stratified societies.' To be sure, that equality was never total and was always at risk. That is the constant refrain of the prophets – themselves testimony to Judaism's underlying egalitarianism with their willingness to confront kings and 'speak truth to power'. Yet Jewry did succeed, more than most, in sustaining the dignity of its members through suffering and poverty. One vignette is revealing – Melvin Urofsky's description of Brandeis's reaction to the East European Jewish immigrants to the United States when he first encountered them in his role as mediator of the New York garment workers' strike of 1910:

> While going through the lofts, he heard numerous quarrels between workers and their bosses, and was amazed that they treated one another more like equals than as inferiors and superiors. In one argument an employee shouted at the owner, '*Ihr darft sich shemen! Past dos far a Yid?*' ('You should be ashamed! Is this worthy of a Jew?'), while another time a machine operator lectured his employer with a quotation from Isaiah: 'It is you who have devoured the vineyard, the spoil of the poor is in your houses. What do you mean by crushing My people, by grinding the face of the poor? says the Lord God of hosts.'

For the Torah, and for post-biblical Judaism no less, society is a moral construct, a place where freedom is a collective reality to which all contribute and by which all have equal access, if not to wealth and power, then at least to human dignity in its most tangible forms: food to eat, clothes to wear, a source of independent livelihood, and a home: Micah's famous vision of a world in which 'Every man will sit under his own vine and his own fig-tree, and no one will make them afraid.' This is not the only version of an egalitarian society, but it is the oldest, the most consistently achieved, and the most humane. It did not happen by chance. Its existence was predicated on collective *memory*. Once a year, every year, every Jew was commanded to relive the experience of Egypt as a constant reminder of the bread of affliction and the bitter herbs of slavery – to know that the battle for freedom is never finally won but must be fought for in every generation.

5

History and Memory

In every generation, each of us must see ourselves as if we personally had come out from Egypt,
as it is said, 'It is because of this that the Lord acted for me *when* I *came out of Egypt.'*

Mishnah, Pesachim

 ll Jews who are at all conscious of their identity as Jews,' wrote the late Sir Isaiah Berlin, 'are steeped in history.' He continued:

> They have longer memories, they are aware of a longer continuity as a community than any other which has survived… Whatever other factors may have entered into the unique amalgam which, if not always Jews themselves, at any rate the rest of the world instantly recognizes as the Jewish people, historical consciousness – sense of continuity with the past – is among the most powerful.

Once, at a dinner, I found myself sitting next to a famous opera singer. 'What I envy you for [he meant, Jews],' he said, 'is your gift of history. I know nothing about my great-grandparents, but you have a history that goes all the way back.' So strong is this sense that Benjamin Disraeli (born a Jew, but baptized by his father as a child) referred to it in one of his most famous replies in Parliament. In 1835, the Irish Catholic politician Daniel O'Connell made a slighting reference to Disraeli's Jewish ancestry. Disraeli replied, 'Yes, I am a Jew, and when the ancestors of the right honourable gentleman were brutal savages in an unknown island, mine were priests in the temple of Solomon.'

Where does it come from, this Jewish consciousness of the past? The prophets of Israel were the first people to see God in *history*. The ancient world – the world of myth – saw the presence of the gods in *nature*, in the unchanging rhythm of the seasons and the fearful dislocations of flood, famine and storm. The revolution of ancient Israel was to see God not in nature but above it, utterly transcendent, yet revealing Himself to mankind in the form of a call to build a different kind of society than any which existed hitherto.

Monotheism was not the only great Israelite discovery. More significant still was the realization that God is not only the Creator but also the Redeemer. As Judah Halevi pointed out in the *Kuzari*, the Ten Commandments do not begin with the words, 'I am the Lord your God who created heaven and earth,' but 'I am the Lord your God who brought you out of the land of Egypt.' He is to be found not only in what Wordsworth described as that 'sense sublime' of 'something far more deeply interfused, whose dwelling is the light of setting suns, and the round ocean and the living air' but also in the great events of history, above all the liberation of a small slave people from the grip of the greatest empire of the ancient world, the Egypt of the Pharaohs.

From earliest times, Israel knew that something unprecedented had happened whose significance would send reverberations far beyond their own time. Speaking to the generation who would soon cross the Jordan and enter the promised land, Moses reminds them of the unique character of the experience they had undergone:

> Ask now about the former days, long before your time, from the day God created man on earth; ask from one end of the heavens to the other. Has anything so great as this ever happened, or has anything like it ever been heard of?... Has any god ever tried to take for himself one nation out of another nation, by testings, by miraculous signs and wonders and wars, by a mighty hand and an outstretched arm, or by great and awesome deeds, like all the things the Lord your God did for you in Egypt before your very eyes? (Deuteronomy 4:32,34)

Israel knew God not by contemplating the sun and the stars but directly through its own past. Where other faiths, ancient and modern, saw religion as the flight from history into a world without time, Judaism saw time itself as the arena where God and mankind met. Three-quarters of the Hebrew Bible is made up of historical narratives. Jews were the first to make the momentous claim that history has meaning. It is not merely a sequence of disconnected events, but the long story of humanity's response to, or rebellion against, the voice of God as it echoes in the conscience of mankind.

It is all the more remarkable, therefore, that biblical Hebrew has no word for history. Modern Hebrew had to borrow a word: *historiah*. The key-word of the Hebrew Bible is not *history* but *memory*. *Zakhor*, the command to remember, occurs time and again in the Torah:

> *Remember* the days of old (Deuteronomy 32:7)
> *Remember* what Amalek did to you (Deuteronomy 25:17)
> O My people, *remember* now what Balak king of Moab plotted against you
> (Micah 6:5)

And with equal insistence, there is the command not to forget:

> Beware lest you *forget* the Lord your God... lest you lift up your hearts

and *forget* the Lord your God who brought you out of the land of Egypt... And it shall come to pass if you indeed *forget* the Lord your God... I bear witness against you this day that you shall utterly perish. (Deuteronomy 8:11,14,19).

The word *zakhor* in one or other of its forms occurs no less than 169 times in the Hebrew Bible. As Yosef Hayim Yerushalmi notes, 'Only in Israel and nowhere else is the injunction to remember felt as a religious imperative to an entire people.' This was Moses' injunction to future generations: 'Only be careful, and watch yourselves closely so that you do not forget the things your eyes have seen or let them slip from your heart as long as you live. Teach them to your children and to their children after them' (Deuteronomy 4:9). Jews were to become a people of memory.

The word *zakhar*, meaning 'male', comes from the same root as *zakhor*, 'remember', suggesting that there are two dimensions of Jewish identity – biological, conferred by the mother, and cultural, conferred by the father in his role as story-teller, guardian of a people's past which he is charged with handing on to his children. There is an identity we acquire at birth. We are the children of Abraham, Isaac and Jacob, Sarah, Rebecca, Rachel and Leah. We are part of the covenantal family. That is the maternal gift. But there is another identity, going back not to the patriarchs and matriarchs but to the revelation at Mount Sinai, whose content we only gradually learn and internalize. That is the function traditionally ascribed to fathers, who are charged with giving children the identity that comes through memory.

The Hebrew verb *zakhor* signifies more than a consciousness of the past. My predecessor, Lord Jakobovits, pointed out that the word *Yizkor*, the name given to the traditional Jewish prayer for the dead, is associated in the Torah with the future. 'God remembered Noah' and brought him out on dry land. 'God remembered Abraham' and rescued his nephew Lot from the destruction of the cities of the plain. 'God remembered Rachel' and gave her a child. We remember for the sake of the future, and for life.

There is a profound difference between history and memory. History is *his* story – an event that happened sometime else to someone else. Memory is *my* story – something that happened to me and is part of who I am. History is information. Memory, by contrast, is part of identity. I can study the history of other peoples, cultures and civilizations. They deepen my knowledge and broaden my horizons. But they do not make a claim on me. They are the past as past. Memory is the past as present, as it lives on in me. Without memory there can be no identity. Alzheimer's Disease, the progressive atrophying of memory function, is also the disintegration of personality. As with individuals, so with a nation: it has a continuing identity to the extent that it can remember where it came from and who its ancestors were.

Yet there is a paradox in the idea of collective memory. How can I *remember* what did not happen to me – an event that took place long before I was born? The answer given by the seder service on Pesach is: through re-enactment, by living again the events of ancient times as if they were happening now. That is the significance of the statement of the sages that on Pesach, 'In every generation, each of us must see ourselves as if we personally had come out of Egypt.' At the beginning of the seder, by lifting the matzah and declaring, 'This is the bread of affliction which our ancestors ate in the land of Egypt,' we make the leap across time and turn 'then' into 'now'. 'It is because of what the Lord did for *me* when *I* came out of Egypt' (Exodus 13:8). In these words tradition heard the continuous present, the past that lives on, the event that speaks to me in the first person singular.

There is something quite distinctive about the biblical approach to time. The historical books of the Bible are the first of their kind by several centuries, long before the Greek writer Herodotus (fifth century BCE), known as 'the father of history'. Yet the biblical narrative is never mere history, a recording of what happened because it happened, whether to entertain or instruct. Nor is it myth, a pre-scientific attempt to explain why the world is as it is. It is nothing less than the sustained attempt to see events through the prism of faith, as the ongoing interaction between heaven and earth, command and response, the Divine word and the human success or failure in hearing and acting on the word. It is saturated by the idea of covenant as the partnership, initiated by God and entered into by mankind, making them partners in the work of redemption.

There is nothing pre-ordained in this narrative. By giving humanity freewill, God has made human beings His co-authors in writing the script of history. Yet it is not open-ended either, 'a tale, told by an idiot, full of sound and fury, signifying nothing'. History, as understood by the Torah, is the story of how human beings, led only by the sound of a voice, a call, began the long journey, not yet complete, to a promised land and a messianic age where people construct a society that honours the image of God in others, sanctifying life, building families of love and trust, shaping communities by the principles of justice and compassion, and living at peace with their neighbours. No religion has conferred on mankind a greater responsibility. We are not, in this narrative, condemned to fail because of hubris or 'original sin'. We are not confined to pure submission to the will of God. Instead, God has entrusted his great creation to our safekeeping, and though the Hebrew Bible tells us that Israel failed often, it also tells us that God has never lost faith in us, though we may sometimes lose our faith in Him.

The concept of covenant is intimately related to time. 'I have chosen him,' says God of Abraham, 'so that he may instruct his children and his household after him to keep to the way of the Lord, by doing what is right and just.' The achievement of a free and just society is not the work of a moment but of many generations. Israel must experience exile before it can fully understand the concept of home. It must undergo slavery if it is to long with all its being for freedom. It must walk through the valley of the shadow of death to know in its bones the sanctity of life. That is why covenant is essentially linked to education and memory, for the journey is long – longer than many lifetimes – and it is only when each generation hands on to the next what it has heard and learned and prayed for, that the journey continues; and only if the journey continues is history redeemed. History has meaning only for those who believe it has meaning. Without that, it is what Harold MacMillan called 'events, dear boy, events'.

In his book *Zakhor: Jewish History and Jewish Memory*, Yosef Yerushalmi makes the fascinating observation that, having seen God in history and written an entire library of historical works, the Jewish people suddenly stopped writing history at the time of the destruction of the Second Temple. The last great Jewish historian was Josephus, who wrote his works in the first century of the Common Era. From then on, throughout the rabbinic literature of the Mishnaic, Talmudic and medieval periods, there is virtually no historical writing with the exception of the sixteenth century when, in response to the Spanish expulsion, several works appeared, trying to make sense of the tragic fate of Jews in the Diaspora.

The great renaissance of historical writing occurred in the early nineteenth century when the 'Society for the Science of Judaism' was formed in Germany and the great works of Zunz, Graetz and others began to appear. What Yerushalmi notes is that this new scholarly enterprise was born, not in a sense of identification with the past, but precisely out of a sense of alienation. In the eyes of its founders, Judaism was a spent force, a relic of the past that had no future in post-Enlightenment Europe. All that remained, in Steinschneider's words, was 'to give it a decent burial'. It is said that Zunz, introduced in his old age to a Hebrew poet visiting from Russia, asked him, 'Tell me, when did you live?' History is the dead past which only memory can revive.

It was Samson Raphael Hirsch who delivered the most cogent critique of history as a substitute for memory:

> Moses and Hesiod, David and Sappho, Deborah and Tyrtaeus, Isaiah and Homer, Delphi and Jerusalem, Pythian tripod and Cherubim-sanctuary, prophets and oracles, psalms and elegy – for us they all lie peacefully in one box, they all rest peacefully in one grave, they all have one and the same human origin, they all have one and the same significance, human, transitory and belonging to the past... We let the old Jews fast on *Tisha B'Av*, we let them say *Selichot* and weep over *Kinot*. But in return we know far better than they do in which century these 'poets' flourished, in what metre these 'poets' composed... Do these departed spirits rejoice in the literary gratitude of our present generation? Whom do they recognize as their true heirs? Those who repeated their prayers, but forgot their names, or those who forgot their prayers but remembered their names?

To be a Jew is to know that over and above history is the task of memory. As Jacob Neusner eloquently wrote: 'Civilization hangs suspended, from generation to generation, by the gossamer strand of memory. If only one cohort of mothers and fathers fails to convey to its children what it has learned from its parents, then the great chain of learning and wisdom snaps. If the guardians of human knowledge stumble only one time, in their fall collapses the whole edifice of knowledge and understanding.' More than any other faith, Judaism made this a matter of religious obligation. Pesach is where the past does not die but lives, in the chapter we write in our own lives and in the story we tell our children.

6

Not One Alone

*Not one alone rose against us to destroy us: in every generation they rise against us
and seek our destruction. But the Holy One, blessed be He, saves us from their hands.*

Haggadah

he first mention in the Torah of Jews as a people is a prelude to persecution. 'A new king, who did not know of Joseph, came into power over Egypt. He said to his people, "Look, the people of the children of Israel (*am bnei Yisrael*) have become too numerous for us. We must deal wisely with them..."' Wisdom in this case means forced labour, followed by enslavement, then the planned murder of every male child. It is the first but not the last attempted genocide in the pages of the Bible. The festival of Purim records a second failed attempt, this time by Haman who persuades the Persian king to issue a decree 'to destroy, kill and annihilate all the Jews – young and old, women and little children – on a single day.'

Ironically, the first two references to Israel outside the Bible are obituaries for the Jewish people. The Merneptah stele from Egypt in the thirteenth century BCE, as we noted in an earlier chapter, states: 'Israel is laid waste, her seed is no more.' The Mesha stele, a basalt slab dating from the ninth century BCE, stands today in the Louvre in Paris. In its inscription, Mesha, king of Moab thanks his deity Chemosh for his victories in war. It includes the following lines: 'As for Omri, king of Israel, he humbled Moab for many years, for Chemosh was angry with his land. And his son followed him and he also said, "I will humble Moab." In my time he spoke thus, but I have triumphed over him and over his house, while *Israel has perished forever*.' At times it is hard to know which is the greater wonder of history: Jewish survival, or the attempts of others to ensure Israel did not survive.

The historian Robert Wistrich calls antisemitism 'the longest hatred', and in a way it is, though it has taken too many forms for it to be described as a single phenomenon with one name. The Greek and Latin writers of classical antiquity were often hostile to

Jews, accusing them of clannishness, strange customs and superstitions. Horace condemns them for trying to make converts. Apion criticizes them for failing to worship the same gods as the Alexandrians. Seneca held that they rested on the seventh day because they were lazy. The worst of the pre-Christian polemicists was the Egyptian priest Manetho (third century BCE) who described the Hebrews as a race of lepers who had been thrown out of Egypt. Many of these calumnies survived to be taken up and adapted in later centuries. That has been the fate of anti-Jewish myths: they may be dormant, but they never die. Yet it would be wrong to describe reactions to Jews in antiquity as universally hostile. There is evidence to suggest that Alexander the Great thought highly of them and rewarded them for their loyalty. Aristotle spoke well of them, as did his successor Theophrastus. Besides, the ancient world was not known for its love of foreigners, whoever they might be.

Something new enters the world with Christianity and with the early decision, following the Council of Jerusalem, that it would become, not a religion directed to Jews but one that sought adherents among the gentiles. A series of fateful judgements was incorporated into Christianity's early texts and developed by the Church fathers: among them that Christianity was 'the new Israel', that God had rejected the 'old' Israel, and that Jews had been guilty of wilful blindness and worse in rejecting the Christian messiah. The proposal of Marcion – that Christianity should be separated completely from Judaism, with the New Testament as its only scripture – failed. From then on, Christianity was locked into an adversarial relationship with Judaism, glaringly apparent in the New Testament and the work of Christian thinkers from the second to the fourth centuries, among them Justin Martyr, Origen, Melito, Tertullian, Eusebius, Gregory of Nyssa, and St John Chrysostom. This *Adversus Judaeos* tradition, often savage in its rhetoric, left a deep mark on the development of Christianity, a fact that became immensely consequential when – with the conversion of the Roman emperor Constantine in 313 – Christianity became a world power, which it was to remain for almost 1,500 years.

Hostility deepened into massacre with the First Crusade (1096), during which, on their way to Holy Land, Christians massacred Jewish communities in northern France and Germany. It was at this time that the line, 'Pour out Thy wrath against the nations that do not know Thee...' first began to appear in Haggadot, the one note of Jewish protest against the Christian slaughter of Jews in the name of God. From then on, the religious anti-Judaism of the Church began to take on a more irrational, demonic character. During the Middle Ages, Jews were accused of ritual murder, poisoning wells, desecrating the host, causing the 'Black Death', and colluding with the Devil. There were periodic forced conversions, public disputations, book burnings, show trials, burnings at the stake, mob attacks and massacres. In the years following the Black Death alone (1347–1350), some two hundred Jewish communities were destroyed. Jews were expelled from Brittany in 1239–40, Anjou and Maine in 1289, England in 1290, France at various periods from 1182 to 1394, and from regions of Germany throughout the fifteenth century. In Spain, where they had experienced a rare

Golden Age, an onslaught took place in 1391, during which synagogues and homes were burned, businesses looted and many Jews murdered. From then on, Spanish Jews faced increasing hostility until their expulsion in 1492. Nor did the tragedy end there. Still to come were Luther's tirade against Jews ('their synagogues should be set on fire… their homes should likewise be broken down and destroyed… they should be deprived of their prayerbooks and Talmuds'), the invention of the ghetto (Rome 1555, by edict of Pope Paul IV) and the Chmielnicki pogroms (1648–58) during which as many as 100,000 Jews died. The experience of Jews in Christian Europe is one of the tragedies of mankind.

Nor was their experience under Islam an especially happy one. There seems to have been an expectation on the part of the first Muslims that Jews would willingly embrace the new faith which, like Christianity, claimed to include and supersede earlier revelations. When this did not happen, reprisals were harsh. Islam began with a massacre of Jews in Medina, and like Christianity incorporated sharply anti-Jewish sentiments into its sacred texts. There were times, especially in its early period of expansion, when tolerance prevailed, though within limits. Jews were given *dhimmi* status as second-class citizens, which meant that they had to pay special taxes and wear distinctive clothing (the yellow star Jews were forced to wear in Nazi Europe had its origins in medieval Baghdad). They were banned from government service and from building new houses of worship, and were subject to periodic public humiliations. At times, extreme Islamic sects made life intolerable. In 1066 the Jewish community of Granada was attacked and three thousand were killed. In 1090 the community was assaulted again by an Islamic sect known as the Almoravids, and during the next century it suffered an onslaught from a new group, the Almohads.

There is no doubt, however, that as a whole Jews fared better during the Middle Ages under Muslim than under Christian rule. What was remarkable, however, was the way in which Christian myths which had no salience in Islamic terms were later adopted by Islam to fuel new and essentially alien forms of anti-Jewish hostility. Of these, the most striking is the Blood Libel. First instigated in Norwich in 1144 and then copied throughout Europe, this accused Jews of killing Christian children to drink or use their blood for ritual purposes. Officially rejected by the Vatican, the myth persisted well into the twentieth century. From the perspective of Judaism, the myth is absurd: the consumption of blood is categorically forbidden. Within Christianity it makes sense: that is what the wine of communion represents. (The playwright Arnold Wesker wrote a play, called *Blood Libel*, for the 850th anniversary of the event in Norwich, and was kind enough to send me a copy of the script. I read it and asked him why it had no Jewish characters – they were all off-stage. He replied that the Blood Libel was a Christian phenomenon, in which Jews were objects, not participants.) Rooted in Christian theology, the Blood Libel none the less spread to Islam, where it appeared in Aleppo (1811, 1853), Beirut (1824), Antioch (1826), Hamma (1829), Tripoli (1834), Dayr al-Qamar (1847), Damanhur (1877) and Damascus (most famously in 1840, but also in 1848 and 1890). In 1983 the Syrian Defence Minister

Mustafa Tlas wrote a book, *The Matzo of Zion*, to prove that the libel was true ('The Jew can kill you and take your blood in order to make his Zionist bread'), and in 1991 the Syrian delegate to the United Nations Human Rights Commission urged its members to read the book, the better to understand the nature of 'Zionist racism'.

These are devastating chapters in the history of the human spirit. It was no wonder, therefore, that Jews vested immense – in some cases almost messianic - hopes in the Enlightenment, which promised the defeat of prejudice in the name of reason, and a new dawn of tolerance. It did not happen. Early on, there were ominous signs. In the 1750s, Voltaire, the great advocate of liberty, described Jews as 'an ignorant and barbarous people, who have long united the most sordid avarice with the most detestable superstitition', though he was gracious enough to add, 'Still, we ought not to burn them.' In 1789, as the French National Assembly proclaimed its Declaration of the Rights of Man, anti-Jewish riots broke out in Alsace.

The great philosophers of modernity did not distinguish themselves by their generosity of imagination. Immanuel Kant spoke of Jews as 'the vampires of society' and called for the 'euthanasia' of Judaism. Fichte argued against giving civil rights to Jews. Hegel took Judaism as his model of a slave morality. Schopenhauer spoke of Jews as 'no better than cattle'. Nietzsche blamed Judaism for the 'falsification' of values. The great logician Gottlob Frege wrote in 1924 that he regarded it as a 'misfortune that there are so many Jews in Germany'. Martin Heidegger, the greatest German philosopher of the twentieth century, was an enthusiastic member of the Nazi party who never subsequently apologized for his admiration of Hitler or his betrayal of Jewish colleagues. I have seen no adequate account – though this may be my ignorance of the literature – of how it was that philosophy, which carried with it the highest hopes of an age of reason, utterly failed to confront antisemitism. Even Jean-Paul Sartre's *Réflexions sur la Question Juive*, written after the war in 1946, is a deeply flawed work, attributing no independent dignity to Jewish existence (his argument was that Jews do not create antisemitism; antisemitism creates Jews).

Reviewing this history, it is clear that antisemitism is not a unitary phenomenon, a coherent belief or ideology. Jews have been hated because they were rich and because they were poor; because they were capitalists and because they were communists; because they believed in tradition and because they were rootless cosmopolitans; because they kept to themselves and because they penetrated everywhere. Antisemitism is not a belief but a virus. The human body has an immensely sophisticated immune system which develops defences against viruses. It is penetrated, however, because viruses mutate. Antisemitism mutates.

In pre-Christian times it took the relatively simple form of hostility to strangers, a *dis*like of the *un*like. In the early Christian centuries it became a religious phenomenon: anti-Judaism. In the Middle Ages it was transmuted into a series of myths whose common theme was that Jews were the cause of all bad things. Following the Enlightenment, religious or mythical justifications were no longer acceptable to secular public discourse, and thus racial antisemitism was born (the word 'antisemitism' itself was only coined in 1879, by the German journalist Wilhelm Marr). The prestige given to prejudice by sacred texts was replaced by the new guarantor of truth: science. A pseudo-science of race was created, designed to prove that Jews were an inferior species. Other quasi-scientific disciplines were enlisted: an anthropology that identified 'old' with 'primitive'; a Darwinian reading of history that saw 'natural selection' as the ruthless elimination of the weak by the strong; and a scientific approach to society (social engineering), including eugenics and other medical ideas, to construct the thought that society could be improved by the surgical removal of 'flawed' individuals and groups. If philosophy failed Jews, so did science: there were all too few protests at these insanities. Inevitably, racial antisemitism was a more deadly form than any of its predecessors, because whereas religious convictions can be renounced, races can only be exterminated.

It is difficult to know what to say in the face of such evil, for evil it is, regardless of the sanctity or high ideals or pseudo-scientific concepts in which it has been clothed. Heaven alone knows whether Jews have been better or worse than other people, but no people who have ever lived have deserved such hate, such persecution. Nor has it ended.

An autobiographical note: I grew up in Christian Britain and went to Christian schools (in those days, Jewish day schools were rare). I experienced nothing but kindness from my teachers and friends. Those days left an enduring impression on me. They taught me admiration for a faith that was not and will never be my own. They showed me that deep and abiding tolerance is possible and has surpassing beauty. They helped me form friendships in later life with Christian leaders and others from other faiths – Muslim, Hindu, Sikh, Buddhist, Jain, Zoroastrian and Bahai – which I cherish. As a child, when I came to the passage in the Haggadah which speaks of hatred through the ages – 'Not one alone rose against us to destroy us' – I felt intuitively that those words referred to an age that had passed. They may have described the experience of my parents' generation, but not mine. As I grew older, that conviction grew. The Holocaust, I believed, had taught humanity the words, 'Never again'.

I was wrong. Antisemitism in a new and virulent form – now focusing on collective Jewish existence in Israel while also attacking individual Jews and Jewish buildings in the Diaspora – has appeared again. With astonishing speed and ease, it has circumvented the immune systems built up by the West during the course of more than half a century of Holocaust education, interfaith dialogue and anti-racist legislation. How did it happen?

Viruses are effective when they persuade the body's immune system that they are part of the body itself. Viruses mutate so as to appear to host cells not as enemies but friends. So great was the impact of the Holocaust that it rendered certain evils taboo: racism, 'ethnic cleansing', crimes against humanity and attempted genocide. The only way antisemitism could penetrate such defences was to turn them against Jews. Starting with the infamous 1975 United Nations resolution equating Zionism with racism, it reached a culmination in the United Nations Conference against Racism in Durban in

September 2001, in which the state of Israel – the sole democracy in the Middle East – was uniquely accused of each of these evils in turn.

The attempt failed, but the language and narrative were established as acceptable forms of discourse in the public domain. A new myth, as powerful as any of its medieval precursors, was born in which the existence of a Jewish state, however small, became the cause of all international disorder, from the destruction of the World Trade Center less than a week after the Durban conference to the 'clash of civilizations' that threatened the twenty-first century's prospects of peace. Thus racial antisemitism mutated into mythological anti-Zionism with the further rider that all Jews are Zionists and thus legitimate targets of violence. Into this new mould, all the old fantasies of hate, from the Blood Libel to the late-nineteenth century forgery, *The Protocols of the Elders of Zion*, were poured and sprang again into life.

One date links medieval, modern and post-modern hostility: Pesach itself. Pesach was the favoured time for Blood Libels, for it was said and apparently believed, at least by the masses, that Jews needed blood to make *matzot*. It was the date chosen by the Nazis for the extermination of the Warsaw ghetto in 1943 (the Nazis deliberately chose Jewish holy days for their most brutal murders: this became known as the 'Goebbels calendar'). It was the day selected by anti-Israel terrorists in 2002 for the suicide bombing in Netanya in which 29 people were killed and hundreds injured as they prepared to celebrate the seder. There is something about the biblical festival of freedom that outrages those who believe – sometimes in the name of God, sometimes in the name of ethically advanced civilization – that freedom must, by definition, exclude Jews.

Why does antisemitism exist? There has been an almost endless set of speculations. Some have seen it in psychological terms: displaced fear, externalization of inner conflict, projected guilt, the creation of a scapegoat. Others have given it a socio-political explanation: Jews were a group who could conveniently be blamed for economic resentments, social unrest, class conflict or destabilizing change. Yet others view it through the prism of culture and identity: Jews were the stereotyped outsiders against whom a group could define itself. There have been voices within the Jewish tradition that see hostility as inevitable: 'Esau hates Jacob', or 'From Sinai, hate [*sinah*] descended into the world.' Yet others, noting the concentration of antisemitism among the very faiths – Christianity and Islam – that trace their descent to Abrahamic monotheism, favour a Freudian explanation in terms of the myth of Oedipus: we seek to kill those who gave us birth. It would be strange indeed if so complex a phenomenon did not give rise to multiple explanations.

My own view, though it does not essentially conflict with any of these hypotheses, is that Jews were hated because they were different. To be sure, every people, race and faith is different. None, however, has insisted with such tenacity on the right to be different, the duty to be different. Alone among the peoples of the Alexandrian and Roman empires, Jews rose up in rebellion – never on political grounds, but simply in defence of their right to practise their faith. Almost alone in Christian Europe, they refused to convert (some did; the majority did not) despite the immense pressures that were placed upon them, sometimes at the cost of life itself. In post-Enlightenment Europe they remained distinctive. They acculturated, integrated, but did not disappear. In the contemporary Middle East, the state of Israel remains an island of Jewish life in an Islamic sea. Jews were different. That, we recall, was Haman's reason for advocating genocide: 'There is a certain people, dispersed and scattered among the peoples... whose customs are different from those of all other people.' It is one thing to be different and an empire, a civilization, a world power; quite another to be different and a minority, whether in one's own land or in dispersion. Jewish existence raises in its most acute form the problem of difference, and always has.

There is something unusual, even unique, about the faith of Judaism. It was the world's first monotheism. Abraham, Moses and the prophets were the first to believe in a single God, creator of heaven and earth, whose authority transcended all earthly powers. Integral to Jewish faith is the proposition that God made (with Noah after the Flood) a covenant with all mankind. It is this covenant, with its insistence on the rule of justice and the sanctity of life, that is the earliest intimation of what today are known as codes of universal human rights (the Torah itself speaks of commands and prohibitions rather than rights). Yet Judaism itself – the way of Torah – is not, and was never seen as, a universal code. Instead, through a series of covenants with the patriarchs, and later the Israelites at Mount Sinai, it was the code of a particular people – one people, not all. From this arises the well known but still remarkable fact that Judaism does not see itself as the only path to God. Malkitzedek, Jethro and the daughter of Pharaoh who rescued Moses are just three of the figures who, outside the covenant of Torah, none the less come to know and fear God. 'The saintly among the nations of the world,' said the sages, 'have a share in the world to come.' The seeming paradox can be stated simply: *the God of Israel is the God of all humanity, but the religion of Israel is not, and is not intended to be, the religion of all humanity*. This is a phenomenon in need of explanation. To understand it is to reach a theological conclusion about antisemitism. It is also a vital clue in deciphering the place of Pesach in the worldview of Judaism.

The Torah is about one people, Israel, its faith, history and land. Yet it does not begin with one people. It opens instead with humanity as a whole: Adam and Eve, Cain and Abel, Noah and the Flood. Each represents a universal message. The story of Adam and Eve tells us that, in Rabbi Akiva's words, 'Beloved is mankind for it was created in the image [of God].' The story of Cain tells us of the universal danger of sibling rivalry, violence and murder. Noah, after the Flood, represents all humanity in covenant with God. These are the universals of the human condition. There then follows a narrative that marks the transition from the universal (Noah) to the particular (Abraham): the story of Babel. It begins with a dramatic statement: 'The entire world had one language with uniform words.' Babel – a reference to the great city states of Mesopotamia – is a symbol of empire, a single civilization imposed by force on a mass of individuals. Today, historians of the ancient world call this type of civilization 'cosmological', meaning that it projected its hierarchy on the heavens. It believed that its social structure mirrored the cosmos. The Torah tells us, without immediately explaining why, that there is something fundamentally wrong with this kind of order. God confuses the speech of Babel's builders and then, in the next chapter, calls on Abraham to make a lonely journey into an unknown future. From then on until the end of days there will be no universal language, culture or civilization. There will indeed be a universal moral code, the code of Noah, but no universal religion.

It is difficult to overestimate the originality and power of this idea. Having made mankind in His image and made a covenant with all humanity, God turns to one individual, one extended family, one people, and asks it to be different *thereby teaching mankind the dignity of difference*. The word *kadosh*, 'holy', in the Torah means just that: different, distinctive, set apart. What is wrong with universal civilizations, the echoes of Babel through the ages, is that they sacrifice the individual to the collective. They make men serve the state instead of making the state serve mankind. They impose an artificial unity on a divinely created diversity. Our humanity exists not despite but precisely because of our individual uniqueness. As the Mishnah puts it in one of rabbinic Judaism's most profound teachings, 'When a human being makes many coins in the same mint, they all come out the same. God makes every person in the same image – His image – but they are all different.' Judaism is a particular covenant with the universal God, because it is only in and through our particularity that we are fully human, and it is only through the institutions of particularity – families, communities, languages and traditions, each with its own local character – that we protect and sustain our humanity.

If Babel is the Bible's first symbol of empire, Egypt is its second. The Egyptians – so the Torah tells us and so we know from independent sources – feared and despised strangers. At one time they had been conquered by them – the Hyksos. It is no wonder therefore that they had negative feelings about the *Ivrim*, 'Hebrews'. The Torah uses a strong word, *to'evah* ('abomination', 'taboo') to describe the Egyptian attitude to nomadic shepherd peoples (Genesis 43:32, 46:34). The opening chapters of the book of Exodus tell an eminently realistic story about the slow slide from discrimination to persecution to enslavement. The Hebrews were different and thus a threat and therefore to be subject to progressive dehumanization, a pattern that Jews experienced more than once in their subsequent history. The Torah leaves us in no doubt whatsoever as to the lesson Israel was to learn from this formative experience, stating it no less than thirty-six times: You shall love the stranger, because you know what it feels like to be a stranger. You shall protect and respect one who is different, for you, more than any other people on earth, know what it is to be different.

To be a Jew, therefore, from the days of Abraham and Sarah to today, is to carry the burden and dignity of difference. Jews never built an empire. They never sought to become a world power, imposing their culture on others. Though the prophets foresaw the day when all mankind would worship the One God, they never foresaw a time when the nations would adopt Israel's covenant, the Torah. The task of the people of the covenant – set out in God's first call to Abraham – is to be true to its own faith while contributing to the good of others: 'through you shall all the nations of earth be blessed.' Abraham fights and prays on behalf of the people of the cities of the plain, though their faith is not his. The biblical *ger toshav*, the non-Jew living within Israel's jurisdiction, has equal rights merely by adopting the universal (Noahide) code, not by embracing the covenant of Israel. Judaism accepts converts; it does not seek them. In charging Israel to be the exemplar of the dignity of difference, therefore, God posed two challenges: one to Israel, the other to the nations of the world. For Israel, the question has always been: do we have the courage to be different? For the nations it has been: do we make space for difference? The failure of the first leads to assimilation; of the second, to antisemitism.

Jews were persecuted because they were different. Under the Alexandrian and Roman empires they resisted Hellenization. Under medieval Christianity and Islam they refused conversion. Under nineteenth century European nationalism they remained a distinctive group. During each of these five civilizations they sought no special rights except the right to be themselves, true to the faith of their ancestors. At each stage, some Jews defected. Most stayed loyal. Their vision was simple, best expressed in the words of the prophet Micah:

> Every man will sit under his own vine and his own fig tree,
> And no one will make them afraid,
> For the Lord Almighty has spoken.
> All the nations will walk, each in the name of its god;
> We will walk in the name of the Lord our God for ever and ever.
>
> (Micah 4:4–5)

I know of no spiritual vision truer to the nature of this created world, with its multiplicity of faiths, languages and cultures; none more generous in its understanding of the myriad forms of the human quest for God; none more vigilant in defence of the particular, the local, the relationships in which our humanity is expressed through covenants of love rather than the coercive force of power. Antisemitism – the paradigm case of the hatred of difference – is more than an assault against Jews. It is a flawed understanding, catastrophic in its consequences, of what it is to be human.

If I am right, three conclusions follow: one for Jews, a second for antisemites, a third for humanity as a whole.

For Jews, the response to antisemitism must be to fight it but never to internalize it or accept it on its own terms. Racial antisemitism, product of a late nineteenth century Europe that saw itself as the summit of civilization, eventually cost the lives of six million Jews. But it left another, less visible scar. One of the mistakes made by good, honourable and reflective Jews was to believe that since Jews were the objects of antisemitism, they were also its cause. They argued that since Jews were hated because they were different, they should try, as far as possible, not to be different. Some converted; others assimilated; yet others reformulated Judaism to eliminate as far as possible all that made Jews and Judaism distinctive. When these things failed – as they did, not only in nineteenth century France, Germany and Austria but also in fifteenth century Spain – some internalized the failure. Thus was born the tortured psychology known as Jewish self-hatred: the result of Jews ceasing to define themselves as a nation loved by God and instead seeing themselves as the people hated by gentiles. It was a tragic error. Antisemitism is not caused by Jews; they are merely its targets. We now know that there can be antisemitism in countries where there are no Jews at all. Hatred is something that can happen to us, but it is not who we are. It can never be the basis of an identity.

One episode, told by a rabbinical colleague, has long lingered in my mind. It took place in Russia in the early 1990s, following the collapse of communism. For the first time in seventy years, Jews were free openly to live as Jews, but at the same time antisemitic attitudes, long suppressed, came to the surface. A British rabbi had gone there to help with the reconstruction of Jewish life, and was one day visited by a young lady in distress. 'All my life,' she said, 'I hid the fact that I was a Jew and no one ever commented on my Jewishness. Now, though, when I walk past, my neighbours mutter *Zhid* (Jew). What shall I do?' The rabbi replied, 'If you had not told me you were Jewish, I would never have known. But with my hat and beard, no one could miss the fact that I am a Jew. Yet, in all the months I have been here, no one has shouted *Zhid* at me. Why do you think that is?' The girl was silent for a moment and then said, 'Because they know that if they shout *Zhid* at me, I will take it as an insult, but if they shout *Zhid* at you, you will take it as a compliment.' That is a deep insight. Beyond eternal vigilance, the best way for Jews to combat antisemitism is to wear their identity with pride.

To antisemites, we must say this: we will never return hate with hate. To be a Jew is to work for peace and justice; revenge belongs to God, not us. Yet there is a truth that must also be spoken, namely that antisemitism is a profound psychological dysfunction, a disease masquerading as a cure. When bad things happen to a person or group, there are two questions it can ask: 'How can I put it right?' or 'Who did this to me?' Asking the first defines me as a subject, a moral agent, a responsible self. Asking the second identifies me as an object, a victim; and a victim can feel only resentment and rage.

There is an immense appeal to the culture of victimhood. It wins sympathy and the suspension of moral judgement. Its cost, however, is higher still, for defining oneself as a victim – antisemites always do – involves the systematic denial of responsibility. Dostoevsky once wrote that 'If God does not exist, all is permitted.' That is untrue. But if *responsibility* does not exist, then all is permitted; and few phenomena have relieved more people of more responsibility than the mythical belief that there exists a group responsible for all the evils in the world, and the simultaneous knowledge, at some other level of consciousness, that it is in fact so vulnerable that it can be attacked with impunity.

It is no accident that throughout history, and no less so today, antisemitism has been the weapon of choice of tyrants, dictators, holders of non-democratic power and rulers of totalitarian states. It appeals because it deflects public unrest at hunger, poverty, ignorance, disease, economic inequalities, bribery, corruption and denial of human rights. It redirects indignation from its proper object to a mythical enemy charged with supernatural powers to control the world. That is why those who care for freedom, democracy and the rule of law must never cease to remind us that in the long run antisemitism harms those who practise it no less than those against whom it is practised. The culture of victimhood, so fashionable today, never liberates, but only perpetuates the condition of the victim.

To humanity, the argument must be simple and direct. Antisemitism – the hatred of difference – is an assault not on Jews only but on the human condition as such. Life is sacred because each person – even genetically identical twins – is different, therefore irreplaceable and non-substitutable. Every language, culture, and civilization (provided that it satisfies the minimum conditions of a universal moral code) has its own integrity and because each is different, each adds something unique to the collective heritage of mankind. Cultural diversity is as essential to our social ecology as biodiversity is to our natural ecology. A world without room for Jews is one that has no room for difference, and a world that lacks space for difference lacks space for humanity itself.

7

Pesach and the
Rebirth of Israel

Now we are here; next year may we be in the land of Israel.
Now we are slaves; next year may we be free.

Haggadah

In January 1895, a young Viennese journalist, Theodor Herzl, reporting on the Dreyfus trial in Paris, was shocked by the sight of crowds shouting *'A mort les juifs'* – 'Death to the Jews'. Antisemitism, he realized, was alive and strong, not only in places like Russia, where in 1881 pogroms had broken out in more than a hundred towns, but in France itself, home of the revolution, the secular state and the declaration of the rights of man. He became a man transformed. Within a year he had written his response, which he called *Der Judenstaat*, 'the Jewish State'. In it he summed up the disillusionment of a century of Jewish life, in which the hopes of European enlightenment and emancipation had proved so false:

> We have sincerely tried everywhere to merge with the national communities in which we live, seeking only to preserve the faith of our fathers. It is not permitted us. In vain are we loyal patriots, sometimes superloyal; in vain do we make the same sacrifices of life and property as our fellow citizens; in vain do we strive to enhance the fame of our native lands in the arts and sciences, or her wealth by trade and commerce. In our native lands where we have lived for centuries we are still decried as aliens, often by men whose ancestors had not yet come at a time when Jewish sighs had long been heard in the country.

There was, he argued, only one solution to antisemitism. If the nation states of Europe were so hostile to Jews, then Jews must have a state of their own. He was not the first secular Jew to reach this conclusion. Judah Leib Pinsker had said the same in 1882 in the wake of the pogroms. Moses Hess, one-time friend and mentor of Karl Marx, has done so even earlier in 1862. But there was something altogether compelling about Herzl. Tall, impressive, persuasive, he threw himself into political activity like a man possessed, travelling around Europe, speaking to statesmen, arguing his case with conviction and charm, never admitting the possibility of defeat. Within a year, in 1897, he had succeeded in convening the first Zionist Congress, writing in his diary on 3 September the famous words, 'At Basle I founded the Jewish State. If I said this out loud today, I would be answered by universal laughter. Perhaps in five years, certainly in fifty, everyone will know it.' Fifty years later, on 29 November 1947, the United Nations General Assembly voted to bring a Jewish state into being, and on 15 May 1948, Israel was born.

Herzl died in 1904, aged forty-four, worn out by his eight years of frenetic activity in the Zionist cause. In 1902 he published a novel, *Altneuland*, setting out the Israel of his dream. In one of the key scenes, he tells how the assimilated Dr Friedrich Loewenberg – Herzl's thinly disguised portrait of himself – rediscovers his religious roots while attending a seder service. This is how Herzl describes it:

> And so the ritual went on, half religious ceremony and half family meal, moving for anyone who had a heart to be moved by ancient custom. For this most Jewish of Jewish festivals reached back farther into ancient times than any living customs of the civilized world. It was celebrated now, exactly as it had been observed for hundreds and hundreds of years. The world had changed, nations had vanished from the face of the earth, others had made their way into the annals of history... and only this one nation was still here, cherishing its ancient customs, true to itself, remembering the sufferings of its ancestors. It still prays in the ancient language and the ancient formulas to the Eternal God, this nation of slaves and now of free men – Israel.

So the story of the first exodus inspired a new return to Zion.

What is it to see the presence of God in history? The question is exceptionally difficult to answer. Ancient societies were interested in the past. They, like we, wanted to know how we came to be here, why society was the way it was, and how the universe was formed. Yet none before ancient Israel saw the unfolding of events as intrinsically meaningful, a narrative of redemption. Indeed, virtually all later societies who came to share this vision did so under the influence of the Hebrew Bible. As the historian J. H. Plumb puts it: 'The concept that within the history of mankind itself a process was at work which would mould his future, and lead man to situations totally different from his past, seems to have found its first expression amongst the Jews.' In and through their religious vision, 'the past became more than a collection of tales, a projection of human experience, or a system of moral examples... It became an intimate part of destiny, and an interpretation of the future.' Nothing more profoundly illustrates this than the way the story of the exodus shaped the Jewish imagination, not only of successive generations of those who lived their lives by faith, but even of profoundly secular figures like Hess, Pinsker and Herzl.

The sequence of exile and homecoming, exodus and redemption seems, from the very beginning, to have been part of the basic structure of Jewish consciousness. Adam and Eve are exiled from Eden. Cain is sentenced to a life of exile. The builders of Babel are scattered throughout the earth. Sin – a disturbance of the order of the universe – leads to exile and displacement. Already foreshadowed in these opening chapters is the possibility of an end of days in which mankind, repenting its sins, experiences a collective homecoming. In Isaiah's words, 'The wolf shall live with the sheep and the leopard lie down with the kid... They will neither harm nor destroy in all My holy mountain, for the earth will be full of the knowledge of the Lord as the waters cover the sea' – a new Eden, in other words, and a benign flood. This, for the Hebrew Bible, is the metaphysical structure of history as a whole: harmony, broken by wrongdoing, followed by exile, then acknowledgement and atonement, and eventual return to harmony.

It is with Abraham and Sarah and their descendants, however, that this pattern becomes vivid in a concrete historical way. One of the most striking facts about the patriarchal families is that they all experience exile. Abraham and Isaac are both forced, through famine, to travel to the land of the Philistines. Jacob suffers exile twice, once to escape Esau, a second time to be rejoined with his son Joseph. In none of these is exile the result of sin, and it is the first instance that provides the interpretive clue to the rest. It occurs in the twelfth chapter of Genesis, almost immediately after God's call to Abraham to leave his land, birthplace and father's house. No sooner has he done so than we read: 'There was a famine in the land, and Abram went down to Egypt...' He senses danger, fearing that the Egyptians will kill him and take Sarah into the royal harem. Sarah, saying that she is Abram's sister, is indeed taken into Pharaoh's palace, which is then visited by a series of plagues. Pharaoh then sends the couple away.

The episode seems to disturb the narrative logic of the patriarchal story. Why, if God wants Abraham to go to the land of Canaan, does He force him to leave almost as soon as he has arrived? Midrash Rabbah, an early rabbinic commentary, gives what is undoubtedly the correct answer:

> The Holy One, blessed be He, said to our father Abraham, 'Go forth and tread out a path for your children.' For you find that everything written in connection with Abraham is written in connection with his children. Of Abraham it is written, *And there was a famine in the land*, and of Israel it is written, *For these two years there has been famine in the land*. Of Abraham: *And Abram went down to Egypt*. Of Israel: *And our fathers went down into Egypt*. Of Abraham: *To sojourn there*. Of Israel: *To sojourn in the land are we come*...

And so on through a long series of linguistic and substantive parallels between Abraham's fate and the later experience of the Israelites. The exiles of Abraham, Isaac and Jacob are, in other words, prefigurations of what would later happen to their descendants. It is as if the patriarchs and matriarchs of the Jewish people had *rehearsed in advance* the fate of their children, not necessarily knowing that they were doing so, but none the less *laying the foundations of future hope*. The Israelites, exiled and enslaved, would be liberated and redeemed, not only because God said so, but because He had *done so* in the past. He had already shown, several times in different ways, that He was with the ancestors of the nation, protecting them and bringing them safely back.

By the time we open the book of Exodus, we already know something of immense significance. History is full of unpredictable reversals. Joseph had given the Israelites a haven in the land of Egypt, but there was always the possibility of 'a new king who knew not Joseph'. A protected minority can become a vulnerable minority. There is nothing in the Bible or Jewish faith that speaks of historical inevitability. To live in time is to be exposed to the hazards of time. But Israel knew from its own history that however long it may seem to be delayed, redemption is at hand. God will bring deliverance in the future because He has done so in the past.

It was this that, at a later stage in Jewish history, formed the basis of the vision of hope that is shared by all the prophets. Israel might suffer exile again, but it would return. 'They will come speedily,' prophesies Hosea, 'flying like birds out of Egypt.' 'I will restore the fortunes of My people Israel,' says Amos in the name of God, 'They shall rebuild deserted cities and live in them, they shall plant vineyards and drink their wine, make gardens and eat their fruit.' Moses himself, in one of his darkest visions, ends with the unshakable assurance: 'Yet in spite of this, when they are in the land of their enemies, I will not reject them or abhor them so as to destroy them completely, breaking My covenant with them. I am the Lord their God. But for their sake I will remember the covenant with their ancestors whom I brought out of Egypt in the sight of the nations to be their God. I am the Lord.' Micah said it simply: 'As in the days when you came out of Egypt, I will show them My wonders.' What was, would be again.

The Exodus was more than an event in the past. It was a precursor of redemption in the future. Israel, as Moses warned, would not dwell securely in its land. It would forget its moral and spiritual vocation. It would be attracted to the pagan culture of its neighbours. By so doing it would lose the reason for its existence and find itself unable, at times of crisis, to summon the shared vision and collective energy needed to prevail against neighbouring imperial powers. It would suffer defeat and exile; it would undergo its dark night of the soul; it would, as Ezekiel said, utter the fateful words *avdah tikvatenu*, 'Our hope is destroyed.' But despair would never prevail. In the past, God brought His people from slavery to freedom and from exile to the land, and therefore He would do so again. The Jewish people never completely lost faith in God, because its prophets knew that God would never completely lose faith in His people. History intimated destiny. What happened once would happen again. That is what lies behind the words with which the Haggadah begins: 'Now we are here; next year in the land of Israel. Now we are slaves; next year we will be free.' The Jewish people kept the vision alive. It is not too much to say that the vision kept the Jewish people alive.

It is difficult at this distance in time to realize the depth of the crisis represented by the destruction of the Second Temple in the year 70 CE, and the later suppression of the disastrous Bar Kochba revolt (132–135 CE). The very foundations of Jewish existence had been destroyed. There was now no Temple or Jewish sovereignty. There were no kings or priests or prophets. Jerusalem had been razed to the ground and rebuilt as a Roman city, Aelia Capitolina, in which Jews were forbidden to live.

More than six centuries earlier, following the destruction of the First Temple, the people had come close to despair. A psalm from that period has left us with an indelible record of their mood: 'By the rivers of Babylon we sat and wept when we remembered Zion... How can we sing the songs of the Lord in a strange land?' That moment, though, brought its own consolation. There were prophets of the stature of Jeremiah and Ezekiel to assure the people that they would return. The exile would be finite, temporary. It would last, at most, a single lifetime; and their intuition proved correct. There was no such assurance in Roman times. To be sure, figures like Rabbi Akiva were confident that redemption would come. But his hopes were invested in Bar Kochba, and when that uprising failed, so too did any hope that Israel's fortunes would be restored in the foreseeable future.

A midrash on Jacob's dream of a ladder and angels tells us something of the mood of those times:

> The Holy One, blessed be He, showed Jacob the angel of Babylon ascending and descending, the angel of Media ascending and descending, the angel of Greece ascending and descending, and the angel of Rome ascending [but not descending]. Jacob was afraid. He thought: Is it possible this one will never descend? The Holy One, blessed be He, said to him: *Fear not, My servant Jacob.*

Every other exile had a finite duration, but the fall of Israel under Rome seemed to extend indefinitely into the future.

What happened next is one of the great, if quiet, dramas of history. The Jewish people, so bound to time and space – seeing God in history and their home in a specific land – reconstituted itself as a nation *outside* time and space. Prayer took the place of sacrifice. The study of Torah replaced prophecy. Repentance became a substitute for the great ritual of atonement performed by the High Priest in the Holy of Holies. The synagogue – a building that could be anywhere – became a fragment of the Temple in Jerusalem. The Jewish people itself, once a nation in its own land, became a virtual community scattered through space, bound now by a mystical sense of collective responsibility (Israel, said Rabbi Shimon bar Yochai, is 'like a single body with a single soul: when one is afflicted, all feel the pain'). In exile everywhere, they were at home in a text. The Torah, said the German poet Heinrich Heine, became 'the portable homeland of the Jew'.

These developments did not happen overnight. In a sense, Jews had been preparing them ever since the Babylonian exile. It was then, beginning with Ezra, that a succession of scribes, scholars and sages began to reshape Israel from the people of the land to the people of the book. The result was that Jews succeeded in doing what no other people has ever done. They sustained their identity and way of life through almost two thousand years of exile. Despite the hostility showed to them – Max Weber once described them as a 'pariah people' – they kept their dignity and self-respect. And through some of the worst sufferings ever experienced by a group, they preserved their hope: 'Next year in Jerusalem; next year free'. There is nothing remotely comparable in history. It was the triumph of faith over circumstance.

But there was a price to be paid, namely the almost complete de-politicization of Judaism. To be sure, from the first to the nineteenth centuries, Jews had self-governing powers. They ran their own communities, arbitrated internal disputes and created not just synagogues but also remarkable educational and welfare institutions. But the disastrous failure of the two rebellions against Rome, in 66 and 132 CE, left their mark. Jews did not thereafter fight for their independence. They did not mobilize for their return to Israel. They had learned at great cost that these initiatives were likely to backfire, bringing devastation in their wake. Instead, following the advice of the prophet Jeremiah in an earlier age they sought 'the peace of the city to which they were exiled', waiting patiently for God to bring His people back to Zion.

The tension of waiting was sometimes unbearable, and this gave rise throughout the Middle Ages to a series of messianic movements in which a would-be saviour appeared, promising deliverance. The most famous of these – Shabbatai Zevi in the seventeenth century – was in fact only one of many (Maimonides mentions several in his father's lifetime alone). But these movements, beginning in fevered hope and ending in disillusionment, only served to underscore how dangerous it was to 'force the end'. Jews believed that they would return to Israel, but there was no natural, non-miraculous route from here to there. Throughout the Middle Ages, individual Jews made the journey to the Holy Land, among them Judah Halevi and Nahmanides. There was always a Jewish presence there, though sometimes small and in dire circumstances. In the eighteenth and early nineteenth centuries, followers of both the Hassidic movement and their opponents, disciples of the Vilna Gaon, made their way to Israel in significant numbers. But they came to wait for redemption, not to initiate it.

Three factors changed Jewish attitudes in the course of the nineteenth century. The first was the rise of European nationalism. If the Italians could win their independence, why not the Jews? There was ferment in the air following the French Revolution. A new political era seemed to be dawning, with messianic possibilities. It was no less a figure than Napoleon who, setting out to conquer the Middle East in 1799, issued a call to Jews: 'Israelites arise! Now is the moment which may not return for generations to claim back the rights you have been deprived of for thousands of years, to live again as a nation among nations.' How serious an offer this was, was never put to the test. Napoleon was forced to abandon his military campaign. But a note had been struck and it was echoed, not least in Britain, during the course of the nineteenth century. Figures like Lord Shaftesbury and Colonel Charles Churchill began to advocate Jewish settlement in the Holy Land, partly as a way of advancing British interests in the region, but also, and no less, out of deep belief in the biblical prophecies and a sense that the time was right. The English novelist George Eliot made the rebirth of Jewish nationalism a central theme of her book *Daniel Deronda* (1876). The Damascus Blood Libel of 1840, in which Sir Moses Montefiore and Adolf Cremieux, the lay leaders of British and French Jewry, successfully intervened, demonstrated for the first time the possibility of international Jewish diplomacy. It was in this context that two rabbis, Yehudah Alkalai and Zvi Hirsch Kalischer, began to sketch the outline of a religious Zionism, based less on a state than on agricultural settlements. What was novel in their work was the suggestion that though, ultimately, redemption rested with God, the first and preliminary steps should be taken by Jews themselves.

The second development was a certain secularization of Jewish history. I use this word with some trepidation, but there is no other. It began with Spinoza, a Jew who broke with Judaism, but who in his *Tractatus Theologico-Politicus* (1670) first raised the possibility that Jews might take hold of their fate and re-establish a Jewish state. Spinoza did not believe in a God of history, and thus thought about religion in purely natural terms. No less significant was the influence of the nineteenth century historian Heinrich Graetz, whose writings did much to stimulate Jewish interest and pride in the past. Hess, Pinsker and Herzl were part of the legacy of this process. Seeing themselves as secular Jews, they did not feel themselves constrained merely to wait and pray for a new birth of Jewish liberty. The earliest of them, Hess, was also the most insightful. He guessed what Herzl later discovered, that support for Jewish nationalism would come not from the culturally integrated Jews of the West but from the religious heartlands of Eastern Europe. It was the meeting of secular and religious that brought about what neither could have done on their own.

The third and decisive factor, however, was the rise in antisemitism in the second half of the nineteenth century. It was this that made the return not merely possible but urgent and necessary. The irony is that this seems to have been foreseen from the beginning. In Babylon in the sixth century BCE Ezekiel had already prophesied: 'You say, "We want to be like the nations, like the peoples of the world…" but what you have in mind will never happen. As surely as I live, declares the Sovereign Lord, I will rule over you with a mighty hand and an outstretched arm and outpoured wrath.' The Mishnaic teacher Rabbi Yehoshua predicted that an evil ruler would arise 'whose decrees will be as harsh as those of Haman' and drive Jews back to their faith and land. What is common to both these teachings is the belief that Jews would not seek to return of their own accord. They might try to assimilate, but they would fail. Love of the land would not be enough to move Jews to action. The hostility of their neighbours would.

So Zionism was born. It would be hard to find any other movement that brought together so many dissonant, competing visions. There were utopian religious Zionists like Rav Kook and practical religious Zionists like Rabbi Reines. Among the secularists were political Zionists like Herzl, cultural Zionists such as Ahad ha-Am, Nietzscheans like Berdichevski, Tolstoyans of the calibre of Aaron David Gordon, and dozens of others, each with their own carefully wrought utopia. They clashed, at times vehemently. Yet out of their clamorous discord came one of the most astonishing achievements of all time.

The creation of the State of Israel was fraught with difficulty. Despite the Balfour Declaration (1917), in which Britain, the new mandatory power in Palestine, promised Jews a national home, there was intense opposition – from the Arab world, other international forces, from politicians in Britain, and at times from Jews themselves. For thirty years, various compromises were proposed, all accepted by Jews and rejected by their opponents. On the day the State was proclaimed, it was attacked on all fronts by its neighbours. Since then it has lived under constant threat of war, violence, terror and delegitimization. Yet it has achieved wondrous things.

Through it Hebrew, the language of the Bible, was reborn as a living tongue. Jewish communities under threat have been rescued, including those like the Jews of Ethiopia who had little contact with other Jews for centuries. Jews have come to Israel from over a hundred countries, representing the entire lexicon of cultural diversity. A desolate landscape has bloomed again. Jerusalem has been rebuilt. The world of Torah scholarship, devastated by the Holocaust, has been revived and the sound of learning echoes throughout the land. Economically, politically, socially and culturally, Israel's achievements are unmatched by any country of its age and size. The sages said that, at the crossing of the Red Sea, the simplest Jew saw miracles that the greatest of later prophets were not destined to see. That, surely, was the privilege of those who witnessed Israel's rebirth and youth. The messiah has not come. Israel is not yet at peace. The Temple has not been rebuilt. Our time is not yet redemption. Yet many, if not all, of the prayers of two thousand years have been answered. No one, reviewing this singular history, can doubt that faith makes a difference; that a nation's history is shaped by what it believes.

Judah Halevi once compared the Jewish people to a seed. In his Kuzari, a fictional dialogue between a rabbi and the king of the Khazars, the king asks the rabbi a pointed question. How is it that, if you are truly chosen by God, you are everywhere subjected to humiliation and persecution? Where is your greatness? The rabbi replies: We are like the seed of a great tree. When first planted in the ground it appears to disintegrate. But it is actually all the while gathering strength to grow. Eventually it will put forth roots and shoots and begin to reach toward heaven.

That is what Pesach was during more than eighteen centuries of exile and dispersion: a seed planted in Jewish memory, waiting to be activated and to grow. Without it Jews would certainly have disappeared. Lacking hope of return – hope tempered by faith into a certainty like steel – they would have made their peace with their condition, merged into their surrounding societies and ambient cultures and vanished, like every other culture deprived of a home. Pesach, like a seed frozen in suspended animation, contained the latent energy that led Jews in the twentieth century to create the single most remarkable accomplishment in the modern world, the rebirth of Israel, the land, the state, the nation and the people. Micah's vision, and Ezekiel's, and Moses', came true.

The Irish historian Conor Cruise O'Brien once remarked that Jews who see themselves as unreligious are sometimes very religious indeed. That was true of Hess, Pinsker, Herzl, Chaim Weizmann, David Ben-Gurion and many other heroes and pioneers of the return to Zion. They were not 'spiritual' nor did they observe many of the commandments. But the vision of the prophets and the covenant of Jewish history flowed through their veins. God works through people; sometimes, so the prophets taught, without their conscious knowledge and consent. It is difficult to reflect deeply on the rebirth of Israel without sensing the touch of heaven in the minds of men and women, leading them to play their parts in a drama so much greater than any individual could have executed, even conceived. The historian Barbara Tuchman, writes, 'Viewing this strange and singular history one cannot escape the impression that it must contain some special significance for the history of mankind, that in some way, whether one believes in divine providence or inscrutable circumstance, the Jews have been singled out to carry the tale of human fate.'

Who then wrote the script of the Jewish drama? God, or the Jewish people? Or was it, as the sages taught, an inextricable combination of both: God as he was heard by the people, and the people as they responded to God? Isaac Bashevis Singer came close when he said, 'God is a writer and we are both the heroes and the readers.' One thing is certain, that without Pesach, celebrated over the centuries, the State of Israel would not have been born. The prophets were right: the exodus of the past contained within it the exodus of the future; and I, born in the same year as the State, can only say, 'Blessed are you, O Lord... who kept us alive and sustained us and brought us to this day.'

8

An Afternoon
in Jerusalem

It happened in Jerusalem, one Shabbat afternoon towards the end of the Gulf War. Our family had gone to the holy city to find peace. Instead we found ourselves in the midst of war. Within weeks of our arrival it became clear that the Middle East was yet again about to be engulfed in conflict. Iraq had invaded Kuwait and a massive international force led by the United States was ready to intervene. Israel was not involved, yet we knew it would be the primary target of Iraqi weapons. So it proved to be. Thirty-nine times during those weeks we heard the sirens wail their warning of SCUD missiles. Each time we put on our gas masks and retreated to our sealed rooms, not knowing where the next attack would land or whether it would contain chemical weapons. It was another reminder that it is not easy to find peace as a Jew.

Yet, as we stepped out into the Jerusalem sunlight there was peace. The city breathed the stillness of Shabbat. The late afternoon sun was turning the houses, of Jerusalem stone, into burnished gold. As we looked across the valley to the walls of the Old City we could understand why, long ago, people had called this the city of peace and why, even when it lay in ruins, Jews were convinced that the Divine presence never left Jerusalem.

We had been invited by one of our neighbours to *seudah shlishit*, the third Shabbat meal, the meal that symbolizes the coming together of God and the Jewish people – 'You are one, and Your name is one, and who is like your people Israel, a nation unique on earth?' When we arrived we discovered that they had also invited a group of Rumanian Jews who had recently come to make their home in Israel. They had made the journey as a group because they were a choir. In Rumania they had sung the songs of Jewish hope and longing. Now, in Jerusalem, they began to sing again around the table, beginning with the twenty-third Psalm that Jews have long been accustomed to sing on Shabbat afternoon: 'The Lord is my shepherd, I shall lack nothing… Even though I walk through the valley of the shadow of death I will fear no evil, for You are with me.' Those words, thousands of years old, caught the mood of the moment. This was peace in the midst of war, a pool of stillness in the turmoil of the world.

Then a rather moving thing happened. As the sounds of the choir reverberated around the alleyways of our quiet corner of Jerusalem, people from the neighbouring houses began to appear, drawn by the music. One by one they slipped in through the open door and stood around and, hesitantly at first, then with growing confidence, joined the singing. Here was an Israeli artist, there a new arrival from Russia, here an American investment banker, there a family from South Africa, and in the doorway a group of tourists who happened to be walking by and had stopped to see what was happening and then found themselves caught up by the embrace of the atmosphere. No one spoke; no one wanted to break the mood. We continued to sing the songs of Shabbat afternoon. As the sun began to set behind the hills, I could feel the Divine presence among us, joining our words to those of a hundred generations of Jews, uniting them into a vast choral symphony, the love song of a people for God, and I sensed something of the mystery and majesty of the Jewish people, and I knew that it was this that I had come to Jerusalem to find.

We had come together, each of us as the result of a long journey, in some cases physical, in others spiritual, and in many, both. We each had stories to tell of how we came to be in Jerusalem that afternoon. But just as our individual voices had united to sing the words of our ancestors' songs, so our stories were part of a larger story. Our personal routes were stages on the most remarkable journey ever undertaken by a people, spanning almost every country on the face of the earth, and four thousand years of time. If we had been able, then and there, to trace back the history of our parents and theirs across the generations, we would have been awestruck at its drama and scope. Was there anything that could remotely compare to the long Jewish journey to Jerusalem? Was this, I thought, not the most vivid testimony imaginable to the power and endurance of faith?

I thought back to the beginning of the journey, when God spoke to Abraham and Sarah and beckoned them towards an unknown land. Then, centuries later, with the Israelites enslaved in Egypt, God called Moses and told him to lead the people to freedom across the desert to the land flowing with milk and honey. I thought of David who consecrated Jerusalem as his capital and brought the ark of the covenant into the city, singing and dancing, and of Solomon who built the Temple and asked God that it should become the home of the prayers of all mankind. I thought of Jeremiah who foresaw its destruction, and Isaiah who told the Israelites that they would one day return, and Ezra and Nehemiah who led the people back. I thought of the Second Temple and its defilement, and of the Maccabees who delivered it once again into Jewish hands, and the terrible devastation that later occurred at the hands of the Romans. I recalled the story of the rabbis of the first century who wept as they saw a fox entering the ruined Holy of Holies, and of Rabbi Akiva who comforted them and assured them that Jerusalem would one day be rebuilt.

For eighteen centuries, Jews were scattered across the world, but they never forgot Jerusalem. They prayed toward it. They mourned it even during their celebrations. Each year, on the Ninth of Av, the anniversary of the destruction, they sat and wept as if they had just been bereaved. Like the survivors of an earlier catastrophe, they said, 'If I forget you, O Jerusalem, may my right hand forget its skill, may my tongue cling to the roof of my mouth if I do not remember you, if I do not consider Jerusalem my highest joy.' Each Pesach at the climax of the *seder* they said *Leshanah haba'ah bi-Yerushalayim*. 'Next year in Jerusalem.' The next year they said the same.

I thought of the Jews of the Middle Ages – among them Judah Halevi, Maimonides and Nahmanides – who journeyed there, often amidst great danger. I thought of my great-grandfather who made the journey there in the 1870s, travelling from Lithuania with a Sefer Torah in his arms, and who wrote one of the great histories of Jerusalem. I thought of those who fought in Israel's wars, in 1948 to defend the newborn state from destruction, and who, in 1967, reunified the divided city. And I thought of us, gathered there that Shabbat afternoon singing songs of faith, finding peace in the midst of battle, and converging from our many countries of origin on the place to which Jews had so long prayed. I understood then that to be a Jew is to be part of that journey, begun by Abraham and Sarah and continued by their children ever since – not just to a place but to a set of ideals, a way of life, a state of collective grace – and that I had caught a glimpse of the eternal people joining their voices across space and time and singing its never-ending song.

At any time in those long centuries the journey might have ended. It might have done so at the very beginning, when Abraham arrived to find the land starved by famine and was compelled to travel to Egypt. It might have done so half-a-dozen times during Moses' leadership when the people, fatigued and frightened by the journey, wanted to turn round and go back. It might have come to a close with the destruction of the First or Second Temples, had there not been prophets and sages to lift Jews from the abyss of despair. In their long centuries of dispersion Jews might simply have abandoned thoughts of return. But Jews are an obstinate people, and were never reconciled to the loss of Jerusalem. They carried with them the pain and the hope, the memory of the ruins and the vision of a city rebuilt. Never, after that afternoon, could I treat lightly the ideas of memory and prayer and faith. Jews never forgot Jerusalem. They prayed for it. They believed they would return. Had even one generation failed to do these things, the journey would have ended and much of Jewish history would have come to nothing. Faith had brought us to that time and place to see the fulfilment of our ancestors' dreams.

Jerusalem is a place, but it is more than a place. It became a metaphor for the collective destination of the Jewish people. A city is what we build together, individually through our homes, collectively through our public spaces. So Jerusalem became a symbol of what Jews were summoned to build by creating a city of righteousness worthy of being a home for the Divine presence. Its stones would be good deeds, and its mortar, relationships of generosity and trust. Its houses would be families, its defensive walls, schools and houses of study. Shabbat and the festivals would be its public parks and gardens. For Jews believed that, even in a violent and destructive world, heaven could be built on earth. It was their most daring vision. The architect of the city would be God. The builders would be ordinary men and women. It would be a Jewish city, but it would be open to all, and people from all faiths would come and be moved by its beauty.

So Jerusalem, the 'faithful city', became the destination of the Jewish journey, which began with Abraham and Sarah and will only be complete at the end of days. This is how the prophet Isaiah envisioned it, in words that for millennia have captured the human imagination:

> In the last days
> The mountain of the Lord's Temple will be established
> As chief among the mountains;
> It will be raised above the hills,
> And all the nations will stream to it.
> Many peoples will come and say,
> 'Come, let us go up to the mountain of the Lord,
> to the house of the God of Jacob.
> He will teach us His ways,
> So that we may walk in His path.'
> The law will go forth from Zion,
> And the word of the Lord from Jerusalem.
> He will judge between the nations
> And will settle disputes for many peoples.
> They will beat their swords into ploughshares
> And their spears into pruning hooks.
> Nation will not take up sword against nation,
> Nor will they train for war any more. (Isaiah 2:2–4)

These words, among the most influential ever written, sum up much of Jewish faith. They epitomize what it might be like to 'perfect the world under the sovereignty of God'. And as they journeyed through the centuries and continents, Jews carried this vision with them, believing that their task was to be true to their faith, to be loyal to God, to exemplify His ways to mankind, and to build a world at peace with itself by learning and teaching how to respect the freedom and dignity of others.

As I remembered all this, I wondered at the tenacity of our ancestors. At times it must have seemed a vain hope. How, given all their suffering through the ages, did they continue to believe in the possibility of a city 'redeemed by justice' whose name was peace? Was their faith blind, or was it something else, a faith so strong that it was capable of surviving catastrophe and still believing that people could change, and therefore the world could change? Perhaps there never was a more revolutionary faith. Certainly no people has ever held to its beliefs with more tenacity.

And as the singing ended, and Shabbat drew to a close, I understood that to be a Jew is to join the journey of our people, the story of Pesach and the long walk across centuries and continents from exile to homecoming. There is no story like it, and the journey is not yet complete.

9

The Universal Story

Observe [these decrees] carefully, for this is your wisdom and understanding in the eyes
of the nations who, will hear about all these decrees and say, 'Surely this great nation is
a wise and understanding people.'   Deuteronomy 4:6

n his 1849 novel *White-Jacket*, Herman Melville made clear how much
the American dream owed to the story of Israel:

> We Americans are the peculiar, chosen people – the Israel
> of our time; we bear the ark of the liberties of the world.
> God has predestined, mankind expects, great things from
> our race; and great things we feel in our souls. The rest of
> the nations must soon be in our rear. We are pioneers of
> the world; the advance-guard, sent on through the
> wilderness of untried things, to break a new path in the
> New World that is ours.

The story of Pesach is intensely particularistic. It tells of how one people, long ago,
experienced oppression and were led to liberty through a long and arduous journey across
the desert. Yet no story has had greater impact on the political development of the West.
Moses knew that the events of his time had a significance that went far beyond those days
and that people; that they would eventually become a source of inspiration to other
nations. So, remarkably, it came to be. When black Americans sang, 'Let my people go',
when South American liberation theologians in the 1960s based their work on the book
of Exodus, when Nelson Mandela entitled his autobiography *The Long Walk to Freedom*,
each was adopting Israel's story and making it their own. More than Plato's *Republic* or
Aristotle's *Politics*, more than Rousseau's *The Social Contract* or Marx's *Das Kapital*, the
Pesach story has been the West's most influential source-book of liberty. 'Since the
Exodus,' said Heinrich Heine, 'Freedom has always spoken with a Hebrew accent.'

Its first major impact was on the politics of England in the seventeenth century and came about as the result of three factors. The first was the Reformation, with its emphasis on the Bible, as opposed to the Church, as a source of authority. The second was the invention of printing in the mid-fifteenth century by Gutenberg in Germany and Caxton in Britain (printing had in fact been invented in China several centuries earlier, but had not spread). For the first time, books were available in large numbers and at a price ordinary people could afford, and an overwhelming proportion of the first books produced were Bibles. A million of them were in circulation in Britain by 1640. The third factor was the translation of the Bible into the vernacular, which had been resisted, even forbidden by law, until then. Tyndale's pioneering translation was published in 1530 and was followed by many others until the King James Bible, one of the great influences on English language and literature, appeared in 1611.

The result was that for the first time, people other than priests came into direct contact with the Hebrew Bible, and its effect was immense. It taught that each individual had dignity as God's image and was entitled to freedom from tyranny, and to equality before the law. It told of how prophets criticized kings and that unjust rulers could be overthrown. The story of the Exodus itself taught the fundamental difference between might and right, power and justice, rule and authority. It introduced an ethical dimension into the politics of power.

The Hebrew Bible exercised a decisive influence on political thinkers in the seventeenth century. John Milton wrote that 'there are no songs comparable to the songs of Zion; no orations equal to those of the prophets; and no politics like those which the Scriptures teach' and called the Bible 'that book within whose sacred context all wisdom is enfolded'. The great political theorists of the seventeenth century, Thomas Hobbes and John Locke, cite it constantly in their works. There are 657 biblical references in *Leviathan* alone. The person, though, who did most to turn it into political reality was Oliver Cromwell, leader of the parliamentary party in England's civil war. The English, he never tired of saying, were the 'new Israel', and in his first parliamentary speech of the protectorship, he described the Exodus as 'the only parallel of God's dealing with us that I know'.

In a square in the centre of Philadelphia, in front of Independence Hall where America's Declaration of Independence and Constitution were drafted, stands one of the great symbols of the nation, the Liberty Bell, visited by more than a million tourists each year. Around the top of the bell are words taken from the twenty-fifth chapter of Leviticus: 'Proclaim liberty throughout the land to all the inhabitants thereof.' The presence of this biblical quotation is no coincidence. It exemplifies the close relationship between the Hebrew Bible and America's founders. More even than in the case of England under Cromwell, America was the great attempt to construct a society on biblical lines, following in the footsteps of Moses.

Already in 1620 the Pilgrim Fathers, seeing themselves as a 'continuation and extension of the Jewish church', pledged themselves in a covenant to create a body politic, inspired by the example of biblical Israel, and frame 'just and equal laws'. In 1776, in Philadelphia itself, Benjamin Franklin and Thomas Jefferson met to design a seal for the new United States. Franklin proposed that it should bear a picture of Moses lifting his staff to divide the Red Sea, together with the motto, 'Rebellion to tyrants is obedience to God.' Jefferson preferred a less aggressive design: the Israelites in the wilderness being 'led by a cloud by day and a pillar of fire at night'. In 1799, delivering a thanksgiving sermon in Massachusetts, Abiel Abbot expressed an idea that by then was widely held: 'It has often been remarked that the people of the United States come nearer to a parallel with Ancient Israel, than any other nation upon the globe. Hence "Our American Israel" is a term frequently used; and common consent allows it apt and proper.' England was Egypt, America the promised land, and the United States the fulfilment of the old-new journey to liberty.

No one expressed more fulsomely the debt owed to the story of Israel than America's second president, John Adams, who in 1809 wrote to a friend:

> I will insist that the Hebrews have done more to civilize men than any other nation. If I were an atheist, and believed in blind eternal fate, I should still believe that fate had ordained the Jews to be the most essential instrument for civilizing the nations. If I were an atheist of the other sect, who believe or pretend to believe that all is ordered by chance, I should believe that chance had ordered the Jews to preserve and propagate to all mankind the doctrine of a supreme, intelligent, wise, almighty sovereign of the universe, which I believe to be the great essential principle of all morality, and consequently of all civilization.

The supreme expression of the American faith was the Declaration of Independence (1776), largely drafted by Jefferson. In one of the most famous of all political affirmations, it stated: 'We hold these truths to be self-evident, that all men are created equal, that they are endowed by their Creator with certain unalienable rights, that among these are life, liberty and the pursuit of happiness.' The striking thing about this sentence is that 'these truths' are anything *but* self-evident. Most societies at most times have held as self-evidently true that men are created *un*equal. Some are born to rule, others to be ruled. Every ancient myth, dogma and creed with the exception of the Hebrew Bible was a justification for inequality and hierarchy, a canonization of the status quo. Plato held that society was stratified into three classes, guardians (philosopher-kings), auxiliaries (soldiers) and the rest; and that whether or not these distinctions were given by birth, people should be taught that they were. Aristotle believed that some people were born to be slaves. Gradations of class were written into the structure of reality. The strong, powerful, wealthy and high-born were meant (whether by nature or God) to exercise supremacy over others. Jefferson's 'truths' were self-evident only to a culture steeped in the Hebrew Bible, from its opening declaration that the human individual is 'the image of God', to its enactment in history in the Exodus and the covenant at Mount Sinai.

We owe to Robert Bellah the idea that America has a 'civil religion' – a set of beliefs and a shared narrative, a faith, that underlie its public and political life. One of the great differences between the United States and Europe is that political, especially presidential, discourse continues to be religious to this day. Every inaugural address, with the sole exception of Washington's second (hardly a speech at all; it contains a mere two paragraphs), contains a reference to God. There is, at it were, a public theology that has been part of America's political culture throughout.

What is fascinating is that this civil religion differs in significant respects from America's congregational life, which is overwhelmingly Christian. American presidents do not tend to speak in explicitly Christian terms. They talk instead of divine providence and the sovereignty of God. They refer to covenant and the moral bonds by which societies are sustained. The liberty of which they speak is biblical rather than libertarian: a matter less of rights than responsibilities, not the freedom to do what one likes, but the freedom to do what is correct and thus contribute to the common good. They invoke an essentially Mosaic narrative of America as the promised land to which successive generations of immigrants have come to find freedom from oppression and build, in John Winthrop's famous phrase, 'a city upon a hill'.

This uniquely American rhetoric deserves more attention than it has received. It is not merely a *façon de parler*, an empty convention, but the way in which successive generations of citizens have understood and rededicated themselves to the terms of their shared project. Regardless of whether individual presidents have been personally religious (Eisenhower once reportedly said, 'Our government makes no sense unless it is founded in a deeply felt religious faith – and I don't care what it is'), they have had to adopt this language in order to keep faith with the past. Its connection with Pesach is direct. The great American political addresses are the most sustained attempt in the modern world to place the themes of exodus, redemption and the presence of God in history at the centre of public life.

The vision was first set out by John Winthrop aboard the *Arabella* in 1630 as it sailed for New England. Speaking in conscious imitation of Moses at the end of his life, he invited his fellow settlers to 'enter into a covenant' with God and to 'follow the counsel of Micah, to do justly, to love mercy and to walk humbly with our God.' If they failed to live up to the covenant 'the Lord will surely break out in wrath against us', but if they were true to its terms, 'The Lord will be our God, and delight to dwell among us, as his own people, and will command a blessing upon us in all our ways.' They would then find 'that the God of Israel is among us'.

American presidents did not use such explicitly biblical language. A hundred and fifty years had passed, and unlike the pilgrim fathers they were not speaking to a sect but to what had become a great and independent nation. Yet their sentiments were the same. In the first inaugural in 1789, George Washington declared, 'It would be peculiarly improper to omit in this first official act my fervent supplications to that Almighty Being who rules over the universe,' and warned that 'the propitious smiles of Heaven can never be expected on a nation that disregards the eternal rules of order and right which Heaven itself has ordained.' In his second inaugural (1805), Thomas Jefferson alluded to the exodus: 'I shall need, too, the favour of that Being in whose hands we are, who led our fathers, as Israel of old, from their native land and planted them in a country flowing with all the necessaries and comforts of life.'

It might be thought that this kind of language would have been confined to those early years of independence, when the sense was still strong that something great, even miraculous, was at work in America. Yet in 1961, John F. Kennedy was still using the same biblical cadences:

> I have sworn before you and Almighty God the same solemn oath our forebears prescribed nearly a century and three quarters ago. The world is very different now. For man holds in his mortal hands the power to abolish all forms of human poverty and all forms of human life. And yet the same revolutionary beliefs for which our forebears fought are still at issue around the globe – the belief that the rights of man come not from the generosity of the state, but from the hand of God... With a good conscience our only sure reward, with history the final judge of our deeds, let us go forth to lead the land we love, asking His blessing and His help, but knowing that here on earth God's work must truly be our own.

Succeeding the assassinated Kennedy, Lyndon Baines Johnson gave a particularly striking account of 'the American covenant':

> They came here – the exile and the stranger, brave but frightened – to find a place where a man could be his own man. They made a covenant with this land. Conceived in justice, written in liberty, bound in union, it was meant one day to inspire the hopes of all mankind; and it binds us still. If we keep its terms, we shall flourish... Under this covenant of justice, liberty and union we have become a nation – prosperous, great and mighty. And we have kept our freedom. But we have no promise from God that our greatness will endure. We have been allowed by Him to seek greatness with the sweat of our hands and the strength of our spirit.

In 2001, the vision still drove George W. Bush. Pledging himself to work for a nation of justice and opportunity, he added:

> I know this is in our reach because we are guided by a power larger than ourselves who creates us equal in His image... Americans are generous and strong and decent, not because we believe in ourselves, but because we hold beliefs beyond ourselves... We are not this [nation's] story's author, who fills time and eternity with his purpose. Yet his purpose is achieved in our duty, and our duty is fulfilled in service to one another.

No other country in the West uses this intensely religious vocabulary. It is particularly striking in view of the fact that the American constitution, in the form of the First Amendment, formally separates religion and state.

It was the great French writer, Alexis de Tocqueville, who in the 1830s, in the course of his classic *Democracy in America*, explained the paradox. There was a separation between religion and state, but not between religion and society. 'Religion in America,' he wrote, 'takes no direct part in the government of society, but it must be regarded as the first of their political institutions.' What he meant was that, though it had no power, it had enormous influence. It sustained families. It bound communities together. It prompted people to join voluntary organizations for the promotion of the common good. It was the basis of a shared morality which, precisely because it was upheld by faith, did not have constantly to be enforced by law. 'In France,' he noted, 'I had almost always seen the spirit of religion and the spirit of freedom marching in opposite directions. In America I found they were intimately united and that they reigned in common over the same country.'

In a strange way civil religion has the same relationship to the United States as Pesach does to the Jewish people. It is, first and foremost, not a philosophy but a story. It tells of how a persecuted group escaped from the old world and made a hazardous journey to an unknown land, there to construct a new society, in Abraham Lincoln's famous words, 'conceived in liberty, and dedicated to the proposition that all men are created equal.' Like the Pesach story, it must be told repeatedly, as it is in every inaugural address. It defines the nation, not merely in terms of its past but also as a moral-spiritual commitment to the future. It is no accident that the founders of America turned to the Hebrew Bible, nor that successive presidents have done likewise, because there is no other text in Western literature that draws these themes – history, providence, covenant, responsibility, 'the exile and the stranger', the need to fight for freedom in every generation – together in a vision that is at once political and spiritual. Israel, ancient and modern, and the United States are the two supreme examples of societies constructed in conscious pursuit of an idea.

There have been four revolutions in the West in modern times: the British and American, and the French and Russian. In Britain and America the source of inspiration was the Hebrew Bible. In France and Russia it was the great alternative to the Bible, namely philosophy. The theorist of the French revolution was Jean-Jacques Rousseau; of the Russian, Karl Marx. The contrast between them is vivid. Britain and America succeeded in creating a free society, not without civil war, but at least without tyranny and terror. The French and Russian revolutions began with a dream of utopia and ended with a nightmare of bloodshed and the suppression of human rights. The great *philosophes*, Helvetius, Rousseau, Fichte, Hegel, Saint-Simon and Marx, created not freedom but its betrayal, what J. L. Talmon called 'totalitarian democracy'.

Why did Britain and America succeed where France and Russia failed? The explanation is surely complex but much – perhaps all – turns on how a society answers the question: who is the ultimate sovereign, God or man? The British and Americans gave the first answer, the French and Russian revolutionaries the second. For the British and American architects of liberty, God was the supreme power. All authority was therefore subject to the transcendental demands of the moral law. For the French and Russian ideologists, ultimate value lay in the state or the collective. The failure of the French and Russian revolutions is the most compelling testimony to the fact that when human beings arrogate supreme power to themselves, politics loses its sole secure defence of freedom. Democracy, in and of itself, is not enough. As Tocqueville and John Stuart Mill warned, it merely replaces the tyranny of a minority with the tyranny of the majority. From ancient Athens to the Third Reich and the Soviet Union, no political system that vested absolute power in its rulers, however elected, has resisted corruption. Societies that exile God lead to the eclipse of man. That is why the Exodus narrative remains the canonical text of liberty. It is only when a society acknowledges God that man is protected from his fellow man. As Lord Acton put it in his description of biblical politics:

> The inspired men who rose in unfailing succession to prophesy against the usurper and the tyrant, constantly proclaimed that the laws, which were divine, were paramount over sinful rulers, and appealed from the established authorities, from the kings, the priests, and the princes of the people, to the healing forces that slept in the uncorrupted consciences of the masses. Thus the example of the Hebrew nation laid down the parallel lines on which all freedom has been won – the doctrine of national tradition and the doctrine of the higher law; the principle that a constitution grows from a root, by process of development, and not of essential change; and the principle that all political authorities must be tested and reformed according to a code which was not made by man.

The Exodus is the inexhaustible source of inspiration to all those who long for freedom. It taught that right was sovereign over might; that freedom and justice must belong to all, not some; that, under God, all human beings are equal; and that over all earthly powers is the supreme power, the King of Kings, who hears the cry of the oppressed and who intervenes in history to liberate slaves. It took many centuries for this vision to become the shared property of the liberal democracies of the West; and there is no guarantee that it will remain so. Freedom is a moral achievement, and without a constant effort of education it atrophies and must be fought for again. Nowhere more than on Pesach, though, do we see how the story of one people can become the inspiration of many; how, loyal to its faith across the centuries, the Jewish people became the guardians of a vision through which, ultimately, 'all the peoples of the earth will be blessed'.

10

The Omer and the Politics of Torah

So teach us to number our days, that we may get us a heart of wisdom
Psalm 90:12

Some of Judaism's most profound truths are to be found, not in texts but in time, in the Jewish calendar itself. Nowhere is this more so than in the case of *sefirat ha-omer*, the counting of the forty-nine days from Pesach to Shavuot. 'From the day after the Sabbath [understood by Jewish tradition as the first day of Pesach], the day you brought the sheaf of the wave offering, count seven full weeks. Count fifty days up to the day after the seventh Sabbath, and then present an offering of new grain to the Lord' (Leviticus 23:15–16).

These words contain no obvious political dimension. The counting of the days has to do with the period of the harvest in the land of Israel. Immediately after the first day of Passover, an offering was made of the first produce of the barley crop. Seven weeks later, on the festival of Shavuot, firstfruits were brought in thanksgiving. The period between was one in which the Israelites were especially mindful of Divine blessing and protection. It was God who had 'brought forth bread from the ground', who sent the rain that made the crops grow and protected them from damage and storm. At no other time was the presence of God in nature – 'the force that through the green fuse drives the flower' – so apparent. So Israel was to count the days, giving thanks for the blessing of each.

But Jewish tradition rightly saw a quite different meaning to the act of counting days. Among the revolutions brought about by the Torah was the shift of consciousness from nature to history. The Jewish festivals are not only about the seasons of the year. They are also about decisive events in the birth of a people. Pesach is about the exodus from Egypt. Sukkot represents the forty years of wandering in the wilderness when the Israelites had only temporary homes. There is no explicit connection between Shavuot and a historical event, but tradition understood it as the anniversary of the giving of the Torah at Mount Sinai. This connection gives an entirely new significance to the counting of the Omer.

The forty-nine days mark the period between leaving Egypt and the day the Israelites stood at the foot of the mountain and received their constitution as a 'kingdom of priests and a holy nation'. According to Maimonides, the people counted the days in longing as they approached the moment of revelation. For the Jewish mystics, the days represent the gradual purification of the Israelites from the corrosive effects of slavery. For Nachmanides, they mean that Pesach and Shavuot are actually a single extended festival. Just as Sukkot is followed seven days later by Shemini Atseret, so Pesach is followed seven weeks later by Shavuot. The days of the Omer are the equivalent of *chol ha-moed*, intermediate days of the festival.

What each of these interpretations implies is that Pesach does not stand alone, because the exodus as an event does not stand alone. Leaving Egypt was only the beginning of freedom. Without a moral code – the commandments heard at Sinai – the Israelites might have gained release from oppression, but they had not yet acquired liberty. The counting of the days expresses the unbreakable connection between Pesach and Shavuot as stages on a single journey from slavery to redemption. Freedom begins with exodus but it reaches its fulfilment in the acceptance of a code of conduct, the Torah, freely offered by God, freely accepted by the people. The counting of the Omer is thus an act of retracing the steps from individual freedom to a free society.

In one of the most influential political essays of the twentieth century, *Two Concepts of Liberty*, the late Sir Isaiah Berlin made a distinction between what he called 'negative' and 'positive' freedom. Negative freedom means freedom *from* coercion and constraint. It is the ability to do what I want. Positive freedom is freedom *to*: to act in my own best interests, or in accordance with my 'true' self, or some other fundamental purpose. Writing in 1957 in the aftermath of the Holocaust, and at a time when the Soviet Union was in full force, Berlin was concerned to argue the case for liberty against totalitarianism. He knew as well as anyone that even the most brutal regime was capable of arguing that it alone gave people true freedom. That was because Jean-Jacques Rousseau and Karl Marx, two prophets of totalitarianism, both claimed to have finally understood the meaning of liberty. For Rousseau, freedom meant merging your individual will with the will of society as a whole. For Marx it meant collective ownership of capital so that the rich could no longer oppress the poor. Marx spoke of freeing the workers from their chains, Rousseau of 'forcing men to be free'. Berlin was rightly concerned with the crimes committed in the name of liberty and therefore argued in favour of negative freedom alone. A society should leave people as free as possible to do what they want. Anything else – any form of positive freedom – opened the doors to tyranny.

Berlin's analysis is impressive but wrong. There are few faiths that have reflected as deeply on the meaning of freedom as Judaism. Pesach is *zman cherutenu*, the 'festival of freedom'. The biblical account of the exodus includes a declaration on the part of God which uses four different words to describe freedom (one of the reasons for the four cups of wine at the seder service): 'I am the Lord and I will *free* you from the burdens of the Egyptians and *deliver* you from slavery to them. I will *redeem* you with an outstretched arm and with mighty judgement. I will *take* you as My people, and I will be your God.' Clearly, for the Torah, freedom is a process, a complex idea that cannot be reduced to simple formulae.

To understand the biblical approach to freedom we have to remember that the Torah describes two disasters, each of which is a symbol of a world gone wrong. The second is slavery in Egypt. The first is the Flood. The second represents totalitarianism. The first was the result, not of too oppressive an order, but the opposite: lawlessness, chaos, violence, the absence of restraints, what Hobbes called the war of 'all against all'. If freedom is the ability to do what we wish, then it means freedom for the violent against the peaceful, the aggressive against the passive, the exploitative against the trusting. It means freedom for the strong but not the weak, the cruel but not the kind, the rich but not the poor. That is why the theorists of liberty in the seventeenth and eighteenth centuries did not call it freedom at all. They called it 'licence'. Negative freedom in Berlin's sense cannot be sufficient for a just and gracious society. It brings individual but not collective liberty. It favours some but not all.

That is what makes the Torah's approach to freedom so rich and subtle. There is a biblical word for negative freedom, namely *chofesh*. That is what a person receives when he or she is released from slavery. They now no longer have someone ordering them to do this or that. They have become their own masters. That, for the Torah, is an essential precondition of human dignity. As we saw in an earlier chapter, many of the institutions of Judaism – from Shabbat to the release of slaves and cancellation of debts in the seventh year and the return of ancestral land in the fiftieth – are about this kind of freedom, about not being enslaved or indebted to someone else. When the poet Naftali Herz Imber sat down to compose *Hatikvah*, the national anthem of the state of Israel, he used this word. He spoke of the Jewish hope to be *am chofshi be'artzenu*, 'a free people in our own land'. *Chofesh* means freedom as personal independence.

But independence is only half of the human situation. The first time the Torah uses the words *lo tov*, 'not good', it is to make this point: 'It is not good for man to be alone.' Human beings cannot survive in isolation. We are, said Aristotle, 'political animals', or as Maimonides put it, more Jewishly, we are 'social animals'. We need the assistance of others for our most basic requirements of food, shelter and defence. The very process of procreation needs partnership. We want to be independent, but we are also and inescapably interdependent. From this flows the whole drama and pathos of the human situation. Hegel once put the problem simply by asking, what do porcupines do in the winter? If they stay apart, they freeze. If they come too close, they injure one another. The art is to find the right balance between closeness and distance. So it is with us.

We need one another to survive. But the very act of forming a partnership with someone else creates potential conflict. I want this; you want that. Whose will is to prevail? If mine, then you suffer. If yours, then I suffer. The human condition is fraught with the tension of clashing interests, desires, passions and pursuits. It happens within marriages, families, communities, societies and between nations, and it leads to violence and sometimes war. The problem of freedom is never as simple as its theorists would like it to be.

The classic solution – it has appeared in almost infinite forms since the birth of civilization – is to use force, centralized in the form of the state. This is the simplest way of preventing one person robbing or injuring another. There are laws, and they are enforced. The significant questions then become: who is the state, and how intrusive is it? The first question preoccupied the ancient Greeks, who distinguished between different forms of government (monarchy, oligarchy, democracy). The second concerned figures like John Stuart Mill, who argued that the state should never interfere with people's lives unless they were directly harming others. Isaiah Berlin belongs to this second tradition.

One of the most original insights of the Hebrew Bible, however, is that force is not the only or even the best way of getting people to co-operate. There is another alternative. Imagine that you and I, different in our interests and strengths, realize that we would both gain if we were to work together. Neither of us wants to use force. That would be an assault on the other's integrity. But neither of us wants to risk betrayal by the other. The alternative to the use of force is *trust*. Trust is created by the use of language. We talk, communicate, share our dreams; we begin to understand one another and realize that we can work together. We can then go further and make a promise to one another. We can enter into a mutual pledge. This is a highly specialized use of language known as *performative utterance*. It means, the use of words to create facts, in this case, mutually binding obligations. What then has to happen for trust to be effective is that I must *keep* my word, and you, yours. The Torah has a special word for a mutual pledge of this kind. It calls it a *brit*, a covenant.

The most basic form of covenant is a marriage. In marriage two people agree to join their destinies to one another, to cherish, support and protect each other, so that neither is condemned to face an uncertain future alone. Marriage is a remarkable institution because, to the extent that it is honoured, it shows that two people, each respecting the integrity of the other, can nonetheless create a collaborative partnership that relies for its strength not on the use of force but on love, loyalty, fidelity, the willingness to undertake responsibilities and keep to them and the readiness to consider another person's interests as sacred as one's own. Not by accident is the book of Genesis largely about families and marriage: Adam and Eve, Noah and his household, Abraham and Sarah, Isaac and Rebecca, Jacob, Rachel and Leah. Knowing the Bible as well as we do, we rarely if ever stop to consider how strange this is. But it is strange to the point of being unique. Every other literature until modern times (the times, say, of Jane Austen) is about epic heroes, gods or demi-gods, figures of legendary strength and power. The stunning originality of the book of Genesis is that its heroes and heroines are ordinary people in ordinary situations, made extraordinary not by their power but by their loyalty to one another and to God.

In moving from Genesis to Exodus the Torah takes the idea further in a radical leap of the imagination. What if covenant might be the basis not only of marriage but of a society as a whole? What if the Israelites, already forged as a people in the crucible of suffering, undertook a pledge with one another and with God, to respect each other's freedom, to value someone else's property and safety with the same vigilance that I do my own, and to see society as an extended family, so that I owe to others the same duty of concern and care that I owe my brothers and sisters? Such a society would be held together not by the use of force – not by rulers, armies, police and courts – but by *the power of words* to bind us to one another in open-ended and mutual commitment. These words would, of necessity, be *sacred*, which is to say, commanding, obligating, binding, to be taken with the same ultimate seriousness as life itself.

That is what happens to the Israelites at Mount Sinai. Accepting only God, and no human power, as their sovereign, they pledge themselves to one another by agreeing to a code of duties to each other and to God. They become the first – and until the birth of the United States the only – nation to be formed by a covenant, whose written constitution was the Torah, and whose force was none other than the word undertaken and honoured as a matter of reciprocal loyalty and binding commitment. Thus Judaism became the first religion of the *word*, whose most sacred object is a book, and whose ultimate reality is God who enters into a covenant with a people (a covenant seen by the prophets as a form of marriage), thus turning love into law and law into love.

What an extraordinary idea of freedom this is. It depends, for its success, not on power, but on moral obligation. Needless to say, this places a greater burden on the educated conscience than any other political system, and therefore requires unique institutions. It needs constant education. The people must know the law; they must hand it on to their children; they must speak of it constantly until it becomes part of their innermost being. It needs regular rehearsal – dramatic enactments like the festivals, through which Israel reminds itself of who it is and how it came to be. But the gain is immense. It means that Israel, if it is loyal to the covenant, will experience a freedom greater than any other people in ancient or even modern times. They will keep the law, not because of fear of arrest, trial and punishment, but because of their love of God, their concern for their neighbours, and their shared sense of past and future. Only once we understand this can we appreciate the strangest fact of all in Jewish history – that without sovereignty and a land, without police or an army, without any of the normal accoutrements of nationhood, the Jewish people kept Jewish law voluntarily in exile for two thousand years. There is nothing else remotely like this in history.

Judaism has a special word for this unique form of freedom. It is *cherut*. In the *Ethics of the Fathers*, the sages explained it by way of a brilliant play on words. Noting the similarity between *cherut* and *charut*, 'engraved', they re-read the biblical text in which Moses descended from Mount Sinai, holding in his hands the two tablets of stone containing the law of God. The verse reads, 'The tablets were the work of God; the writing was the writing of God, *engraved* on the tablets.' The rabbis said, 'Read not *charut* but *cherut*, not *engraved* but *freedom*, for there is no one so free as one who occupies himself with the study of Torah.' What they meant was that if the law is engraved on the hearts of its citizens, it does not need to be enforced by police. True freedom – *cherut* – is the ability to control oneself without having to be controlled by others, accepting voluntarily the moral restraints without which liberty becomes licence and society itself a battle-ground of warring instincts and desires.

That, therefore, is the journey the counting of the omer represents: from *chofesh*, the negative freedom of Pesach and the release from slavery, to *cherut*, the substantive freedom of the covenant and the revelation at Mount Sinai. Freedom means more than losing your chains. It involves developing the capacity to think, feel and act for the benefit of others. That needs families, schools, places of worship, conversations between the generations, rituals, prayers and the telling of stories. It needs 'habits of the heart', and it takes time – which is why, between Pesach and Shavuot, we become conscious of time by counting days. Pesach is the beginning of the journey, not the end.

Covenantal politics stand as the great alternative to three other systems: hierarchical, organic and contractual. Hierarchical politics are built on divisions of class or caste. Organic politics, of which nationalism and fascism are examples, are predicated on the idea that the individual has meaning only as part of the whole. Contractual politics take the opposite view, that the individual is supreme, and that politics is the pursuit of self-interest. I gain by handing over some of my powers to a government which, by securing the rule of law, the defence of the realm, and providing certain services, makes me better off than I would be otherwise.

Covenantal systems are unique in placing ethics at the heart of society. They place a high value on loyalty and trust. They cherish the family as the birthplace of virtue. They speak about respect for parents and responsibility to children. They emphasize community, the bonds of belonging, voluntary work and service. They assume no conflict between responsibility for oneself and others (Hillel's 'If I am not for myself, who will be? But if I am only for myself, what am I?'). They assume, not as a fact but as a value to be constantly worked for, the equal worth of all, especially the dependent and vulnerable. And they depend on belief in a set of ethical principles beyond the autonomous will. In a covenantal society, 'I ought' does not mean 'I want'. Covenantal societies are not based on abstract principles but concrete historical memories. They are about *this people* and how it came to be, and what led its founders to make this particular pledge in pursuit of that vision, these ideals. Covenants create societies, not states. A covenant is, in this sense, pre-political rather than political. The children of Israel did not become a state until it chose a king in the days of Samuel. Until then it had been a loose collection of tribes. But it became a society – a republic of faith under the sovereignty of God – at Mount Sinai, several centuries before.

As I intimated in the previous chapter, the greatest covenantal society in modern times has been the United States. The early colonies were formed by covenant. Presidential inaugurals regularly invoke both the word and the idea. America's definitive covenantal document is the Declaration of Independence (1776), constructed eleven years before its Constitution. What John Schaar writes about the political beliefs of Abraham Lincoln applies to America as a whole:

> We are a nation formed by a covenant, by dedication to a set of
> principles and by an exchange of promises to uphold and advance

certain commitments among ourselves and throughout the world. Those principles and commitments are the core of American identity, the soul of the body politic. They make the American nation unique, and uniquely valuable, among and to the other nations. But the other side of the conception contains a warning very like the warnings spoken by the prophets to Israel: if we fail in our promises to each other, and lose the principles of the covenant, then we lose everything, for they are we.

At the heart of the politics of the Hebrew Bible is the understanding, achieved through painful experience of exile and exodus, that liberty depends on a shared moral code, and on the education of new generations to internalize its values. Much of the Bible is a commentary on the historic difficulties faced by the Israelites as they tried, and often failed, to realize the social vision of the covenant. A period of disorder in the days of the Judges ('In those days there was no king in Israel; each person did what was right in his own eyes.') was followed by a succession of sometimes corrupt and tyrannical kings. The ideal of the Torah – lofty but not utopian – is of limited government accompanied by personal self-government, the law of the state taking second place to the law of the heart. Only a self-disciplined people will be able to sustain for long the political framework of liberty. For without moral restraint, society is condemned to oscillate between anarchy and oppression, too little government and too much, and sometimes both at once.

One of the ironies of the post-modern West is that the triumph of freedom over totalitarian regimes has gone hand in hand with an erosion of the moral bases of freedom. Morality has been relativized into self-fulfilment. Responsibilities have taken second place to rights. The very idea of objective standards of right and wrong has become suspect. If history teaches any lesson at all it is that this, if unchecked, is a prelude to disaster. The man who said so best was an unlikely figure, Bertrand Russell. Russell, hardly a religious man, thought that the two great ages of mankind were to be found in ancient Greece and Renaissance Italy. But he was honest enough to admit that the very features that made them great contained the seeds of their own demise:

> What had happened in the great age of Greece happened again in Renaissance Italy: traditional moral restraints disappeared, because they were seen to be associated with superstition; the liberation from fetters made individuals energetic and creative, producing a rare fluorescence of genius; but the anarchy and treachery which inevitably resulted from the decay of morals made Italians collectively impotent, and they fell, like the Greeks, under the domination of nations less civilized than themselves but not so destitute of social cohesion.

To win freedom is one thing; to sustain it, another. Judaism taught this truth in the simplest of ways, by counting the days between Pesach and Shavuot, exodus and revelation. Freedom begins with the defeat of tyranny, but it is preserved by a code of virtue – the Torah, Israel's 'constitution of liberty' – which lies beyond the realm of democratic vote, individual preference or passing fashion. Judaism's early sages asked, 'Who is mighty?' They answered: not one who is strong enough to defeat his opponents, but one who is strong enough to practise self-restraint. Moral virtue needs a different and more difficult strength than military courage. That is what we learn on the journey from Pesach and Shavuot, from individual to covenantal freedom.

11

Time as a Narrative of Hope

The unappeased memory of a future still to be fulfilled.
Harold Fisch, *A Remembered Future*

In his monumental work *The Wealth and Poverty of Nations*, Harvard economic historian David Landes asks a fascinating question. China in the Middle Ages was more advanced than Europe. Long before the West, it had invented paper, printing, gunpowder, the compass and porcelain. By the eleventh century it had developed blast furnaces, fuelled by coal and coke, for smelting iron. By the twelfth it had already produced a water-driven machine for spinning hemp. In many fields it was centuries ahead. Yet the industrial revolution took place, not in China, but in Europe. Why was it that in China, technological progress moved so far but no further?

There are multiple explanations, but one, suggests Landes, is that Europe had something that China lacked, namely the Western sense of time. The Chinese did not see time as the arena of change; the Europeans did. To create a revolution, first you have to be able to imagine it. You need the ideas that make historical transformation possible and desirable. What Europe possessed, and what proved critical to its economic and political success, was a Judeo-Christian concept of time.

We tend to take time for granted. It is, we assume, the same for everyone everywhere – one of the few things that is. There are sixty minutes in an hour, twenty-four hours in a day, seven days in a week, regardless of how rich or poor we are, or where we live on the surface of the world. One of the few differences between ourselves and our ancestors is that we can measure it more accurately, using oscillating quartz crystals instead of the sundials and water-clocks, hourglasses and calibrated candles of the ancient world. But time is not simply something we measure. It is also something to which we bring some of our deepest assumptions about the nature of reality and mankind's place in the universe. The understanding of time differs from culture to culture and from age to age. Historians are generally agreed that with the Hebrew Bible a quite new concept of time appeared. It is not too much to say – many scholars have – that this was one of Judaism's greatest contributions to the West.

The most obvious sense of time is given by nature. That is how the ancients thought, and many moderns also. Any understanding of time on the basis of nature is bound to be cyclical. Things change, but they come back to their starting point. The planets revolve in their courses. The climate passes through its seasons: spring, summer, autumn, winter. Life has its own rhythms: birth, growth, decline, death, and rebirth. That is how time appears to those for whom nature, myth or science are the primary realities. Time, like the slow turning of a wheel, describes a circle, periodically returning to where it began. That which was, will be again. Nothing ultimately changes.

That was time in the world of myth. In modernity, it was given its most famous expression by Nietzsche. The sum total of energy in the universe, he argued, is finite. But time is infinite. Therefore any possible configuration of elements has already happened, and will happen again in the future. The Hebrew Bible itself contains a book dedicated to this theme – the strange work called *Kohelet*, Ecclesiastes. 'What has been will be again, what has been done will be done again; there is nothing new under the sun.' *Kohelet* draws the inevitable conclusion: 'Meaningless, meaningless, everything is meaningless.'

It is difficult to grasp the immensity of the leap that occurred when first Abraham, then Moses and the Israelites, and later the prophets, began to see time differently. It was one of the greatest revolutions in the history of ideas, and it has still not been made by all cultures. It came when the religious visionaries of Israel heard God in history instead of seeing God in nature. If God transcends nature, then He is free. Unlike the gods of the ancient world He is not bound by the laws of nature. God acts, not because He must, but because He wills and chooses.

The fateful corollary is that, having been made in God's image, we too are free. Though we are part of nature – we have bodies, we feel hunger and cold, we age and die – there is something within us that is not part of nature, namely self-consciousness, the ability to stand back from our immediate situation and pass judgement on it. The Greeks called this 'the soul'. The second chapter of Genesis calls it 'the breath of God'. The combination of language and self-consciousness means that human beings have a sense of time to be found nowhere else in creation. All animals have a sense of cyclical time hardwired into their brains. Some migrate, others hibernate, at particular points in the year. What is unique to humans is the sense of a *distant* past and future: 'there was' and 'there will be'. It took a radical imaginative leap to see that if we are free, not wholly determined by nature, the world of 'there will be' might be altogether different from that of 'there was'.

Human beings can choose. They can learn by error and experience and act differently next time. The future, therefore, is not destined to be like the past. History is not an endless series of eternal recurrences or *deja vus*. Instead it is like a journey, with a starting point and a destination, or like a book with a beginning and middle and distantly glimpsed end. This is the sense of time that makes its appearance in the Hebrew Bible. Until Christianity borrowed it from Judaism, it existed nowhere else. The Greek writer Herodotus, for example, is widely known as 'the father of history', but he had no thought of history as an overarching narrative. It was simply the record of events. History, for him, was interesting simply because it happened and because it contained exemplary cases of courage and folly, success and failure, but it added up to no larger pattern. Jews thought otherwise.

It began with Abraham's journey from Ur. But the decisive event was the exodus. In Egypt, the Israelites first sensed the intervention of God in history on a massive scale. The Egypt of the pharaohs was the oldest, most stable and seemingly impregnable of the empires of the ancient world. It embodied timelessness. With the solitary exception of the Hyksos invasion three centuries before, Egypt was the supreme example of civilization-as-order, power immune to change. The seasons, life and death, pharaohs themselves, came and went, but the social structure, like Egypt's monumental buildings, defied time.

The overthrowing of this structure and the unprecedented release of a whole nation from slavery showed that societies are *not* immutable. They belong, not to nature but to culture. They are made by men and women; therefore they can be unmade and remade by men and women. Injustice, oppression, dominance, exploitation, the enslavement of the weak by the strong, are not written into the constitution of the universe, for beyond them is the voice of the transcendent God, the 'ought' beyond the 'is', summoning us to shape a more gracious and humane world. That is where the Israelites' journey began. To those who hear the voice, it continues still.

The historian Eric Voegelin suggests that it was not by accident that God chose the desert to reveal the plan of a new kind of society: 'When the world has become Desert, man is at last in the solitude in which he can hear thunderingly the voice of the spirit.' Voegelin does not make the verbal connection between the Hebrew terms for 'desert', *midbar*, and 'word', *dabar*, but there is one. The desert is the place of human silence in which the Divine word can be sensed in its fullness and power. 'What emerged from the alembic of the Desert,' he concludes, 'was not a people like the Egyptians or Babylonians, the Canaanites or Philistines, the Hittites or Arameans, but a new genus of society, set off from the civilizations of the age by the divine choice. It was a people that moved on the historical scene while living toward a goal beyond history.'

For the first time an abyss opened up between the past and the future, Egypt and the promised land. The journey through space, across the wilderness, came to symbolize a journey through time, whose destination is something new, unprecedented, a tomorrow radically unlike yesterday. In this context we begin to understand the Israelites' constant complaints and their expressed desire, on several occasions, to go back to Egypt. The psychologist Erich Fromm coined the phrase 'fear of freedom', and when the Israelites first experienced it, it must have been fearful indeed – the loss of everything secure, predictable, unchanging, and in its place only uncertainty and a destination always beyond the horizon. An open future – the essential negation of cyclical time – can be terrifying. Only God's promise, and the Israelites' trust in that promise, made it bearable. It is worth noting that it is this concept of time that makes the Hebrew word *emunah*, usually translated as 'faith', utterly distinctive in the religious language of mankind. It does not mean certainty; it means, to the contrary, *the courage to live with uncertainty*, knowing that the future is radically unpredictable, but that it can be faced without fear because we are not alone. God and His word are with us.

Voegelin is particularly acute when he says that Israel was a 'people that moved on the historical scene while living toward a goal beyond history.' The destination of the Jewish journey was much more than a place, Canaan, the land 'flowing with milk and honey'. It was an ideal future, the 'time to come', an era of justice and peace. Moses spoke of it in his majestic closing speeches that we know as the Book of Deuteronomy. Isaiah foresaw it in the surpassing visions that form the closing chapters of the book that bears his name. Almost all the prophets have their own formulations. Joel speaks of a day in which God will 'pour out My spirit on all people. Your sons and daughters will prophesy, your old men will dream dreams, your young men will see visions.' Jeremiah envisions a future in which, in God's words, 'I will put My law in their minds and write it on their hearts… No longer will a man teach his neighbour, or a man his brother, saying "Know the Lord", because they will all know Me, from the least of them to the greatest.' Eventually it became known as the messianic age.

No concept has been more debated, contested and fraught with controversy than the messianic age. It led, in Jewish history, to a series of false messiahs, each of whom left disruption in their wake. In more modern times it created a deep rift between Zionists and their opponents, between those who believed that redemption could or should be initiated by man and those who argued that, to the contrary, it could only be brought by God, so that any attempt to hasten the end by human intervention was heresy. Had it not been for the Holocaust, that debate might still divide the Jewish world. Gershom Scholem argued on secular grounds that the messianic idea had caused more harm than good. It led, he said, to '*a life lived in deferment*, in which nothing can be done definitively, nothing can be irrevocably accomplished.' Because, for centuries, Jews were suspended between a remote miraculous past (the biblical era) and an equally remote miraculous future (the messianic age), the present was systematically devalued; suspended animation.

The concept of messianic time *is* dangerous, because it can lead to two alternative possibilities: a refusal to act in the present because all redemption is in the hands of God, or, to the contrary, a readiness to act recklessly in the present because redemption is at hand and God will ensure success. The very existence of Israel depends on the ability to keep these two tendencies in check. My own interpretation of the Messianic idea, however, is that it stands in relation to Jewish history as the stars did to ancient navigation. As Kenneth Minogue notes, 'when you steer by a star you don't aim to arrive there.' The perfect world – the world we rehearse every Shabbat – is beyond history; but history itself is the attempt, never wholly successful, but marked none the less by real and significant advance, to come ever closer to that ideal. God alone can bring about a world of perfect justice, but we are not wrong to keep that vision constantly before us as we seek to create a society less random and cruel than those in the past.

The messianic idea gave Jewish sensibility its unique restlessness, its striving, its principled orientation to the future, unlike almost every other civilization known to mankind, whose golden age is in the distant, usually mythical past. Moses spent his life travelling toward a land he was not allowed to enter. 'It is not given to you to complete the task,' said Rabbi Tarfon, 'but neither are you free to desist from it.' Jewish time sees us as travellers on the road to a destination not yet reached; wayfarers on a journey begun by our ancestors, to be continued by our children. At best we see the promised age as Moses saw the land of Israel at the end of his life – distantly, as from a mountain top. But that is enough. All of history tells us that we are not wrong to travel, to take risks, to see poverty, hunger, disease and injustice as things we are called on to fight, not accept. Not all of mankind's dreams are destined, as they were for the Greek dramatists, to end in tragedy. With God's help, and that of other people with whom we are bound in covenant, we can change the world.

Thomas Cahill gives us a sense of the impact of this idea on the imagination of the West:

> The Jews gave us the Outside and the Inside – our outlook and our inner life. We can hardly get up in the morning or cross the street without being Jewish. We dream Jewish dreams and hope Jewish hopes. Most of our best words, in fact – *new, adventure, surprise; unique, individual, person, vocation; time, history, future; freedom, progress, spirit; faith, hope, justice* – are the gifts of the Jews.

The name usually given by historians to this new concept is linear (as opposed to 'cyclical') time. This, though, is a profound mistake. Linear time is, in fact, the quite different idea that took shape between the seventeenth and twentieth centuries when the religious view of time, born in the Hebrew Bible and re-introduced into the West by the Puritans, was secularized. Now it was no longer God, or the Bible, or faith that would drive history forward, but reason and experimentation. Through science, humanity would conquer ignorance. Through reason, it would banish prejudice. Through trade it would develop the wealth of nations. Through technology, it would dominate nature. That was the view shared by thinkers as diverse as Saint-Simon, Comte, Hegel and Marx, economists like Adam Smith, biologists like Darwin, and the historians and anthropologists of the nineteenth century. Condorcet put it as well as any when he wrote, 'Nature has set no term to the perfection of our human faculties; that the perfectibility of man is truly indefinite, and that the progress of this perfectibility, from now onwards independent of any power that might wish to halt it, has no other limit than the duration of the globe on which nature has cast us.'

This is not biblical time but a translation of it into a quite different frame of reference. Instead of seeing history as an interactive drama between heaven and earth,

God's word and mankind's response, it sees it as an arena dominated by man alone. In place of ethics it enthrones science; instead of a journey full of risk, it sees history as continuous, unbroken advance; it deletes the word 'redemption' and replaces it with the word 'progress'.

These were powerful ideas, and for almost three centuries they were effective. They led to the development of science, improvements in medicine, the industrial revolution, the spread of democracy, and the growth of tolerance as an ideal. By now, though, we know its limitations. The Enlightenment failed to prevent the Holocaust. Technology has given us the power to destroy life on earth. The growth of consumption threatens the ecological system whose air we breath. We have moved from modernity to 'post-modernity', meaning that we have lost confidence in the upward march of time. As Robert Bellah notes, 'Progress, modernity's master idea, seems less compelling when it appears that it may be progress into the abyss.'

Jewish time is not linear but something more profound. I call it *covenantal time*. This is time, not as continuous advance, but as a narrative with a beginning and a distant end, in whose midst we are and whose twists and turns continue to surprise us. The terms of the drama are set. There are two characters, God and mankind. There are continuing themes: exile and redemption, wanderings in the wilderness, backslidings and lapses, atonement and forgiveness, returns and rededications, epiphanies and moments when man looks for God and fails to find him. Nothing in this narrative is as simple as linear time. There is no guarantee of progress. There are constant digressions, false turns, wanderings in the wilderness. There is no 'historical inevitability' – that modern idea which, as Karl Popper and Isaiah Berlin remind us, has been the source of so much brutality and bloodshed in the modern world ('progress', like every other false god, has called forth the blood of human sacrifice in abundance). Above all, covenantal time is conscious of *limits* in our dealings with nature and our fellowmen. The prophets of linear time have always been convinced that there are no limits: that nature is infinitely bountiful, economic growth open-ended, and humanity – through revolution, or social engineering, or eugenics, or selective cloning – ultimately perfectible. Whenever mankind loses a sense of limits, disaster follows as surely as does night, day.

The deepest difference between linear and covenantal time is that whereas the first gives rise to *optimism*, the latter leads to *hope*. These two concepts, often confused, are in fact utterly different. Optimism is the belief that things will get better. Hope is the belief that, together, we can make things better. Optimism is a passive virtue, hope an active one. It takes no courage – only a certain naivety – to be an optimist. It takes great courage to sustain hope. No Jew – knowing what we do of the past, of hatred, bloodshed, persecution in the name of God, suppression of human rights in the name of freedom – can be an optimist. But Jews have never given up hope. 'Even youths grow tired and weary, and young men stumble and fall,' says Isaiah, 'but those who hope in the Lord will renew their strength.' 'Restrain your voice from weeping,' urges Jeremiah, 'there is hope for your future.' To be a prophet is to find a vestige of hope in the wreckage of despair. Jewish time – this is the secret of the influence of the Pesach story on the Western imagination – is the supreme narrative of hope.

It is worth adding, because I have not seen it said, that this is why the British and American revolutions succeeded while the French and Russian revolutions failed. There is a fundamental difference between philosophy – the gift of the Greeks to Western civilization – and the Hebrew Bible – the gift of Israel. Philosophy (that 'series of footnotes to Plato' as Alfred North Whitehead called it) sees *truth as system*. The Bible sees *truth as story*. Philosophical systems are essentially timeless. They speak either of truth as eternal, or (in the case of Hegel and Marx) of history as inexorable, predetermined. In Judaism, by contrast, time is of the essence, which is why its vision can only be told in the form of narrative (first this, then that; 'it came to pass after these things'; chronological, rather than logical sequence). Two things only stand outside of time: the beginning of days (Eden) and the end (the messianic age). Between them lies the long journey to redemption.

More than any other system, the Hebrew Bible teaches that it takes time to realize moral ideals. Pesach, 3,300 years ago, was the definitive protest against slavery, yet the West did not abolish slavery until the nineteenth century, and in America, only at the cost of civil war. The opening chapter of the Torah, with its statement that the human person is 'the image of God', was the first articulation of the sanctity of the individual and thus of human rights. It was not until 1948 that the United Nations issued its Universal Declaration of Human Rights. Isaiah and his younger contemporary Micah were the first to envision peace as an ideal. Humanity has not reached it yet. Nor has any society yet realized the vision of a world without hierarchy and manipulation, experienced by Jews one day in seven, every Shabbat. The messianic age is not now. There is still a way to go.

Because of its systemic failure to understand time, philosophy (an immense gift to civilization, and still our best way of thinking about thinking) has always been, and will always be, disastrous when applied to the political realm, which is what happened in revolutionary France and communist Russia. Philosophy as political ideology constantly holds forth the promise of a shortcut to utopia – and there is no short-cut. It took forty years for the Israelites to get from Egypt to the banks of the Jordan, a journey that should have taken days. That, says Maimonides, was no accident. A generation born in slavery was not ready for the responsibilities of freedom. Hope is the ability to combine aspiration with patience; to be undeterred by setbacks and delays; to have a sense of the time it takes to effect change in the human heart; never to forget the destination even in the midst of exile and disaster. The politics of progress, from Plato to Marx (what J. L. Talmon calls 'secular messianism') is always impatient because it lacks more than a superficial understanding of time. Judaism has never ceased to wrestle with time ('I will not let you go until you bless me,' said Jacob to the angel, as Jews have always said of time and fate). Because of this it yields a different kind of aspiration, one that I call *the politics of hope*.

Jews are a tiny people, less than a quarter of a per cent of the population of the world. They always were. ('Not because you had greater numbers than all the other nations did God embrace you and choose you,' said Moses at the end of his life, 'You are among the smallest of all the nations'). Because of this, it has often found it difficult to understand its place in the totality of mankind. Sometimes it has thought too little of itself (the verdict of Moses' spies comes to mind: They are giants, we are grasshoppers). At others it has thought too much ('When I felt secure,' says David in Psalm 30, 'I said "I shall never be shaken."'). Which was it: the pariah people or the chosen people? Caught between these extremes, and despite its almost endless preoccupation with its own identity, it found it hard to arrive at a realistic estimate of its role among the nations. As we saw in the chapter on antisemitism, that same difficulty has existed when other nations tried to form an evaluation of Jews and Judaism. They found themselves caught between contemptuous dismissal and an exaggerated view of Jewish power, sometimes believing both at once.

My own view, arrived at after long reflection, is that Jews have been called on to bear witness – in their faith, history and way of life – to certain fundamental truths of the human condition: that we are free, and thus responsible, and therefore charged with becoming God's partners in the work of redemption; that life is sacred and therefore human rights are non-negotiable; that civilizations become invulnerable only when they care for the vulnerable; that freedom depends on education and the emotional intelligence that comes from strong families and communities held together by the bonds of shared memory and responsibility; and that all achievement in the social realm takes time and can only be sustained by a narrative of hope.

These are not the only truths of the human situation, and therefore Judaism does not hold a monopoly on wisdom ('If they tell you, there is wisdom among the nations, believe it,' said the rabbis. They even composed a special blessing on seeing a non-Jewish sage). Not all truths are compatible. That is why there can be no ultimate global harmony within history (= unredeemed, non-messianic time). For principled reasons, for example, Jews did not develop the visual arts (they believed in a God who could be heard, not seen). The Greeks did. Nor did Jews cultivate the forms of inner peace practiced by some oriental mysticisms, for this involves a sense of the unreality of pain and suffering, which Judaism, with its striving for this-worldly justice, cannot accept. For that reason Judaism has a dual concept of peace: the end-of-days peace envisioned by the prophets, the more modest here-and-now peace articulated by the sages in their concept of *darkhei shalom*, a set of rules for friendly coexistence with those with whom you disagree.

Judaism, as I have argued, teaches the *dignity of difference*: the diversity of the created world and the irreducible multiplicity of human attempts to express the infinite. In such a world, the most important process is *conversation* – a willingness to speak and listen to others, knowing that you have something unique to teach, but others do also (Who is wise? asked Ben Zoma, and answered: One who learns from everyone). Because of its unique experience of the exodus, Jews learned more than most the importance of loving the stranger, of being true to one's own faith while being a blessing to others, of contributing to the human project as a whole without making the mistake that we are all the same. Judaism is the great counter-voice in the conversation of mankind.

I have tried to show how the modern history of the West – especially Britain in the seventeenth century, and America from then till now – was shaped by the new encounter with the Hebrew Bible, brought about by the Reformation and the invention of printing. Jews themselves suffered a more tempestuous exposure to modernity, which began with the promise of Enlightenment and ended in the Holocaust and the transfer of Jewish hopes to a reborn Israel. Antisemitism has not ended, but the Jewish situation has been transformed. For the first time in two thousand years, the Jewish people has a home, a place where it can construct a macro-society on the basis of Judaic principle (not a theocratic state: that is something altogether different). For the first time ever, outside Israel, Jews have the chance of making a substantive contribution to the shaping of the liberal, pluralist democracies of the West. The Pesach story is therefore more salient than ever: no longer a mere hope but a real and present challenge.

It is fair to say that we have not yet risen to that challenge. The Jewish religious imagination, still suffering the effects of trauma and dislocation, has not yet recovered its poise, scope, intellectual breadth or prophetic depth. In the past half-century it has produced too few prophets – men and women sufficiently gifted in the arts of listening to time and eternity, the particularity of Jewish existence and the universality of human concern, to hear in God's word for all time the specific cadences of the word for *this* time. Yet this too will come, and I have tried in these chapters to signal the territory from which it will come and the themes it will embrace. The Pesach story influenced not only Jews but non-Jews also, as Moses foresaw – knowing as he did that the God who rescued Israel from Egypt is the God, not of Israel only, but of the world, and therefore that the exodus contains a message not only for Jews, but for all who seek, on this troubled planet, to construct a society that is a worthy dwelling place for God, whose image we are.

The Sages at Bnei Brak

It happened that Rabbi Eliezer, Rabbi Joshua, Rabbi Elazar the son of Azariah, Rabbi Akiva and Rabbi Tarfon sat all night in Bnei Brak telling the story of the going out from Egypt, until their students came to tell them that it was time for the recitation of the morning Shema.

Haggadah

The story of the five sages at Bnei Brak who spent the night discussing the Exodus, and only stopped when their disciples came to tell them that it was morning, has long intrigued commentators and scholars. What were they talking about?

One suggestion, made by the late Cecil Roth among others, has attracted considerable interest, namely that they were discussing the Bar Kochba rebellion against the Romans. Bnei Brak was the home of Rabbi Akiva, who was known to be a supporter of Bar Kochba, and who eventually went to a martyr's death in the course of the revolt.

It is a fascinating suggestion, but there is no evidence for it. There is no intimation in the text that this was the subject of their conversation. Nor was it likely that the sages would have turned their attention from the religious duty of the night – telling the story of the going out from Egypt – to discuss contemporary politics.

The Bar Kochba rebellion was a tragic error. It led to one of the greatest ever devastations of Jewish life. The Roman historian Dio estimates that 580,000 Jews died in the fighting 'and countless numbers by starvation, fire and the sword'. 985 towns were destroyed and the countryside was laid waste. Jerusalem was razed to the ground and rebuilt as Aelia Capitolina, a Roman city, which Jews were forbidden to enter. The many sages who opposed Rabbi Akiva were, on this occasion, right. Their views are recorded in the Talmud. Had this been the subject of their conversation, the passage would have given us some indication of the fact. My conclusion is that Roth was wrong.

There *was* a drama at Bnei Brak that night, but it was a different kind of drama, with an altogether happier outcome. We can reconstruct, with some degree of certainty, what happened. But first we need to engage in a journey of discovery to understand the background of that evening and what was at stake.

The first thing to note is the halakhic significance of the episode. We have just said in the Haggadah, 'Even if we are all wise, all people of understanding, all elders, and all well versed in the Torah, we are nonetheless commanded to tell the story of the going out of Egypt, and whoever does so at great length is to be praised.' Three points are being made here. [1] The duty of reciting the Haggadah is not only to teach it to children; we must also teach it to ourselves. [2] We must recount it each year even though we already know the story. [3] The command has no fixed limit. Unlike, for example, the story of Purim which we recount by reading the Megillah, in the case of Pesach the duty of recounting the Exodus is not confined to reciting the text. The more deeply we enter into it, reflecting, expounding, adding new insights, the more we are worthy of praise.

How do we know these things, especially the last? In many cases the rabbis brought a proof from a biblical verse. But in some, they brought a proof from precedent, from the actions of the sages. The technical phrase for such a proof is *maaseh rav*, 'The force of precedent is great.' A sage may, for example, advance a halakhic opinion speculatively (*halakhah velo lema'aseh*). This is how the law appears to him. Nonetheless he may not always be willing to act – or instruct others to act – on the basis of this opinion until it has been tested against and approved by his contemporaries. When a sage acts in a certain way, this is a far stronger demonstration of the law. It shows that he not merely believes the law to be thus; he is prepared to put it into practice. Thus, *maaseh rav* – 'an act is a strong proof of the law' when it is an act performed by an acknowledged halakhic authority.

The opening word of the passage about the sages in Bnei Brak, *Maaseh*, 'It happened', is therefore not a mere introduction. It is a statement that the event to be related has halakhic force. It tells us what the law is. The fact that five of the greatest sages of the Mishnah stayed up all night telling the story of the Exodus is a proof of all three rules in the previous paragraph. We now know what is at stake in the episode. Whether or not this was their conscious intent, the sages of Bnei Brak were establishing an important set of laws which apply to us, especially the duty to tell the story 'at great length'.

Secondly, we note that there is no other version of this gathering in the rabbinic literature. There is, however, a parallel passage, full of interest and dating from approximately (possibly, as we shall see, exactly) the same time. It appears in an appendix to the Mishnah, known as the Tosefta (*Pesachim* 10:12). Reading it, we see several significant differences between it and the account in the Haggadah:

> It happened that Rabban Gamliel and the elders were reclining in the house of Boethus ben Zonin at Lod, and they were occupied in studying the laws of Pesach all that night until the cock crowed. They lifted the table, made themselves ready and went to the House of Study [to pray].

The differences are these. [1] This seder takes place in Lod, not Bnei Brak. [2] Rabban Gamliel is present here, but not at Bnei Brak. [3] None of the sages at Bnei Brak are mentioned here. [4] The subject of their conversation was not 'the going out of Egypt' but 'the laws of Pesach'. Each of these details will turn out to be significant.

There is one further passage we must note. It will prove to be the key that unlocks the entire mystery. It has to do with seating plans, and belongs to *hilkhot derekh eretz*, the rules of etiquette:

> The Exilarch [lay head of Babylonian Jewry] said to R. Sheshet: 'Although you are venerable rabbis, yet the Persians are better versed than you in the etiquette of a meal. When there are two couches, the senior guest takes his place first and then the junior one above him. When there are three couches, the senior occupies the middle one, the next in rank takes the place above him, and the third one below him.'... R. Sheshet said: 'I know only a *Baraita* [supplementary teaching] in which it is taught: What is the order of reclining? When there are two couches, the senior reclines first, and then the junior takes his place below him. When there are three, the senior takes his place first, the second next above him, and then the third below him.' (*Berakhot* 46b)

The subject at issue is the seating arrangement when there are several guests, and when all are reclined in the ancient manner on couches or *chaises longues*, with individual tables in front of each. That is a form of seating still known in the orient, and we recall it on Pesach when we recline to drink the wine and for other parts of the service. The question is: how are the guests arranged? The answer, common to both Persian and rabbinic practice, is that the senior person present sits in the centre. It is this fact which leads us to a crucial observation about the episode in Bnei Brak.

The order of the names tells us the seating arrangement that night. It reveals the surprising fact that, though he was neither the eldest nor the most learned of those present, *the senior guest that night, sitting in the centre, was Rabbi Elazar ben Azariah.* The next senior, sitting directly above him, was Rabbi Joshua. Below him was Rabbi Akiva. We can now date the episode precisely. It belongs to the period – a brief one – when *Rabbi Elazar ben Azariah was Nasi, religious head of the Jewish community.* The placement of the sages is exactly what we would expect at that time and no other. Rabbi Elazar ben Azariah has the seat of honour in virtue of his official position. Next to him is Rabbi Joshua, his deputy. On his other side is Rabbi Akiva, the host. Bnei Brak was Rabbi Akiva's town, where he was the local chief rabbi (*mara de'atra*). Flanking them were Rabbi Eliezer and Rabbi Tarfon, two elder statesmen of the halakhic community (Rabbi Tarfon was Rabbi Akiva's first teacher), neither of them, however, holding office within the community. Not only can we now date the episode, but we can set it in historical context.

For almost a century the Jewish community in Israel had been in a state of disarray. There were profound religious divisions. Josephus tells us that the nation was divided into three groups: the worldly and powerful Sadducees, the religious and popular Pharisees, and the sectarians known as the Essenes, among whom were the Qumran community known to us through the Dead Sea Scrolls. The Pharisees themselves were divided. Under Roman rule the Great Sanhedrin, the supreme Jewish court, had been disbanded. This left the religious community without an ultimate authority. The sages, split between the disciples of Hillel and Shammai, taught in separate 'schools'. Tradition records the sense of people at that time that 'the Torah was becoming two Torahs'. The overwhelming impression conveyed by the documentary evidence of the time is that the Jewish community was hopelessly factionalized.

It could not have happened at a worse time. Relations with Rome, the ruling power, were bad. A series of inept governors had offended Jewish sensibilities. There were sporadic protests and revolts. These culminated in the fateful 'great rebellion' of 66 CE. If it were to succeed, Jews would need to summon all their powers in an agreed and concerted effort. Rome was the world power of the day. Its armies were highly trained and disciplined. In retrospect the rebellion was fated to failure. Jews had immense fighting spirit. What they lacked in weapons they more than made up for in morale and determination. But what doomed the enterprise was internal disagreement. Josephus, who was an eye witness of the key events, draws a vivid picture of life within the besieged capital of Jerusalem. At times Jews were more intent on fighting one another than the Romans outside the walls. Looking back on the tragedy the Talmud says, 'Jerusalem was only destroyed because of *sinat chinam*, the internal conflict between Jews.' It was an immense and epoch-making defeat. The Temple went up in flames, the second time it had been destroyed. The rebellion was suppressed, the last outpost – at Massada – committing suicide rather than being taken captive alive. Outwardly Jews had been defeated by the Romans. Inwardly they knew they had defeated themselves. A thousand years later, in a letter written to the sages of Marseilles, Maimonides put it simply. The Jews of the time had not learned the lessons of government and military command. They had not learned how to maintain unity.

It is against this background that a key figure emerges, Rabban Gamliel the second. Tradition tells us that Rabban Yochanan ben Zakkai, in secret negotiations with the Roman general Vespasian, secured a concession. 'Grant me,' he said, 'Yavneh and its sages.' The town of Yavneh was the site of an important rabbinical academy. Yochanan ben Zakkai now turned it into a kind of surrogate capital in place of the ruined Jerusalem. But Jews needed more than a place. They needed a leader. What Yochanan did, in effect, was to restore and even strengthen the role of *Nasi*, the religious head of the community. With the breakdown of political structures, the *Nasi* could now emerge as more than a scholar and judge. He became the representative of the people in its relations with Rome. As the Chatam Sofer noted in one of his responsa, the *Nasi* became a kind of king in an age when Jews lacked any other recognized lay authority. Rabban Yochanan never held this title himself. The man who did so at Yavneh was

Rabban Gamliel. His deputy was R. Joshua.

The Talmud records three occasions on which they disagreed. Each became a *cause célèbre*. On one occasion R. Joshua and Rabban Gamliel gave conflicting rulings on a firstborn animal whose lip became blemished (*Bekhorot* 36a). Not content to override his deputy, Rabban Gamliel made him stand in disgrace in the presence of the scholarly assembly. The other sages protested – not against Rabban Gamliel's ruling but rather against the high-handed manner in which he enforced it.

A second occurred when Rabban Gamliel fixed the New Moon on the basis of eye-witness testimony which other sages regarded as suspect (*Mishnah, Rosh Hashanah* 2:9). R. Joshua took the side of the doubters. Rabban Gamliel then ordered him to appear before him on the day which, according to R. Joshua's calculation, was Yom Kippur, carrying his staff and money-belt. This was a brutal humiliation. On this occasion, however, R. Joshua's colleagues advised him to submit to *Nasi*. The fixing of the calendar depended on the authority of the court, and if R. Joshua called Rabban Gamliel's ruling into question, the whole judicial system might collapse. R. Joshua complied, but the episode added to the sense of unease.

Finally a question arose as to the halakhic status of the daily evening prayer. Was it obligatory or optional? R. Joshua held that it was optional. Rabban Gamliel ruled that it was obligatory. R. Joshua was prepared to withdraw his opinion, but once again Rabban Gamliel ordered him to remain standing while the House of Study was in session, as a gesture of submission to the *Nasi*. This last provocation proved too great. The assembled scholars voted to have Rabban Gamliel removed from office. In his place they appointed R. Elazar ben Azariah. Eventually Rabban Gamliel acknowledged his defeat, apologized to R. Joshua, and was restored to office, though R. Elazar remained, at least nominally, his junior partner. It was during this brief period of R. Elazar ben Azariah's leadership that the seder at Bnei Brak took place. We now understand why he was seated at the centre and why Rabban Gamliel was absent. It may even be that the seder of Rabban Gamliel, at the house of Boethus in Lod, took place at the same time. This would explain why none of the other leading sages was there. Rabban Gamliel was temporarily in disgrace. The other scholars had gone elsewhere, to the home of R. Akiva, the supreme Torah sage of the time.

Inevitably, Rabban Gamliel earned the reputation of being a high-handed and excessively authoritarian leader. To a degree, though, this is unjust. His task, as *Nasi* at Yavneh, was to re-unite a religious leadership traumatized by the divisions of the past. 'There can be only one leader in a generation,' said the sages, 'not two.' If the rabbis were to emerge as the guiding force of a Jewry devastated by defeat and the loss of the Temple, they had to speak with a single voice. The ruthlessness with which Rabban Gamliel suppressed dissent has less to do with his character than with the need of the hour. In the end, though, the rabbis decided as a collective body that this would not do. Rabbinic leadership must be based on collegiality and mutual respect, and a willingness to give an honorable audience to conflicting views. Until Rabban Gamliel was ready to accede to these principles, he was unfit to lead.

This is the background to the drama that was about to unfold at Bnei Brak. The atmosphere was fraught. Seeking unity, the sages had found themselves having to take the unprecedented step of deposing their own head. Huge responsibility now lay on R. Elazar ben Azariah and his colleagues to heal the wounds and restore amicable relations. Unfortunately, at this very moment, a major controversy was in the making – and it was almost certain to come to a head on the seder night itself.

Until when may one tell the story of the going out of Egypt? It depends on the answer to another question. Until when, in Temple times, could you eat the Paschal lamb? The Torah states, 'And you shall tell your child on that day, "It is because of *this* that the Lord did for me when I went free from Egypt."' The word 'this' implies that one is pointing at something while telling the story. From this, the rabbis inferred that one may only recount the story of the exodus 'while the matzah and maror [and in Temple times, the paschal lamb] are present [on the table] before you.' So the two times are linked. While the food is there, one may and should recount. Once it has been eaten, the time for telling the story is over. What is the final deadline?

On this the sages disagreed – precisely those sages present at Bnei Brak. About the eating of the Paschal lamb, R. Elazar ben Azariah and Rabbi Eliezer ruled that it must be done by midnight. R. Akiva and R. Joshua held that it could be done until dawn (*Berakhot* 9a). Elsewhere (*Mekhilta, Bo; Tosefta Pesachim* 10:11) it is clear that what applies to eating applies to telling. R. Eliezer, who holds that the eating must be done by midnight, also holds that one may discourse only until midnight. Other sages, who held that the eating can be done until dawn, also maintained that one may and should talk about Pesach 'all night'.

This, then, was the situation at Bnei Brak. The rabbis, needing above all a period of peace and unity, were about to collide. Four of the five sages present that night held opposing views on how long they could continue their discussion. R. Elazar ben Azariah and R. Eliezer held that it had to cease at midnight. R. Akiva and R. Joshua were of the view that they should carry on through the night until dawn. The question was bound to arise and generate disagreement. Moreover, it set the newly appointed *Nasi* against both his deputy, R. Joshua, and his host, R. Akiva. It was just the kind of conflict they had hoped to avoid, but it was unavoidable. Or was it?

The Talmud (*Rosh Hashanah* 29b) records a fascinating confrontation some years before. Rabban Yochanan ben Zakkai had, as we saw, transferred the centre of Jewish power from the Temple at Jerusalem to the academy at Yavneh. How far could Yavneh become a second Jerusalem? The question arose the first year after the destruction of the Second Temple that Rosh Hashanah fell on Shabbat. In the Temple the shofar was blown on Shabbat, but nowhere else. Could the shofar now be blown on Shabbat at Yavneh? Rabban Yochanan said Yes. A more traditionalist group, known as the Bnei Beterah, said No. Yavneh was not Jerusalem. The academy was not the Temple. The following dialogue then ensued:

Rabban Yochanan ben Zakkai said to them, 'Let us blow.' They replied,

'Let us discuss.' He said, 'Let us blow first and then discuss.' [They agreed.] After the shofar had been blown, they said, 'Now let us discuss.' He replied, 'The shofar has already been heard at Yavneh, and after the act has already been done, there is nothing to discuss!'

It was a brilliant coup. Rabban Yochanan won the argument by creating a *fait accompli*. That is precisely what now happened at Bnei Brak. R. Akiva and R. Joshua engaged the others in conversation and debate so enthralling that they lost all sense of time.

Unlike Rabban Gamliel in Lod, who spent the evening discussing 'the laws of Pesach', this was the one subject they were determined to avoid. Any discussion about law would have led them directly to the question of the time limit of the seder, and thus to potentially explosive disagreement. Instead they spoke about 'the going out from Egypt' – *aggadah*, not *halakhah*; the narrative rather than the law. Their aim was to make R. Elazar ben Azariah and R. Eliezer forget the time. Not only would they thereby avoid any conflict. They would also establish the law itself, that 'the more one discusses, the more one is to be praised' – without any limit on time. The fact that the five leading sages of the generation continued their discussions until dawn would create a binding precedent under the rule of *maaseh rav*, that 'an act is proof of the law'.

It worked brilliantly. So engrossed were R. Elazar and R. Eliezer that they failed to notice when their deadline of midnight passed. They were still talking when the disciples arrived to tell them, 'Masters, the time has come to say the morning Shema.' Dawn was approaching. The evening had passed without the question of time limits arising, and R. Akiva and R. Joshua had succeeded in establishing the law according to their reading of it. Tradition is silent on what the other two sages said when they finally realized the *fait accompli* so skillfully achieved against them. My guess is that they acknowledged defeat graciously. It would not have taken them long to realize not only what had been done, but also why. R. Akiva and R. Joshua were not interested in personal victory. They cared about the integrity of the Jewish people and its spiritual leadership. They knew that the rabbis could not afford yet another dispute of the kind that had split the schools of Hillel and Shammai and in their own time led to the removal of Rabban Gamliel from office. It was a victory not only for truth but also for peace, and it was a necessary one at that time and place.

Who knows whether that Pesach, isolated from his colleagues, Rabban Gamliel himself might not have reconsidered his position and come to the decision that he must make amends with R. Joshua and his other erstwhile colleagues. At any rate he did so soon afterward, and was restored to office. The fraught moment passed, and friendships were remade. The sages became the acknowledged leaders of the Jewish people, a role they held for many centuries thereafter. It might have been otherwise. That is the significance of the seder night at Bnei Brak, and of the healing power of conversation about the going out from Egypt.

13

Women and the Exodus

In reward for the righteous women of that generation, Israel were redeemed from Egypt.
Babylonian Talmud, Sotah

The human hero of the exodus was Moses. It was he who saw the suffering of his people and came to the defence of a man being beaten by an Egyptian taskmaster, and it was he who heard the call of God, confronted Pharaoh and led the Israelites out of Egypt into the desert on the long journey to the promised land. Moses dominates the biblical story – prophet, leader and lawgiver, the epic figure standing between God and the people, wrestling with both.

Yet the opening chapters of Exodus tell another story, no less fascinating, perhaps more so. A close reading of the text reveals that alongside the hero, matching his strength in the face of tyranny, was a series of heroines. The human face of the Exodus is the story of six remarkable women. Without Moses there might have been no exodus. But without the heroism of women there would have been no Moses. Who were they?

The first was Yocheved, Moses' mother. I try to imagine the courage of a woman willing to have a child once the decree has been issued that 'every boy that is born shall be thrown into the Nile.' The scene is Germany, 1939. Anti-Jewish edicts are in force. There is a sense of impending tragedy. To have a child at that time is a supreme act of hope in the midst of despair. That is the bravery of Yocheved.

What do we know about her? Surprisingly little. Her first appearance in the text is conspicuously anonymous: 'A man from the house of Levi went and married a daughter of Levi.' At this stage neither of Moses' parents, Amram and Yocheved, is named. We soon see Yocheved's resourcefulness. For three months she hides the child. When she can do so no longer, she makes a rush basket and sets him afloat on the Nile, hoping that he will be noticed and saved. Like many biblical women, she is a person of action, determination and courage. What else do we know about her?

Only this, that she gives birth to three children destined for greatness: Miriam, the prophetess, Aaron, Israel's first high priest, and Moses, its greatest leader. She endows her children, genetically or by example, with the gift of leadership. We can infer something more. She and her husband are both from the tribe of Levi. A few chapters earlier, the Torah has told us in connection with Levi, Jacob's third-born child, that their father did not see him destined for great things. Together with Shimon, he had rescued their sister Dina at the cost of what Jacob thought was excessive violence. On his death bed he delivers both a prediction and a curse: 'Shimon and Levi are brothers; their wares are instruments of violence. Let my soul not enter their council, my heart not join their company, for in their anger they killed men, and hamstrung oxen as they pleased. Cursed be their anger for it is fierce, and their fury, for it is cruel.'

We hear little subsequently about Shimon. But the children of Levi defy Jacob's low opinion. From their ranks will eventually come, not only the three leaders of the exodus, but Israel's priests and levites, its spiritual ministers, for all time. There is more than a hint that something in Yocheved – her capacity for hope or her faith in life – transforms, in her children, violence into courage, and aggression into an unshakable determination to rescue people and set them on the path to liberty. She has the subtle gift of transforming vice into virtue. She becomes the mother of Israel's leaders.

The second woman is Miriam, Yocheved's daughter, Moses' elder sister. What we know about her is no less impressive. She takes the risk of following the rush basket containing the baby as it floats down the Nile. She sees it taken out of the water by an Egyptian princess. Not content with witnessing its rescue, she takes a remarkable initiative. She goes up to the princess and offers to find a Hebrew woman to nurse the child. The result is that Moses, against all odds, is taken home and brought up in his own family. Miriam is the child slave who has the confidence to be undaunted in the presence of royalty, the courage to speak openly to the daughter of her people's oppressor, and the resourcefulness to think of a way of bringing the baby back to its home. We sense in her qualities of character of a high order. Without her, Moses might never have known his identity. He would have grown up not knowing that he was an Israelite. As if sensing what was at stake, Miriam performs a role that in retrospect was crucial for Israel's redemption – one of the few instances in the Bible (David's encounter with Goliath is another) in which heroism is attributed to a child.

Jewish tradition, however, ascribes to her a gesture more remarkable still:

> Amram was the most eminent man of his generation. Aware that Pharaoh had decreed, 'Every son that is born shall be cast into the river,' he said, 'In vain do we labour,' and was the first to divorce his wife. After that, all the Israelite men divorced their wives. Then his daughter said to him, 'Father, your decree is more cruel than Pharaoh's. He has decreed only against the males; you decree against both males and females. Pharaoh decreed only concerning this world, while you decree concerning both this world and the next. Since Pharaoh is a wicked man, there is doubt whether his decree will be fulfilled or not; but since you are a righteous man, your decree is sure to be fulfilled.' At once, he went and took back his wife, and so did all the others. (*Babylonian Talmud, Sotah* 12a)

What are we to make of this strange suggestion?

Rabbinic commentaries of this kind are sometimes described as 'legends'. That is not what they are. In filling the gaps of the biblical text – reading between its lines – Israel's early rabbinic sages were doing two things. Firstly, they were listening (the word 'reading' is inadequate) to the nuances of the biblical text. In the wake of the destruction of the Second Temple, *midrash*, or biblical exposition, became the rabbinic substitute for prophecy. God was 'hiding His face'. He was no longer manifest in Israel's fate. But He had left something of His presence behind: the Torah, the covenant, His 'marriage contract' with the Jewish people. When two lovers are present, they rejoice in one another's company. When one disappears and the other awaits his return, she reads and rereads the letters he wrote her, sensitive to every detail, discovering aspects of his character she had not noticed before, and bringing back a vestige of presence in the midst of absence. That is *midrash* : the close reading of Torah, in the wake of national tragedy, as God's love letters to His people.

Listening to the biblical passage (*Deuteronomy* 26:5–8) that forms the centre-piece of the Haggadah, the sages heard in the phrase, 'He [God] saw our affliction,' an echo of other contexts in which the word 'affliction' appears and has a specific sexual connotation. 'Affliction', as we say in the Haggadah, refers to 'the separation of husbands and wives'. From this hint they reconstructed the following scenario: once Pharaoh had decreed that all male babies were to be murdered, the Israelites decided not to have children. To bring a child into the world with a fifty-fifty chance of being killed was taking an unwarranted risk with life. For that reason the men separated from their wives. How then was Moses born? Something and someone must have changed the Israelites' mind, specifically in the case of Amram, Moses' father. That must have been either Yocheved or Miriam, the only other figures to feature in the narrative at this point. Of the two, Miriam is the obvious candidate. The text says nothing more about Yocheved than that she bore a child, whereas Miriam's resourcefulness shines from every word written about her. It must, therefore, have been Miriam who persuaded her father that he was wrong, that his decision, logical and ethical though it was, lacked one thing, namely faith itself. That is the textual basis for the story.

Midrash is a child of prophecy, though, in another sense. The prophets were interpreters of history. They spoke to their generation and their times. Lacking prophecy, the rabbis turned to biblical text to hear, within the word spoken for all time, the specific resonance for *this* time. Unlike *peshat*, the 'plain, simple, or accepted meaning', *midrash* is the hermeneutic quest for the meaning of the text as if it were spoken, not then but now. *Midrash* is interpretation in the context of *covenantal time*, the word spoken in the past but still active in the present. It is an exercise in conscious and deliberate anachronism (the secular equivalent would be a performance of a Shakespeare tragedy in modern dress, the better to feel its force as contemporary, rather than classical, drama). It is prophetic in the sense of interpreting current events in the light of the Divine word. *Midrash* is the attempt on the part of the sages to understand their own times as a continuation of the narrative of the covenant. In what historical context can we place the story they told of Miriam?

One of the most traumatic of all periods in Jewish history was the failure of the Bar Kochba rebellion and its brutal suppression by the Roman emperor Hadrian. Israel was devastated and most of its leading rabbis put to death. The practice of Judaism – including the teaching of Torah and the act of circumcision – was proscribed on pain of death. A Talmudic passage (*Baba Batra* 60b) reveals the depth of despair the surviving rabbis felt at that time:

> From the day that a government has come to power which issues cruel decrees against us and forbids to us the observance of the Torah and the precepts, and does not allow us to enter into the 'week of the son', we ought by rights to bind ourselves not to marry and have children, so that the seed of Abraham our father would come to an end of itself. However, let Israel go their way: it is better that they should err in ignorance than presumptuously.

This is a passage of intense pathos. The rabbis are saying nothing less than that it would have been reasonable at that point to let the Jewish people cease to be. They had been defeated by the Romans. Their last hope of recovering national sovereignty had failed. The thing that mattered above all – the practice of Judaism – was now banned. Here, therefore, is the historical context of the story the rabbis told about Miriam and Amram. It was not just in Egypt in the age of Ramses II, but in Israel in the days of Hadrian, that Jews contemplated a decision not to bring future generations into being.

The Talmudic passage ends on a curious note: 'Let Israel go their way...' The rabbis are saying that were they to issue the decree that seemed warranted by the circumstances – no more Jewish marriages or children – people would not listen. That is how Jews and Judaism survived. Ordinary people, suggests the Talmud, sometimes have more faith than their spiritual leaders. This is an astonishing admission, but it is not the only time they made it. Commenting on one of Moses' first challenges to God, 'They [the Israelites] will not believe in me,' they said, 'God replied: they are believers, the children of believers, but there will come a time when you yourself will not believe.'

We now sense the full depth of the encounter between daughter and father as the sages understood it. Amram was, they conjectured, 'the most eminent man of his generation'. According to one tradition he was head of the Sanhedrin, the rabbinic supreme court. Yet it is not he but his daughter who rightly understood the spiritual demand of the moment: not despair, but faith in the future. The sociologist Peter Berger calls hope a 'signal of transcendence'. There is nothing that logically justifies hope: if there were, it would not be hope but something else – confidence, certainty, assurance, foreknowledge. Hope is the narrow bridge across which we must walk if we are to pass from slavery to redemption, from the valley of death to the open spaces of new life. That hope, said the sages, is more likely to come from the young than the old, women (the bearers of new life) than men. It is no small testimony to their depth of self-knowledge that the rabbis attributed more faith to a young girl than to Amram, leader of his generation.

The third figure is Pharaoh's daughter, who rescued Moses, knowing that he was a Hebrew child. Again it is impossible not to be moved by this act of compassion by one who knew all too well what was at stake. To raise an Israelite child in the palace of the very ruler who had issued the decree of death took moral determination of a high order. A midrash states that when her handmaids saw that she was set on rescuing the baby, they said, 'It is the way of the world that when a king issues a decree, even if the whole world does not obey it, his own children and household do.' For any Egyptian to protect a Hebrew child was hazardous; to do so in the royal palace doubly so. In Jerusalem today in Yad Vashem, the Holocaust Museum, there is an avenue of remembrance for the righteous gentiles who saved Jewish lives during the Nazi years. Pharaoh's daughter created the precedent.

It is notable that she gives Moses his name (*Mses* – as in Ramses – is in fact an Egyptian word meaning 'child'). Names, in the Torah, are given by parents and in rare cases ordained or changed by God. Moses is the exception. Again a *midrash* emphasizes the point: 'This is the reward for doers of kindness: although Moses had many names, the only one by which he is known through the Torah is that given to him by Pharaoh's daughter. Even the Holy One, blessed be He, did not call him by any other name.'

Pharaoh's daughter is not mentioned by name. There is, however, a reference in the Book of Chronicles (I 4:18) to a certain 'Bityah, the daughter of Pharoah', and tradition identified her with Moses' rescuer. The name *Bityah* means 'daughter of God' and the rabbis speculated that this was not her original name, but one given to her by God in recognition of her kindness: 'Moses was not your son,' He said, 'yet you called him your son. You, too, are not My daughter, but I shall call you My daughter.'

The fourth heroine is Moses' wife, Zipporah, daughter of the Midianite priest Jethro. The first thing that strikes us about Zipporah is that she was willing to accompany Moses on his return to Egypt, despite the hazards of the journey, the risk of the mission, and the fact that the Israelites were not her people, even if she had adopted their faith. There is however one moment during the return journey when Zipporah saves Moses' life. The passage is cryptic in the extreme:

> During the journey, while they were encamped for the night, God confronted Moses and wanted to kill him. Zipporah took a stone knife, cut off her son's foreskin, throwing it down at Moses feet. Then she said: 'Blood bridegroom by circumcision.' (Exodus 4:24–5).

These two verses contain multiple ambiguities. God was angry with Moses, evidently because he had not circumcised his son. According to some, Moses delayed the operation because of the debilitating effect of the journey. According to others he had agreed with his father-in-law that one at least of his children would be brought up, not as an Israelite but as a Midianite. Whatever the interpretation, Zipporah's prompt action saved a life. One midrash attributes to her the level of righteousness of the matriarchs, Sarah, Rebecca, Rachel and Leah.

The fifth and sixth are the midwives, Shifra and Puah, whom Pharaoh instructed to kill every male Hebrew child. The Torah then reports:

> The midwives feared God and did not do what the Egyptian king had commanded. They allowed the infant boys to live. The king of Egypt summoned the midwives and said to them, 'Why did you do this? You let the boys live.' The midwives replied, 'The Hebrew women are not like the Egyptians. They know how to deliver. They can give birth even before a midwife gets to them.' God was good to the midwives, and the people increased and became very numerous. Because the midwives feared God, He made them houses [of their own].

Who were Shifra and Puah? The truth is, we do not know. One midrash identifies them with Yocheved and Miriam, using a midrashic technique of relating the unknown to the known. However, in describing them the Torah uses an ambiguous phrase. It calls them *hameyaldot ha'ivriyot*, which could mean either 'the Hebrew midwives' or 'the midwives to the Hebrews.' On the second interpretation, they may not have been Hebrews at all, but Egyptians. This is the view taken, among others, by Abrabanel and Samuel David Luzzatto. Luzzatto's reasoning is simple: could Pharaoh realistically have expected Hebrew women to murder their own people's children? Rather than decide one way or the other, it seems clear that the Torah's ambiguity on this point is deliberate. We do not know who they were or which people they belonged to because their particular form of moral courage transcended nationality and race. In essence, they were being asked to commit a 'crime against humanity', and the fact that they refused to do so tells us something about the ethical parameters of humanity as such. Though Shifra and Puah are seemingly minor figures in the narrative, they are giants in the story of humanity, and since their behaviour has bearing on more recent events, it is a tale that deserves to be set in its full historical context.

One of the landmarks of modern international law was the judgement against Nazi war criminals in the Nuremberg trials of 1946. This established that there are certain crimes in relation to which the claim 'I was obeying orders' is no defence. There are laws higher than those of the state. 'Crimes against humanity' remain crimes, whatever the law of the land or the orders of a government. There are instructions one is morally bound to disobey, times when civil disobedience is the morally necessary response. This principle, attributed to the American writer Henry David Thoreau in 1848, inspired many of those who fought for the abolition of slavery in the United States, as well as the late Martin Luther King in his struggle for black civil rights in the 1960s. At stake in the principle of civil disobedience is a theory of the moral limits of the state.

Until relatively modern times rulers had absolute authority, tempered only by the concessions they had to make to other powerful groups. Not only was this true in ancient times. It remained the case until the late seventeenth century, when figures like John Locke began to develop theories of liberty, social contract and human rights (see page 55, The Universal Story). Much, even most, religious thought until then was dedicated to justifying existing structures of power. That was the function of myth, and later of the concept of the 'divine right of kings'. In such societies, the idea that there might be moral limits to power would have been unthinkable. To challenge the king was to defy reality itself.

Against this background, biblical monotheism was a revolution thousands of years in advance of the culture of the West. The exodus was more than the liberation of slaves. It was a redrawing of the moral and political landscape. If the image of God is to be found, not only in kings but in the human person as such, then all power that dehumanizes is ipso facto an abuse of power. Slavery, seen by all ancient thinkers as part of the natural order of things, becomes morally wrong, an offence not only against man but against God. When God tells Moses to talk to Pharaoh of, 'My son, My firstborn, Israel', He is announcing to the most powerful ruler of the ancient world that though these people may be your slaves, they are My children. The story of the plagues in Egypt is as much political as theological. Theologically it affirms that the Creator of nature is supreme over the forces of nature. Politically it declares that over every human power stands the sovereignty of God, defender and guarantor of the rights of mankind.

In such a worldview, the idea of civil disobedience is not unthinkable but self-evident. The very notion of authority is defined by the transcendence of right over might, morality over power. Even when wrongfully challenged, leadership has to justify itself. Hence Moses' words to God during the Korach rebellion: 'I have not taken so much as a donkey from them, nor have I wronged any of them.' In one of the world-changing moments in history, social criticism was born in Israel simultaneously with institutionalization of power. No sooner were there kings in Israel, than there were prophets mandated by God to criticize them when they abused their power.

Not only is this true of Israel's internal politics. It applied equally when Jews found themselves in exile under foreign powers. The books of Daniel and Esther – the classic exilic texts – are variations on the theme of civil disobedience. Hananiah, Mishael and Azariah refuse to bow down to Nebuchadnezzar's golden image. Daniel disobeys Darius' command to worship him alone. Mordekhai will not bow down to Haman. A 'stiff-necked people' may sometimes find it hard to worship God, but it will certainly worship nothing less. As the Talmud puts it: 'If there is a conflict between the words of the master and the words of the disciple, whose words should one obey?' No human order, whoever issues it, overrides the commands of God.

This is further evidence of the case I have argued in chapters 9–11, that the Western tradition of liberty is built less on the foundations of ancient Greece than on the Hebrew Bible. What Greece lacked was a theory of the moral limits of power. As Lord Acton noted, Athenian democracy failed because the Greeks believed that 'there is no law superior to that of the State – the lawgiver is above the law'. The result, he writes, was that 'the possession of unlimited power, which corrodes the conscience, hardens the heart, and confounds the understanding of monarchs, exercised its demoralising influence on the illustrious democracy of Athens,' as it has so often since. Greek political thought assumes the sovereignty of the state. Jewish political thought assumes the sovereignty of God, and hence the moral limits of the state. That is why the Torah is the foundational text of liberty and human rights, rather than the Greek political classics.

How moving it is, therefore, that the first recorded instance of civil disobedience – predating Thoreau by more than three millennia - is the story of Shifra and Puah, two ordinary women defying Pharaoh in the name of simple humanity. We know nothing else about them, not even which nation they came from. All we know is that they 'feared God and did not do what the Egyptian king had commanded.' In those fateful words, a precedent was set that eventually became the basis of the United Nations Declaration of Human Rights. Shifra and Puah, by refusing to obey an immoral order, redefined the moral landscape of the world.

One further note is in place. Though Greek literature does not know of the concept of civil disobedience, it does contain one famous case where an individual defies the king, not in the name of justice but in loyalty to established custom and family feeling – Sophocles' Antigone, who buries her brother in defiance of King Creon's order that he stay unburied as a traitor. The contrast between Sophocles and the Bible is fascinating. *Antigone* is a tragedy: the eponymous heroine pays for her defiance with her life. The story of Shifra and Puah is not a tragedy. It ends with a curious phrase. God 'made them houses'. What does this mean? The Italian commentator Samuel David Luzzatto offers an insightful interpretation. Sometimes women become midwives when they are unable to have children of their own. That, he suggests, was the case with Shifra and Puah. Because they saved children's lives, God rewards them – measure for measure – with the blessing of their own children ('houses' = families). In Judaism the moral life is not inescapably tragic, because neither the universe nor fate is blind.

'In reward for the righteous women of that generation, our ancestors were redeemed from Egypt.' There are many midrashic traditions about the faithfulness of women during the days of oppression in Egypt and subsequent journey to the promised land (according to the sages, they neither joined in worship of the golden calf, nor in the doubts that led to the episode of the spies). I have chosen these six examples, however, because they are explicit in the biblical text. Each is a vignette of courage in the face of power, and faith in the presence of despair. The story of the exodus as we tell it at the seder table is about God, not about human beings. Even Moses is mentioned only once in the Haggadah, as an aside. Yet there was a human aspect to the story, and it is about one great man and six outstanding women.

Moses became a hero because he had 'greatness thrust upon him'. He led Israel, not because he chose to, but because he was commanded by God. Yocheved, Miriam, Bitya, Zipporah, Shifra and Puah were not commanded. They acted because they had a strong moral sense, indomitable humanity and an intuitive grasp of what heaven asks of us on earth: they 'feared God'. The monument the Torah erects to freedom, the sovereignty of God and the sanctity of life bears the names of those women who by their courage showed that though tyranny is strong, compassion is stronger still.

14

The Missing Fifth

any commentators, among them the Vilna Gaon, have drawn attention to the influence of the number four in connection with the Haggadah. There are four fours:

1. The four questions
2. The four sons
3. The four cups of wine
4. The four expressions of redemption: 'I will *bring you out* from under the yoke of the Egyptians and *free* you from their slavery. I will *deliver* you with a demonstration of My power and with great acts of judgment. I will *take* you to Me as a nation.'   (Exodus 6:6–7)

It may be, though, that just as an X-ray can reveal an earlier painting beneath the surface of a later one, so beneath the surface of the Haggadah there is another pattern to be discerned. That is what I want to suggest in this chapter.

The first thing to note is that there is, in fact, another 'four' on the seder night, namely the four biblical verses whose exposition forms an important part of the Haggadah:

1. 'An Aramean tried to destroy my father...'
2. 'And the Egyptians ill-treated us and afflicted us...'
3. 'And we cried to the Lord, the God of our fathers...'
4. 'And the Lord brought us out of Egypt...'
   (Deuteronomy 26:5–8)

There are, then, not four fours, but five.

In early editions of the Talmud tractate *Pesachim* (118a) there is a passage that perplexed the medieval commentators. It reads: 'Rabbi Tarfon says: over the *fifth* cup we recite the great Hallel.' The medieval commentators were puzzled by this because elsewhere the rabbinic literature speaks about four cups, not five. The Mishnah, for example, states that a poor person must be supplied with enough money to be able to buy four cups of wine. In both the Babylonian and Jerusalem Talmuds the discussion revolves around the assumption that there are four cups on seder night. How then are we to understand the statement of Rabbi Tarfon that there is a fifth cup?

Among the commentators three views emerged. The first was that of Rashi and the Tosafists. According to them, there are only four cups on the seder night, and it is forbidden to drink a fifth. The statement of Rabbi Tarfon must therefore be a misprint, and the texts of the Talmud should be amended accordingly.

The second was that of Maimonides. He holds that there is a fifth cup, but unlike the other four, it is optional rather than obligatory. The Mishnah which teaches that a poor person must be given enough money to buy four cupfuls of wine means that we must ensure that he has the opportunity to fulfil his obligation. It does not extend to the fifth cup which is permitted but not compulsory. Rabbi Tarfon's statement is to be understood to mean that those who wish to drink a fifth cup should do so during the recitation of the great Hallel.

The third view, that of Ravad of Posquières, a contemporary of Maimonides, is that one *should* drink a fifth cup. There is a difference in Jewish law between an obligation, *hovah*, and a religiously significant good deed, *mitzvah*. The first four cups are obligatory. The fifth is a *mitzvah*, meaning, not obligatory but still praiseworthy and not merely, as Maimonides taught, optional.

Thus there was a controversy over the fifth cup. Rashi said that we should not drink it; Maimonides that we may; Ravad that we should. What does one do, faced with this kind of disagreement? Jewish law tries wherever possible to propose a solution that pays respect to all views, especially when they are held by great halakhic authorities. The solution in the present case was simple. A fifth cup is poured (out of respect for Ravad and Maimonides) but not drunk (out of respect for Rashi).

When a disagreement occurs in the Talmud which is not resolved, the sages often used the word *Teyku*, 'Let it stand'. We believe that such disagreements will be resolved in the time to come when Elijah arrives to announce the coming of the Messiah. One of his roles will be to rule on unresolved halakhic controversies. An allusion to this is to be found in the word *Teyku* itself, which was read as an abbreviation of *Tishbi Yetaretz Kushyot Ve'ibbayot*, 'The Tishbite, Elijah, will answer questions and difficulties.' This therefore is the history behind 'the cup of Elijah' – the cup we fill after the meal but do not drink. It represents the 'fifth cup' mentioned in the Talmud.

According to the Jerusalem Talmud, the reason we have four cups of wine is because of the four expressions of redemption in God's promise to Moses. How then could Rabbi Tarfon suggest that there are not four cups but five? *The fascinating fact is that if we look at the biblical passage there are not four expressions of redemption but five.* The passage continues: 'And I will *bring* you to the land I swore with uplifted hand to give to Abraham, to Isaac and to Jacob. I will give it to you as a possession. I am the Lord.' (Exodus 6:8)

There is a further missing fifth. As mentioned above, during the course of reciting the Haggadah we expound four biblical verses, beginning with, 'An Aramean tried to destroy my father'. In biblical times, this was the declaration made by someone bringing first-fruits to Jerusalem. However, if we turn to the source we discover that there is a fifth verse to this passage: 'He *brought us to this place* [the land of Israel] and gave us this land, a land flowing with milk and honey' (Deuteronomy 26:9). We do not recite or expound this verse at the seder table. But this is strange, since the Mishnah states explicitly, 'And one must expound the passage beginning, "An Aramean tried to destroy my father" *until one has completed the whole passage.*' In fact we do not complete the whole passage, despite the Mishnah's instruction.

So there are three 'missing fifths' – the fifth cup, the fifth expression of redemption, and the fifth verse. It is also clear why. All three refer to God not merely bringing the Jewish people out of Egypt but also *bringing them into the land of Israel.* The Haggadah as we now have it and as it evolved in rabbinic times is, in Maimonides words, 'the Haggadah as practised in the time of exile', meaning, during the period of the Dispersion. The missing fifth represented the missing element in redemption. How could Jews celebrate arriving in the land of Israel when they were in exile? How could they drink the last cup of redemption when they had said at the beginning of the seder, 'This year slaves, next year free; this year here, next year in the land of Israel'?

The fifth cup – poured but not drunk – was like the cup broken at Jewish weddings. It was a symbol of incompletion. It meant that as long as Jews were dispersed throughout the world, facing persecution and danger, they could not yet celebrate to the full. One great sage of the twentieth century, the late Rabbi Menahem Kasher, argued that now that there is a State of Israel, many exiles have been ingathered and Jews have recovered their sovereignty and land, the fifth cup should be re-instated. That remains for the halakhic authorities to decide.

What, though, of the four questions and the four sons? There *was* a fifth question. The Mishnah states that a child should ask: 'On all other nights we eat meat that is cooked, boiled or roasted; but this night only roasted meat.' This text can still be found in the early manuscripts of the Haggadah discovered in the Cairo genizah. It refers to the time when the Temple stood and the food eaten at the seder night included the paschal offering, which was roasted. After the Temple was destroyed and the practice of eating a paschal lamb was discontinued, this question was dropped and another (about reclining) substituted.

Was there a fifth child? The late Lubavitcher Rebbe suggested that there is a fifth child on Pesach. The four children of the Haggadah are all present, sitting round the table. The fifth child is the *one who is not there*, the child lost through outmarriage and assimilation. Rabbinic tradition tells us that in Egypt, many Jews assimilated and did not want to leave. The Torah uses a phrase to describe the Israelites' departure from Egypt, *Vachamushim alu bnei Yisrael miMitzrayim* (Exodus 13:18). This is normally translated as 'The Israelites went up out of Egypt armed for battle.' However Rashi, citing earlier authorities, suggests that *hamush* may not mean 'armed.' Instead it may be related to the word *hamesh*, 'five'. The sentence could therefore be translated as, 'Only a fifth of the Israelites left Egypt.'

The rest, he explains, perished in the plague of darkness. The plague itself was less an affliction of the Egyptians than a way of covering the shame of the Israelites, that so many of their number did not want to leave. Certainly the loss of Jews through assimilation has been an ongoing tragedy of Jewish history. How do we allude to it on seder night? By silence: the fifth child – the one who is not there.

So beneath the surface of the Haggadah we find, not four fours, but five fives. In each case there is a missing fifth – a cup, an expression of deliverance, a verse, a question and a child. Each points to something incomplete in our present situation. In the half-century since the Holocaust the Jewish people has emerged from darkness to light. The State of Israel has come into being. The Hebrew language has been reborn. Jews have been brought to safety from the countries where they faced persecution. In the liberal democracies of the West Jews have gained freedom, and even prominence and affluence.

But Israel is not yet at peace. In the Diaspora assimilation continues apace. Many Jews are estranged from their people and their faith. Something is missing from our celebration – the fifth cup, the fifth deliverance, the fifth verse, the fifth question and the fifth child. That is a measure of what is still to be achieved. We have not yet reached our destination. The missing fifths remind us of work still to be done, a journey not yet complete.

15

The Art of Asking Questions

And when your children ask you...
Exodus 12:26

Socrates (469–399 BCE), **the great Greek philosopher** and mentor of Plato, was in the habit of asking disconcerting questions. To this day, persistent questioning in search of clarity is known as the Socratic method. For this habit, among other things, he was put on trial by the Athenians, accused of 'corrupting the young', and sentenced to death. Nothing could be less like Judaism, in which teaching the young to ask questions is an essential feature of Pesach, so much so that the Haggadah – the narration – must be in response to a question asked by a child. If there is no child present, adults must ask one another, and if one is eating alone, one must ask oneself. In Judaism, to be without questions is not a sign of faith, but of lack of depth. 'As for the child who does not know how to ask, you must begin to teach him how.' Many of the customs of seder night (dipping the parsley and removing the seder plate are two examples) were introduced solely to provoke a child to ask 'Why?' Judaism is a religion of questions.

Abraham Twerski, the American psychiatrist, remembers how, when he was young, his teacher would welcome questions, the more demanding the better. When faced with a particularly tough challenge, he would say, in his broken English: 'You right! You hundred prozent right! Now I show you where you wrong.' The Nobel prize-winning Jewish physicist Isidore Rabi once explained that his mother taught him how to be a scientist. 'Every other child would come back from school and be asked, "What did you learn today?" But my mother used to ask, instead, "Izzy, did you ask a good question today?"' In the yeshiva, the home of traditional Talmudic learning, the highest compliment a teacher can give a student is *Du fregst a gutte kasha*, 'You raise a good objection.'

Where did it come from, this Jewish passion for questions? Clearly it owes much to the fact that three times in the Torah, Moses speaks of children asking for an explanation of religious practice, and in another place it says, 'On that day you shall tell your son…' Together, these four verses serve as the basis for the 'four sons' of the Haggadah. Education is not indoctrination. It is teaching a child to be curious, to wonder, reflect, enquire. The child who asks becomes a partner in the learning process. He or she is no longer a passive recipient but an active participant. To ask is to grow.

But questioning goes deeper than this in Judaism – so deep as to represent a *sui generis* religious phenomenon. The heroes of faith asked questions of the God, and the greater the prophet, the harder the question. Abraham asked, 'Shall the judge of all the earth not do justice?' Moses asked, 'O Lord, why have You brought trouble upon this people?' Jeremiah said, 'You are always righteous, O Lord, when I bring a case before You, yet I would speak with You about Your justice: Why does the way of the wicked prosper? Why do all the faithless live at ease?' The book of Job, the most searching of all explorations of human suffering, is a book of questions asked by man, to which God replies with four chapters of questions of His own. The earliest sermons (known as the *Yelamdenu* type) began with a question asked of the rabbi by a member of the congregation. One of the classic genres of rabbinical literature is called *She'elot uteshuvot*, 'questions and replies'. Questioning is at the heart of Jewish spirituality.

Religious faith has often been seen as naive, blind, accepting. That is not the Jewish way. Judaism is not the suspension of critical intelligence. It contains no equivalent to the famous declaration of the Christian thinker Tertullian, *Certum est quia impossibile est*, 'I believe it because it is impossible.' To the contrary: asking a question is itself a profound expression of faith in the intelligibility of the universe and the meaning-fulness of human life. To ask is to believe that somewhere there is an answer. The fact that throughout history people have devoted their lives to extending the frontiers of knowledge is a compelling testimony to the restlessness of the human spirit and its constant desire to go further, higher, deeper. Far from faith excluding questions, questions testify to faith – that history is not random, that the universe is not impervious to our understanding, that what happens to us is not blind chance. We ask, not because we doubt, but because we believe.

There are three kinds of question, each corresponding to a different aspect of God, humanity and the intellectual quest. The first belongs to the sphere of *chokhmah*, 'wisdom', and includes scientific, historical, and sociological inquiry. Rashi interprets the phrase on the creation of man 'in Our image, according to Our likeness' to mean 'with the power to understand and discern'. *Homo sapiens* is the only being known to us capable of framing the question, 'Why?' Maimonides includes scientific and philosophical understanding as part of the commands to love and fear God, because the more we understand of the universe, the more awe-inspiring it and its Architect reveal themselves to be. The sages coined a special blessing for seeing a sage distinguished for his or her worldly knowledge ('Blessed are You… who have given of His wisdom to flesh and blood'). The first request we make in the daily *Amidah* prayer is 'favour us with knowledge, understanding and insight'. Human dignity is intimately related to our ability to fathom the workings of the universe, natural and social. *Chokhmah* is an encounter with God through *creation*. Making man in His image, the creative God endowed mankind with creativity.

Second are the questions we ask about Torah, like the four that open the seder: 'Why is this night different? Why do we do this, not that? What is the reason for the law?' It is one of the most striking features of biblical Hebrew that though the Torah is full of commands – 613 of them – there is no biblical word that means 'obey'. Instead the Torah uses the word *shema*, meaning, 'to hear, listen, reflect on, internalize and respond'. God wants not blind obedience, but understanding response. Moses tells the Israelites that the commands are 'their wisdom and understanding in the eyes of the nations', implying that they are amenable to human reason. In one of the historic moments of adult education, Ezra, returning from Babylon, assembles the people in Jerusalem and reads publicly from the Torah with the assistance of Levites whose task was 'to make it clear and explain the meaning so that the people could understand what was being read.' The saintly Hillel, known for his gentleness to all, none the less said 'An ignorant person cannot be pious'. The more we ask, search and understand the Torah, the better able we are to internalize its values and apply them to new situations. Torah is a meeting with God in *revelation*.

Undoubtedly, though, the most unique of Judaism's questions and the one most associated with the prophetic tradition is about justice: why bad things happen to good people, why evil seems so often to triumph, why there is so much undeserved suffering in the world. Karl Marx once called religion 'the opium of the people'. He believed that it reconciled them to their condition – their poverty, disease and death, their 'station in life', their subjection to tyrannical rulers, the sheer bleakness of existence for most people most of the time. Faith anaesthetized. It made the otherwise unbearable, bearable. It taught people to accept things as they are because that is the will of God. Religion, he argued, was the most powerful means ever devised for keeping people in their place. It spread the aura of inevitability over arbitrary fate. So, argued Marx, if the world is to be changed, religion must be abandoned.

Nothing could be less true of Judaism – the faith born when God liberated a people from the chains of slavery. The question that echoes through the history of Judaism – from Abraham to Jeremiah to Job to rabbinic *midrash* to medieval lament to Hassidic prayer – is not acceptance of, but a protest against, injustice. There are some questions to which the response is an answer. But there are other questions to which the response is an act. To ask, 'Why do the righteous suffer?' is not to seek an explanation that will reconcile us to the slings and arrows of outrageous fortune. It is to turn to God with a request for action, and to discover, in the very process of making the request, that God is asking the same of us.

There are three scenes in Moses' early life. He sees an Egyptian attacking an Israelite, and he intervenes. He sees two Israelites fighting, and he intervenes. He sees non-Israelite shepherds mistreating the non-Israelite daughters of Jethro, and he intervenes. To be a Jew is to be prepared to act in the face of wrongdoing. When Rabbi Chaim of Brisk was asked, What is the role of a rabbi? he replied, 'To redress the grievances of those who are abandoned and alone, to protect the dignity of the poor, and to save the oppressed from the hands of their oppressor.' Judaism is God's question-mark against the random cruelties of the world. It is His call to us to 'mend the world' until it becomes a place worthy of the Divine presence, to accept no illness that can be cured, no poverty that can be alleviated, no injustice that can be rectified. To ask the prophetic question is not to seek an answer but to be energized to action. That is what it is to meet God in *redemption*.

The three types of question are therefore inter-related. When we use our understanding of creation in conjunction with the commands of revelation, we help to bring redemption – an act at a time, a day at a time, knowing that it is not given to us to complete the task, but nor may we stand aside from it.

There are three conditions, though, for asking a Jewish question. The first is that we seek genuinely to learn – not to doubt, ridicule, dismiss, reject. That is what the 'wicked son' of the Haggadah does: ask not out of a desire to understand but as a prelude to walking away.

Second is that we accept limits to our understanding. Not everything is intelligible at any given moment. There were scientists at the beginning of the twentieth century who believed that virtually every major discovery had already been made – not suspecting that the next hundred years would give rise to Einstein's relativity theory, Heisenberg's uncertainty principle, Gödel's theorem, proof of the 'Big Bang' origin of the universe, the discovery of DNA and the decoding of the human genome. In relation to Torah, there were many German and American Jews in the nineteenth century who could not understand Jewish prayers for a return to Zion, and deleted them from the prayer book. These facts should induce in us a certain humility. Not every scientific orthodoxy survives the test of time. Not everything in Judaism that we do not understand is unintelligible. The very features of Jewish life one generation finds difficult, the next generation may find the most meaningful of all. Faith is not opposed to questions, but it is opposed to the shallow certainty that what we understand is all there is.

Third is that when it comes to Torah, we learn by living and understand by doing. We learn to understand music by listening to music. We learn to appreciate literature by reading literature. There is no way of understanding Shabbat without keeping Shabbat, no way of appreciating how Jewish laws of family purity enhance a marriage without observing them. Judaism, like music, is something that can only be understood from the inside, by immersing yourself in it.

Given these caveats, Judaism is a faith that, more than any other, values the mind, encouraging questions and engaging us at the highest level of intellectual rigour. Every question asked in reverence is the start of a journey towards God, and it begins with the habit which, on Pesach, Jewish parents teach their children: to ask, thereby to join the never-ending dialogue between human understanding and heaven.

16

What Does the Wicked Son Say?

*What does the wicked son say? 'What does this service mean to you?' By saying 'you', not
'me', he excludes himself and thereby denies a basic principle of our faith. You in turn
should set his teeth on edge and say to him, 'Because of what God did for me when I came
forth from Egypt' – for me, not him. Had he been there he would not have been redeemed.*

Haggadah

The section of the Haggadah that speaks of the 'four sons' is a brilliant
example of the subtlety and creativity of rabbinic interpretation. It is
based on the fact that in four places in the Torah (three in Exodus
12–13, one in Deuteronomy 6), reference is made to parents instructing
their children on the meaning of Jewish practice by relating it to the exodus. True to
their conviction that no word in the Torah was superfluous, they did not see these
passages as mere repetition. Each teaches something new. Passionate about education
and ultra-sensitive to nuances in the biblical text, the rabbis sensed that the four verses
were about different kinds of child. Three included questions, but were of varying
levels of sophistication and therefore signalled children of different temperaments and
abilities. The fourth, which made no reference to a question, must refer to the child
who has not yet reached the stage of asking. The passage as it stands testifies to the
centrality of education in Jewish life, and especially to the role of parents as teachers.

From the evidence of parallel passages in the rabbinic literature, it seems likely that
the text as it appears in the Haggadah was the result of several centuries of debate and
a long process of editing. There exist, in writings from the Mishnaic period and also
from the Jerusalem Talmud, sources which read like early drafts on which the
Haggadah text was based. Of great interest, though, is the fact that in two sources we
find reference not to the 'four sons' but to the 'wicked son' alone:

> And when your children say...' (Exodus 12:26). [This implies that] in
> the future, some may say, 'What does this service mean to you?' One

who says 'to you' is a wicked person who excludes himself from the community. [In reply] you too should exclude him from the community by saying, 'Because of what God did for me' – meaning 'He did this for me – not you. (*Mekhilta de-Rabbi Shimon bar Yochai*)

And you shall tell your son on that day, "It is because of what the Lord did for me..."' (Exodus 13:8). Why does it say this [and not "because of what the Lord did for us"]? Because it earlier says, 'What does this service mean to you?' This refers to a wicked son who excludes himself from the community – and because he excludes himself, so too should you exclude him [by saying], 'It is because of what the Lord did for me when I went free from Egypt' – 'me' not 'you' [implying] 'had you been there you would not have been redeemed. (*Mekhilta de-Rabbi Ishmael*)

The two men – Rabbi Ishmael ben Elisha and Rabbi Shimon bar Yochai - from whose schools these teachings come, lived in the second century CE, through one of Judaism's most turbulent and tragic eras. They witnessed the ferocity of Rome in suppressing Jewish life. They saw Jews defect from Judaism – some to ally themselves with Rome itself, others to join the new Christian sect. Rabbi Ishmael and Rabbi Shimon were different personality types, the former a rationalist, the latter a mystic, but they were both intensely loyal to Jewish identity and destiny and shared a sense of distress, verging on anger, at Jews who left the fold. We can now place their comments on 'the wicked son' in a specific historical context. It was not Pesach as such, nor were they speaking about young children. They were talking about Jews who, seeing the fall of Jerusalem and the rise of Rome, changed sides and allied themselves to forces that were in the ascendant. This was, for the rabbis, a kind of betrayal.

Another *midrash* gives us an idea of what defecting Jews argued. As always with rabbinic interpretation, we have to realize that when they spoke about their own time, they did so obliquely, by commenting on earlier times, in this case the Babylonian exile in the days of the prophet Ezekiel:

So you find that Israel sought to free itself from the yoke of its oath in the days of Ezekiel. Men from among the elders of Israel came 'to seek the Lord'. They said to him [Ezekiel], If a slave is purchased by a priest, may he eat *terumah* [food set aside for priests]? He replied, He may. Then they asked, If the priest sold him back again to an Israelite, has he then left the priest's domain? He said to them, He has. Then they said [to Ezekiel], So it is with us. We have left [God's] domain and we shall become like the heathen nations. (*Midrash Tanchuma, Nitzavim, 3*)

The argument (it was restated by Spinoza in the seventeenth century when he abandoned Judaism) is that God's covenant with Israel was conditional on their independence. God was their sovereign, precisely because they were not ruled over by anyone else. Therefore, when they went into exile – in the time of the Babylonian conquest and again in the days of Rome – they lost their independence and became subjects of another king. God could have no further claim on them. He had sold or abandoned them to another power. The covenant was at an end.

This is, it should be said, a powerful case, not to be dismissed lightly. It tells us how profound the crisis was when Jews came under foreign rule. The very survival of Jews and Judaism depended on rejecting it, but that took immense religious courage and determination. Writing in the fourth century from a Christian perspective, Augustine cannot restrain himself from a note of astonishment at the tenacity of Jewish faith: 'It is in truth a surprising fact that the Jewish people never gave up its laws, either under the rule of pagan kings or under the dominion of Christians. In this respect it is different from other tribes and nations; no emperor or king who found them in his land was able to prevent Jews from being differentiated, by their observance of their Law, from the rest of the family of nations.' The persistence of Judaism depended on a leap of faith: that despite everything, the covenant was still in force. God had not abandoned His people and would one day redeem them. It should be added that Augustine was right: no other people in history demonstrated so tenacious a loyalty to their past and future. Virtually without exception, every other people who had been conquered adopted the culture of their conquerors.

The Roman era was not the first time, nor was it to be the last, when the very future of Judaism lay in the balance. It had happened before under Babylon, and again in days of the Greeks. It happened again in fifteenth century Spain, when Jews came under almost unbearable pressure to convert to Christianity. There is an astonishing admission by one of the outstanding figures of the Middle Ages, the scholar and statesman Don Isaac Abrabanel, as to the depth of despair he felt at the time of the Spanish expulsion. There was a time, he writes, when he felt like saying: 'all the prophets who prophesied about my redemption and salvation are all false... Moses, may he rest in peace, was false in his utterances, Isaiah lied in his consolations, Jeremiah and Ezekiel lied in their prophecies.' Nor was he alone. 'Let the people remember,' he adds, 'all the despairing things they used to say' in the days of 1492.

Yet Abrabanel, like Rabbi Ishmael and Shimon bar Yochai thirteen centuries earlier, was convinced that defection, conversion or assimilation were wrong. Not only were they the ultimate betrayal of the covenant of Jewish identity; they would not even succeed in sparing Jews from antisemitism:

> Many of our brethren have forsaken the religion of their forefathers as a result of persecution and wished to be like the nations of the world, thinking that thereby they would remove from them the providence of God and the duty of keeping His Torah, and would prosper in their works just like other nations and would no longer belong to the body of their people. But [they are mistaken, because] though they and their

descendants would do all in their power to assimilate, they would not succeed. They would still be called Jews against their own will, and would be accused of Judaizing in secret and be burnt at the stake for it.

370 years later, in 1862, Moses Hess wrote in almost identical terms about the German Jews of his time: 'Because of the Jew-hatred which surrounds him, the German Jew is only too eager to cast aside everything Jewish and to deny his race.' This too, says Hess, will fail: 'Even baptism itself,' he writes, will 'not save him from the nightmare of German Jew-hatred.' Tragically, history proved both Abrabanel and Hess right.

Behind the simple paragraph about 'the wicked son' is a long and painful history of Jews who, faced with persecution on the one hand and the blandishments of the ruling power on the other, chose to abandon Judaism. Viewing this history it is hard not to feel the irony of the fact that ancient Greece and Rome, two civilizations that prided themselves on their tolerance, and medieval Christianity which claimed to worship the God of love, showed surprisingly little tolerance and love when it came to Jews. Their principle often seemed to be that Jews were to be tolerated and loved, *provided* that they relinquished their Judaism. There can, however, equally be no doubt – it is reflected in the harshness of the reply to 'the wicked son' – that Jews themselves felt betrayed by those of their number who, at times of crisis, went over to the other side, to the persecuting power.

That is the history behind 'the wicked son'. Nowadays, however, the situation is somewhat different. Throughout the Diaspora, Jews are again assimilating and outmarrying. As in the days of Rome and Spain the Jewish people faces a crisis of continuity. This time, however, the cause is not persecution but something else: indifference, perhaps, or ignorance, or the sheer pressure of an age and culture in which long term commitments are becoming rarer and harder to understand. Each age brings its own challenges, and because ours is new, I am inclined to offer a radical re-interpretation of the passage, 'What does the wicked son say?'

I do so for the following reasons. First: has any Jewish parent ever truly believed that his or her son is 'wicked'? The Torah contains a law about 'a stubborn and rebellious son', brought to court by his parents for punishment. The Talmud records the statement by one of Israel's sages that 'there never was nor ever will be a stubborn and rebellious son'. To be a parent is to have compassion for one's child. The Hebrew word for compassion, *rachamim*, comes from the word *rechem*, meaning 'a womb'. No parent can write off a child as irretrievably wicked. That is why, when we plead for God's forgiveness, we call him *Avinu*, 'our parent'.

Second: is the dismissive response – 'set his teeth on edge' – the best way of dealing with a rebellious child? The biblical Jacob did not rebuke his children, Reuben, Shimon and Levi, until he was on his death-bed. According to tradition, he reasoned, 'If I rebuke them during my lifetime, they will leave me and go to my brother Esau.' When, in the early twentieth century, a distressed father wrote to Rav Abraham Kook, about how he should treat his son who had abandoned Judaism, Rav Kook replied, 'If you loved him before, love him even more now.'

Third (a rabbinic objection, this): how *old* is the 'wicked son'? Either he is older than bar mitzvah age (thirteen) or younger. If he is younger, then his question is correct, not dismissive: 'What does this service mean *to you*?' which might well mean, 'I, who have not yet reached the age of commandedness, do not know what it means to be commanded. You, however, do. Please therefore explain it to me.' If however he has reached the age of thirteen, then Jewish law states, 'One who chastises his adult son is to be excommunicated, for he has transgressed the prohibition against "placing a stumbling block before the blind."' Among the prohibitions included under the rule of the 'stumbling block' is provoking someone else to sin. A child over the age of thirteen who strikes his parent is guilty of a major offence. Therefore a parent is forbidden to provoke such a child by acting in such a way as to give rise to retaliation.

Fourth: why does the Haggadah use the strange phrase, 'set his teeth on edge'? Classical Hebrew contains many words meaning instruction, chastisement, correction, remonstration and reproof. The Haggadah is a rabbinic document, and the rabbis tended to prefer plain speaking to circumlocutory metaphors. Why, therefore, 'set his teeth on edge' instead of the plain 'rebuke'?

The last question provides the clue. The phrase, 'set his teeth on edge', is in fact a biblical allusion. It is cited by two of the prophets, Jeremiah and Ezekiel, as a well-known proverb: 'The fathers have eaten sour grapes and the children's teeth are set on edge.' By using this unusual locution the sages were hinting at something profound. Children do not always rebel of their own accord. The parent of a rebellious child should ask himself or herself: did I do something to cause it? Was it my 'sour grapes' that set my child's 'teeth on edge'? Taking this as a key to the whole passage, I suggest the following re-interpretation:

What is the child whom others see as wicked – the adolescent, the rebel, the breakaway – really signalling by his conduct? We know what he says. But what is the question *beneath* the words, the inarticulate cry? 'Father, mother, what does Judaism mean *to you*? You sent me to Hebrew school. You gave me a bar mitzvah. You hired teachers for me. I know what Judaism is supposed to mean. I listened to the lessons. I read the books. But all the time I was growing up, you sent me mixed messages. When I neglected my secular education, you were angry, but when I missed Hebrew lessons, you never seemed to mind. I learned about the laws of Jewish life, but you did not seem to keep them, or if you did so, you did it selectively. What you *said* was that Judaism mattered, but what you *did* seemed to show that it did not matter very much. At my bar mitzvah, you were more concerned about the catering than about how much I understood of the words I said in synagogue. As I grew older, you seemed more interested in which college I went to and which career I pursued than whether I was continuing to study and practice Judaism. You wanted me to marry a Jewish girl, but you never gave me a real reason why. I know what Judaism is supposed to mean to me – but you are my parents. I am Jewish only because you are. So I ask you from the depth of my soul: what does Judaism mean *to you*?'

This is a deep question and it brooks no evasion. The only answer one can give –

the existential response which alone is capable of reaching from soul to soul - is to say what Judaism means *to me* – not to him. We must *own* Judaism before we can pass it on. We must live it if we are to inspire those who will live on after us. The Torah says, 'You shall love the Lord your God with all your heart and with all your soul and with all your might... And you shall teach these things to your children.' Rabbi Moses Alshekh, explaining the connection, said simply: we can only teach to our children what we ourselves love.

What prompts such honesty? The knowledge that without it, 'Had he been there, he would not have been redeemed.' No parent can leave a child unredeemed. Therefore to be a parent is to be willing to take one's child and walk, hand in hand, part-way on the Jewish journey, showing that we are prepared to live by the faith we want him or her to continue. On this reading, the 'wicked child' is not wicked, merely confused, and it is we, his parents, who have confused him. To end his confusion we must first end ours by asking, in the depths of self-knowledge, what Judaism means to us.

17

Begin with the Shame,
End with the Praise

[When telling the story of the going out of Egypt] begin with the shame, but end with the praise.
Mishnah

If you want to understand a people, listen to the way it tells its stories.

In the literature of humanity there are many kinds of story. There are those – we know them from childhood – that end with the words 'And they all lived happily ever after.' We call them fairy stories, fantasies, myths. In the artificial reality they conjure up, the evil dragon is slain, the wicked witch defeated, the curse lifted, the conflict resolved. Judaism has no such stories because it does not believe in myth. In the Jewish narrative, the battle against evil is never complete. The messianic age has not yet come. Until then we live in a universe in which, though there is liberation from Egypt, after Pharaoh comes Amalek, and after Amalek, other tyrants. Injustice must be fought in every generation. The legacy of the exodus is not a world in which 'they all lived happily ever after.' There is no closure, no 'sense of an ending'. Instead there is something more real and at the same time more radical: Shabbat – a world of rest which is temporary but no less utopian, where one day in seven we experience pure, unmediated freedom and gain the strength to continue the journey, take up the struggle.

Beyond myth, there is a second great literary genre which we owe to the Greeks, namely *tragedy*. Tragedy tells the story of human beings, with their aspirations and ambitions, in a world governed by impersonal forces. To be human is to wish, to plan, to dream. But our dreams are destined to crash against the rocks of a reality fundamentally indifferent to our existence. They are *hubris*, and are always punished by *nemesis*. Oedipus and the other great figures of Greek drama fail to defeat the forces of fate, as they were bound to do. Tragedy is the consequence of a vision of the sheer abyss between humanity and the gods. Zeus, like other ancient deities, had no special affection for human beings. They disturbed his peace. They threatened to steal his secret knowledge. The gods of polytheistic cultures tended to be at best mildly irritated by, at worst actively hostile to human beings. A tragic universe is a place where bad things happen for no particular reason; where there is no ultimate justice and no expectation of it; where we learn to accept, with Stoic courage, the random cruelties of circumstance. As Aristotle put it, a tragic hero is one whose fortunes change 'from happiness to misery; and the cause of it must not lie in any depravity, but in some great error on his part.' Or as Jean Anouilh wrote:

> In tragedy nothing is in doubt and everyone's destiny is known. That makes for tranquillity. There is a sort of fellow-feeling among characters in a tragedy: he who kills is as innocent as he who gets killed: it's all a matter of what part you are playing. Tragedy is restful; and the reason is that hope, that foul, deceitful thing, has no part in it.

There is – there can be – no tragedy in Judaism. That is not because there are no disasters, crises, catastrophes. Manifestly there are. Jewish history, as often as not, has been written in tears. Nor is it because in a Jewish story there is always a happy ending. That, to repeat, is the structure of myth, not Judaism. But there is always hope, grounded hope, justified not by optimism, innocence, or a 'Whiggish theory' that sees history as constant progress, but by the terms of the covenant between heaven and earth. *Judaism is the principled rejection of tragedy in the name of hope.*

In the lexicon of civilization, there are deep commonalities but no less profound differences. Every culture makes music but only some produce symphonies. Every people tells stories but not all create novels, let alone those of Dickens or Tolstoy. Each individual has memories but only in certain ages and societies do they write autobiographies. Every map of the human condition must find a place for emotion, but not every culture generates, or even finds meaningful, the emotion called hope. In the West, we tend to take it for granted as if it were a universal phenomenon. It is not. It has deep conceptual preconditions which are, if anything, exceptional rather than normal. What must we believe if we are to hope?

Hope is born when people first come to believe the following: that there is an author of the universe; that He is not merely the first cause, prime mover, initiator of the big bang, but that He is actively involved in history; that He is personal, meaning one who understands us; that He brought the world into existence not out of mere curiosity or for some reason unfathomable to us, but out of love, as a parent gives birth to a child; that, despite the chasm between God and us, the infinite and the miniscule, the eternal and the fleeting, there is communication, that God speaks; that God binds Himself to the same rules of ethics He gives to us; and that therefore, having given His word, He will not fail to honour it. These are massive beliefs. They constitute the metaphysics of Judaism and have left their trace on its daughter monotheisms, Christianity and Islam. But without them, there is no hope, and with them, though there may be misery, injustice and pain, there is no tragedy in the Greek sense, for tragedy means the absence of hope.

'Begin with the shame, but end with the praise' – in this quintessentially anti-tragic formula the rabbis specified how the Pesach story should be told. They disagreed on details. According to some, the narration should be along the lines of the reply to the wise son in the book of Deuteronomy (6:21), 'We were slaves to Pharaoh in Egypt, but God brought us out...' According to others it should echo Joshua's final address to the Israelites, 'Long ago your ancestors – Terach, the father of Abraham and Nachor – lived on the other side of the Euphrates and worshipped other gods' (Joshua 24:2). I explain in the Commentary what is at stake between these two views; and in fact, we do both. However, all agree that in telling the story we must start with the bad news (slavery, idolatry) and end with the good (liberation, revelation). In this simple rule, the rabbis were doing more than outlining the form of the Haggadah narrative. They were summarizing the structure of the Jewish imagination. A nation's emotional tonality is expressed in how it tells its story.

The book of Genesis, for example, is dominated by sibling rivalry, but it ends on a note of reconciliation between Joseph and his brothers ('You intended evil against me, but God turned it into good'). The land promised to the patriarchs is still not theirs. Genesis comes to a close with their descendants in Egypt. But again there is a chord of expectation. Joseph says, 'I am about to die, but God will surely come to your aid and take you up out of this land to the land He promised on oath to Abraham, Isaac and Jacob.' The Mosaic books close with Moses forbidden to enter the land to which he had led his people for forty years, but God leads him up the mountain so that he can see it from afar. The Hebrew Bible as a whole ends (2 Chronicles 36) with Cyrus, king of Persia, giving permission to the Jews to return to Israel and rebuild the Temple. There is no closure to these endings, no guarantee of what will happen next. But there is a confidence, born of covenant, whose name is hope. There will be difficulties ahead, but they will not be insurmountable. There will be grief, but it will not be paralyzing or final. Terrible suffering may lie in wait around the corner, but something and someone will survive. There may be exile but eventually there will be homecoming, return. Defeat is never ultimate, nor do we face the uncertain future alone. 'Though I walk through the valley of the shadow of death, I will fear no evil, for Thou art with me.' Wherever we are, there is a way back to the promised land, the good society, the destination which lies beyond our field of vision but which we know is there.

There is nothing in the empirical character of the events themselves that dictate this way, rather than that, of telling the story. *History does not give rise to hope; hope gives rise to history.* As the philosopher-critic Ernst Cassirer put it, the 'meaning of historical time is built not solely from recollection of the past, but no less from anticipation of the future. It depends as much on the striving as on the act, as much on the tendency toward the future as on the contemplation and actualization of the past.' The Hebrew Bible narrates history the way it does because it sees the relationship between God and man the way it does. We can see this by a simple thought experiment.

Imagine the Hebrew Bible rewritten as Greek tragedy. The same events might be recounted, but the division of books would be different. The book of Genesis would run on into the first chapters of Exodus, with the hopes of Abraham and his children dashed in the face of slavery. The Mosaic books would have come to an end, not with Deuteronomy but with Joshua and Judges and its closing verse, heavy with disillusionment and the sense of chaos: 'In those days Israel had no king; everyone did as he saw fit.' The Bible as a whole might have ended with the Babylonian exile and the book of Lamentations. The difference between hope and tragedy lies not in what happens but in how we interpret and respond to what happens. The moral imagination is shaped not only by events but also, and even primarily, by how we tell the story of those events; where we begin and where we end; how we frame our telling, structure the narrative.

The Pesach story – 'Begin with the shame, end with the praise' – is the archetype of the Jewish reading of history, its insistence on rescuing a thread of meaning from catastrophe, its refusal, at times heroic, to be demoralized by defeat, to give in to the siren call of despair. It is the rejection of myth and tragedy, optimism and pessimism alike. The Jewish narrative does not ask us to believe in a world in which there are simple happy endings. Nor does it allow us to take refuge in the cynical belief that every aspiration ends in failure (it is worth remembering that the first 'cynics', from whom we get the word, were Greek philosophers). Anouilh was right: tragedy is restful; Judaism is restless. There is nothing peaceful about hope. Far simpler to believe nothing, expect nothing, reconcile oneself to the meaninglessness of a universe endlessly revolving in silence around a void, and therefore accept the inevitability of fate. Far harder to strive for justice against oppression, freedom against tyranny, knowing that even victory is never final before the end of days and that until then we must fight the battle in every generation, just as the story of the exodus must be told every year. Yet to be a Jew is to choose what Levinas calls 'difficult liberty' over easy necessity. Israel, says the Torah, is the people whose name means 'one who struggles with God and with man and who prevails.' Far from being simple or naïve, hope demands, creates and is the expression of indomitable moral courage.

Viktor Frankl was a Jew who survived Auschwitz and, on the basis of his experiences, founded a new school of psychiatry he called Logotherapy. Survival, he argued, whether in the concentration camps or through trauma, grief, depression and loss, is a matter of 'man's search for meaning'. If we can find meaning in our suffering, we can emerge, if not physically, then at least psychologically, intact. There was, he discovered, one freedom left in Auschwitz, when every other vestige of liberty and humanity had been destroyed:

> We who lived in concentration camps can remember the men who walked through the huts comforting others, giving away their last piece of bread. They may have been few in number, but they offer sufficient proof that everything can be taken from a man but one thing: the last of the human freedoms – to choose one's attitude in any given set of circumstances, to choose one's own way.

I am awestruck at the courage of successive generations of Jews, survivors of the Crusades, blood libels, inquisitions, expulsions, ghettoes and pogroms, who wrestled with God in prayer and lamentation, who did not accept their fate passively or silently, giving way either to blind submission ('such is the will of God') or to a bleak, Greek view of fate, but who continued – in the fine phrase of Nadezhda Mandelstam – to 'hope against hope'. Jews are not blind to the existence of evil. We feel it, taste it, each year afresh, in the bread of affliction and the bitter herbs of slavery. But we refuse with every fibre of our being to be resigned to it. To understand the Jewish people, one must listen to the way it tells its story. A people whose narrative 'begins with the shame and ends with the praise' is one which, knowing in its bones the reality of evil, did not cease wrestling with the angel of death until it discovered the path from suffering to hope.

18

Ben Zoma and the Sages

Rabbi Elazar son of Azariah said: I am like a man of seventy years old, yet I never understood why the story of the going out of Egypt should be told at night until Ben Zoma explained it [on the basis of the biblical phrase], 'so that you remember the day you left Egypt, all the days of your life'. 'The days of your life' means during the daytime; 'all the days of your life' includes the nights. However the other sages said, 'the days of your life' means during this world; 'all the days of your life' includes the messianic age.

Haggadah

This passage, though it forms part of the Haggadah, is not concerned with Pesach. It was almost certainly added to the Haggadah because of its connection with the previous paragraph in which Rabbi Elazar son of Azariah figured prominently (see page 79, The Sages at Bnei Brak). It is, in fact, part of the Mishnah (*Berakhot* 1:5) which deals with the daily evening prayer.

It is not only on Pesach that we recall the exodus. The Torah states, 'so that you remember the day you left Egypt all the days of your life' (Deuteronomy 16:3), and from this the sages derived the rule that the exodus is to be mentioned – though not expounded at length – every day. This is done by reciting the third paragraph of the Shema ('I am the Lord your God who brought you out of the land of Egypt') and the subsequent blessing before the Amidah. The question arose as to whether this should be done in the evening service as well. There were some communities in Mishnaic times that did; some that did not. The predominant custom – universal today – was to do so. The Mishnah explains the logic of the two views.

Rabbi Elazar says that though he is 'like a man of seventy' he was unable to find a justification for the common practice until Ben Zoma explained it to him. The basis for Ben Zoma's view is the principle, generally accepted by the sages, that the Torah contains no superfluous word. Every apparent redundancy has a purpose. It serves as the basis for a law that we could not have established otherwise. In the present case, the Torah could have said, 'the days of your life'. The addition of the word '*all* ' was to teach that not only must we recall the exodus every day, but also every night. The sages agreed with Ben Zoma's principle that the word 'all' was significant. They held, though, that it did not come to teach a law about nights, but about the messianic age.

It now follows that Ben Zoma and the sages did not disagree only about the structure of the evening prayers. They also disagreed about the future – the character of the messianic age. All agreed that in messianic times there would be a second exodus. Just as God redeemed the Israelites from Egypt, so in the future He would gather them from the countries of their dispersion and bring them back to the land of Israel. So the prophets had foretold, and so all Jews believed. That was not at issue. The question was, however, whether the future redemption would eclipse memories of the past or not. Would we still mention the exodus from Egypt in the Messianic age?

The Haggadah quotes only the first stage of the debate. The continuation is reported in the Talmud:

> Ben Zoma said to the sages: Will the exodus from Egypt be mentioned in the Messianic age? Was it not long ago said, 'Behold the days are coming, says the Lord, when they shall no more say: As the Lord lives who brought the children of Israel out of the land of Egypt; but, As the Lord lives who brought up and led the children of the house of Israel out of the land of the north and from all the countries where I have driven them' (Jeremiah 23:7–8)?

> The sages replied: This does not mean that the mention of the exodus from Egypt will be discontinued. What it means is that the deliverance from the other kingdoms will be primary and the exodus from Egypt will be secondary. (*Babylonian Talmud, Berakhot* 12b)

Jeremiah had prophesied that the future redemption would be more remarkable even than the exodus that took place in the days of Moses. This was agreed by both parties to the debate. The one question over which they divided was whether it would *eclipse* memories of Egypt or merely demote them into second place. Such was the debate in the first half of the second century CE.

There are rare moments when one is privileged to see a prophecy come true. It happened at the beginning of the Gulf War in January 1991. I was in Israel with our family during the whole of the confrontation. In its early stages an Anglo-Jewish solidarity mission came to Israel, and they asked me to address them on the significance of the events through which we were living. We met on Friday night, on the Shabbat when we read the portion of *Beshallach* (Exodus 13:17 onward) which begins with the departure of the Israelites from Egypt.

I quoted the Mishnaic and Talmudic passages about the argument between Ben Zoma and the sages, explaining that all agreed that the future redemption, when God would gather Jews 'out of the land of the north and from all the countries where I have driven them' and bring them back to Israel, would be yet more remarkable than the exodus from Egypt. How, I asked, could this be so? The biblical exodus had been accompanied by signs and wonders, miracles the like of which had long ceased. What could be more wondrous than those days?

I then quoted the opening verse of that week's portion: 'When Pharaoh let the people go, God did not lead them on the road through the land of the Philistines, though it was shorter, for God said: If they face war, they may change their minds and return to Egypt.' The meaning of the verse was clear. Even though the Israelites were fleeing slavery, and despite the fact that they had witnessed miracles, God was concerned that if they were to face war, they would turn round and go back.

I then said to the mission: 'You have just witnessed something more remarkable still. You will have noticed, on your arrival, that Ben Gurion airport was almost empty (during the war, commercial flights ceased and all the airlines closed their desks. The airport was in direct danger of attack from Iraqi SCUD missiles). Only one service has continued to operate on a regular basis without interruption – the flights bringing Russian *olim*, new immigrants, to Israel; perhaps the only time in history that a country has been under missile attack and yet people have continued to travel there, seeking to make it their home. In the days of Moses, when the Israelites left Egypt, God feared that if they saw war they would return. *Today the Russian Jews ('out of the land of the north') have seen war and still they continue to come.* This week we have seen with our own eyes the fulfilment of Jeremiah's prophecy that one day there would be an ingathering of exiles in some respects more miraculous than the exodus from Egypt.'

Despite the grief and pain of modern Jewish history, there have been moments – especially in relation to the State of Israel – that can only be compared with the wonders of the Bible. Perhaps we are too close to be able to see their miraculous character. One day, though, historians will look back at the second half of the twentieth century and wonder at how a people who in the Holocaust had come face to face with the angel of death, responded by reviving a land, recovering their sovereignty, rebuilding Jerusalem, rescuing threatened Jews throughout the world, and proving themselves as courageous in pursuit of peace as in defending themselves in war. The echoes of exodus continue to reverberate through Jewish history, undiminished through time, as wondrous now as in those days long ago.

19

The First Pesach

ashi (Rabbi Shlomo ben Yitzhak, 1040–1105) is the greatest and best loved of all the commentators on the Torah. In the nineteenth chapter of Genesis, however, he makes a comment about Pesach that seems to defy understanding.

God has just sent three messengers – angels in human form – to Abraham. He greets them at the entrance to his tent, and he and Sarah offer them hospitality. They have come to tell Sarah that at long last she will have a child. After they leave, God tells Abraham that He is about to destroy Sodom and Gomorrah and the other cities of the plain. Theirs is an evil civilization, and the cry of their wrongdoing has reached heaven. Abraham protests on their behalf in one of the most powerful of all recorded dialogues between man and God: 'Will You sweep away the righteous with the wicked?... Shall the Judge of all the earth not do justice?' God agrees that if there are even ten righteous people, He will not destroy the cities. Meanwhile, two of the messengers have gone to visit Lot who has made his home in Sodom.

He greets them and offers them hospitality. They decline, but he insists. The next verse states: 'He prepared a meal for them and baked unleavened bread [*matzot*] and they ate' (Genesis 19:3). What is the significance of the reference to unleavened bread? Abraham and Sarah had made 'cakes' for the visitors. By contrast, Lot makes *matzot*. On this, Rashi makes his strange comment. *Pesach haya*, he writes: 'It was Pesach.'

What does Rashi mean? The actual exodus lay more than two hundred years in the future. Abraham had already received the prophecy that 'your descendants will be strangers in a country not their own' (Genesis 15:13), but Lot had not. Nor was Lot a prophet: that much is clear. He was unable to foresee even the immediate future, that within twenty-four hours his home and town would be destroyed. How could he have the foresight to know that the date of the angels' visit was – or more precisely, would become – the festival of Pesach? And why should he be observing its laws generations before it became a reality? Rashi's comment is opaque, to say the least. I want to offer a novel interpretation.

The Torah states that early in their stay in the land of Canaan, Abraham and Lot became wealthy. Their flocks were so large that there was not enough grazing land for them both. There were intermittent quarrels between their herdsmen. Abraham, ever a man of peace, urges Lot to separate. 'Let there not be a quarrel between you and me, or between your herdsmen and mine, for we are brothers.' He tells Lot to choose whichever part of the country he prefers. Lot looks out over the plain of the Jordan valley and sees that it is fertile, 'like the garden of the Lord', and decides to live there. Characteristically, he is more moved by economic considerations than moral ones. The inhabitants are evil, but that does not discourage him. He decides to live in the region of Sodom. Abraham, meanwhile, keeps his distance. He is willing to fight battles for the people of the region (Genesis 14) and to pray on their behalf, but he is concerned to preserve his way of life, the lonely path of loyalty to God.

What happens next is predictable and tragic. By the time the angels visit Lot he is 'sitting in the gateway of the city'. The city gate is where the elders sat in ancient times and, among other things, settled disputes. It was, in effect, a court of law. Rashi comments, 'That day they [the inhabitants of Sodom] had appointed him a judge.' His daughters had married local men – the first case of out-marriage in the Torah. In contemporary terms, Lot had began to assimilate.

The angels tell him that the time has come for him to leave. The city is about to be destroyed, and he is in great danger. He must gather his family and immediately depart. Lot hesitates. He goes to discuss the proposal with his sons-in-law. They laugh. At this point, with acute irony, the text states that 'Lot was, in their eyes, like one making a joke.' Surely, they said, he could not be serious. They dismiss him. The angels urge him again: 'Hurry, or you will be swept away.' Lot hesitates. There is a universe of significance in his hesitation.

Tradition has placed over this word an unusual musical notation, called a *shalshelet*. The tune rises and falls, rises and falls, and seems unable to get on to the next word. The sixteenth century commentator, Rabbi Joseph ibn Caspi, correctly observes that this cantillation is a musical way of signalling inner struggle, profound ambivalence. This is Lot's state of mind at that moment. After a lifetime as a nomad, he had arrived. He had made his home in an affluent town and had achieved social recognition. He has been appointed a judge. His daughters have found husbands from the local population. He has become, or so he believes, accepted as part of Sodom and he cannot bring himself to leave. Despite the repeated warnings from his visitors, he delays, risking his life and the lives of his family in the process. Why should he leave the peace and security he thinks he has found merely because two visiting strangers have issued an alarm?

Biblical narrative is immensely subtle, full of resonance to those able to decode its nuances. A few verses earlier, it provides an ironic counter-commentary to Lot's social ambitions. No sooner has word spread around the town about Lot's visitors, than the inhabitants surround his house, demanding that he bring them out 'that we may know them'. Lot refuses, saying that honour demands that he protect his visitors from harm.

The people of Sodom reply, 'Get out of our way... This fellow came here as an alien, and now he wants to play the judge! We'll treat you worse than them' (Genesis 19:9). Despite the story Lot has told himself – that he is accepted, integrated, acculturated – he remains, in the eyes of the locals, an alien. In thinking he belongs, he is engaging in tragic self-deception.

This very sequence of events was repeated in Egypt, this time on a national scale. The Israelites had settled there and grown affluent. One of their ancestors, Joseph, had risen to greatness and become second-in-command to Pharaoh himself. To be sure, a new Pharaoh had ascended to the throne who 'knew not Joseph' and had begun to afflict them, first conscripting them into forced labour, then carrying out a programme of deliberate genocide, drowning male children in the Nile. But when Moses began the long task of liberation, the Israelites themselves complained. His interventions, they said, had only made things worse. 'You have made us a stench to Pharaoh and his servants and have put a sword in their hand to kill us' (Exodus 5:21). They resented his attempts to rescue them.

The late Rabbi Joseph Soloveitchik made an insightful comment about the opening of the book of Exodus. The first verse reads, 'And these are the names of the children of Israel who were coming (haba'im) to Egypt.' The verse uses the present tense rather than the past. In fact the Israelites had come generations before, but in the eyes of the Egyptians it was as if they had just arrived. They remained immigrants, foreigners, outsiders. The new Pharaoh, announcing his programme of persecution, justifies it with the words: 'If there is war, they will join our enemies and fight against us.' In the eyes of the Egyptians, they were not citizens but aliens, just as the people of Sodom had seen Lot. The Israelites for their part – despite the death-bed reminders of Jacob and Joseph that they would return to the promised land and were not to stay indefinitely in Egypt – 'acquired property there', implying that they intended to make Egypt their home. It was not easy for Moses to get them to leave. In the end they were 'driven out' by the Egyptians (Exodus 12:39), just as Lot was physically dragged by the angels from Sodom (Genesis 19:16).

Sadly, this was often the fate of Jews. Facing danger, they were slow to see it – in Spain in the fifteenth century, in Europe in the twentieth. They had found a place where they prospered, and could not bring themselves to believe that they were not regarded by their neighbours as fellow-citizens. How could a country to which they had contributed so much turn against them? How could they, who had lived there for so long, not be accepted? This delay – the recurrence of Lot's ambivalence – was fraught with risk. The people of history was sometimes deaf to the warning-signals of history. This too, tragically, is part of the Pesach story. Where did it begin? With Lot in Sodom. Rashi's comment is profound: without knowing it, Lot was living through the first Pesach.

20

The Unasked Question

Pesach is a night of questions, but there is one we do not ask, and it is significant. Why was there a Pesach in the first place? Why the years of suffering and slavery? Israel was redeemed. It regained its freedom. It returned to the land its ancestors had been promised centuries before. But why the necessity of exile? Why did God not arrange for Abraham or Isaac or Jacob simply to inherit the land of Canaan? If the Israelites had not gone down to Egypt in the days of Joseph, there would have been no suffering and no need for redemption. Why Pesach?

The question is unavoidable, given the terms of the biblical narrative. The Torah indicates that there was nothing accidental about the events leading up to Pesach. Centuries before, Abraham had been told by God in the 'covenant between the pieces', 'Know for certain that your descendants will be strangers in a country not their own, and they will be enslaved and ill-treated for four hundred years' (Genesis 15:13). We make repeated reference in the course of the Haggadah to the fact that the whole sequence of events was part of a pre-ordained plan. God 'had already calculated the end' of suffering. When Jacob went down to Egypt he was, we say, *anus al pi ha-dibbur*, 'forced by divine decree'. God himself told Jacob, 'Do not be afraid to go down to Egypt, for I will make you into a great nation there' (Genesis 46:3) without giving him an intimation of the sufferings his children would endure. The sages say that at the end of his life, when Jacob wanted to tell his children what would happen to them 'at the end of days', the gift of prophecy was taken from him. Without knowing it, the Israelites were part of a narrative that had been scripted long before.

A *midrash* – one of the few places in which the sages expressed their disquiet about this strange stratagem of providence – expresses the problem very acutely:

> The Holy One blessed be He sought to bring about the decree He had spoken of to Abraham, that 'your descendants will be strangers in a country not their own'. So He arranged that Jacob should love Joseph

more than his other sons, that the brothers would be jealous and hate Joseph, that they would sell him to the Ishmaelites who would bring him down to Egypt, and that Jacob would hear that Joseph was still alive and living there. The result was that Jacob and the tribes went to Egypt and became enslaved. Rabbi Tanhuma said: To what can this be compared? To a herdsman who wishes to place the yoke on a cow, but the cow refuses to have it placed on her. What does the herdsman do? He takes a calf from the cow and leads it to the field where ploughing is to take place. The calf begins to cry for its mother. The cow, hearing the calf cry, rushes to the field, and there, while its attention is distracted and it is thinking only of its child, the yoke is placed upon it. (*Tanhuma, Vayeshev*, 4)

The script God writes for His people is sometimes circuitous and terrifying. The sages applied to it the pointed phrase 'How awesome is God in His dealings with mankind' (Psalm 66:5). Why did He want His people to experience slavery? Why was exile in Egypt the necessary prelude to their life as a sovereign nation in the promised land?

The Book of Jonah tells a strange story. Jonah has been asked by God to convey a warning to the people of Nineveh. Their ways are corrupt; the city will be destroyed unless they repent. Jonah flees from his mission, and in the course of the book we learn why. He knew, he says, that the people of Nineveh, hearing the words of the prophet, would repent and be forgiven. For Jonah, this was unjust. When people do wrong, they should suffer the consequences and be punished. This was particularly so in the case of Nineveh, a city of the Assyrians who were to be the cause of so much suffering to Israel. God's forgiveness conflicted with Jonah's sense of retributive justice. God decides to teach Jonah a moral lesson. He sends him a gourd to give him shade from the burning sun. The next day He sends a worm that makes the gourd wither and die. Jonah is plunged into suicidal depression. God then says to him: 'You have been concerned about this gourd, though you did not tend it or make it grow. It sprang up overnight and died overnight. But Nineveh has more than a hundred and twenty thousand people who cannot tell their right hand from their left, and many cattle as well. Should I not be concerned about that great city?' (Jonah 4:10–11).

God teaches Jonah to care by giving him something and then taking it away. Loss teaches us to value things, though usually too late. *What we have, and then lose, we do not take for granted.* The religious vision is not about seeing things that are not there. It is about seeing the things that are there and always were, but which we never noticed, or paid attention to. *Faith is a form of attention. It is a sustained meditation on the miraculousness of what is, because it might not have been.* What we lose and are given back, we learn to cherish in a way we would not have done had we never lost it in the first place. Faith is about not taking things for granted.

This is the key to understanding a whole series of narratives in the book of Genesis.

Sarah, Rebecca and Rachel long to have children but discover that they are infertile. Only through God's intervention are they able to conceive. Abraham goes through the trial of the binding of Isaac, only to discover that God, who has asked him to sacrifice his child, says 'Stop' at the last moment. This is how the covenantal family learns that having children is not something that merely happens. It is how the people of Israel learned, at the dawn of their history, *never to take children for granted*. Jewish continuity, the raising of new generations of Jews, is not natural, inevitable, a process that takes care of itself. It needs constant effort and attention. The same is true of freedom.

Freedom in the biblical sense – responsible self-restraint – is not natural. To the contrary, the natural order in human societies, as in the animal kingdom, is that the strong prey on and dominate the weak. Nothing is rarer or harder to achieve than a society of equal dignity for all. Merely to conceive it requires a massive disengagement from nature. The Torah tells us how this was achieved, through the historical experience of a people who would ever afterward be the carriers of God's message to mankind.

Israel had to lose its freedom before it could cherish it. Only what we lose do we fully pay attention to. Israel had to suffer the experience of slavery and degradation before it could learn, know, and feel intuitively that there is something morally wrong about oppression. Nor could it, or any other people, carry this message in perpetuity without reliving it every year, tasting the harsh tang of the bread of affliction and the bitterness of slavery. Thus was created, at the birth of the nation, a longing for freedom that was at the very core of its memory and identity.

Had Israel achieved immediate nationhood in the patriarchal age without the experience of exile and persecution, it would – like so many other nations in history – have taken freedom for granted; and when freedom is taken for granted, it has already begun to be lost. Israel became the people conceived in slavery so that it would never cease to long for liberty – and know that liberty is anything but natural. It requires constant vigilance, unceasing moral struggle. Israel discovered freedom by losing it. May it never lose it again.

21

One Only Kid

One only kid, one only kid, that father bought for two small coins.
Haggadah

This strange and haunting song, like many other elements of the seder, is simple on the surface but suggestive of hidden depths. Originally an adaptation of a children's nursery rhyme, it entered the Haggadah, probably from Germany, in the late middle ages. It exemplifies the statement made by Hillel who once saw a skull floating on the water and said: 'Because you drowned others, they drowned you. And those who drowned you will in the end themselves be drowned' (*Avot* 2:7).

The theme is the destructive cycle of vengeance and retaliation. On one interpretation the kid is Israel. The 'father' who bought it for two small coins is God, who redeemed Israel from Egypt through His two representatives, Moses and Aaron. The cat is Assyria, who conquered the northern kingdom of Israel. The dog is Babylon, who defeated the southern kingdom of Judah. The stick is Persia, who replaced Babylon as the imperial power in the sixth century BCE. The fire is the Greeks, who defeated the Persians in the days of Alexander the Great. The water is Rome, who superseded ancient Greece. The ox is Islam, who defeated the Romans in Palestine in the seventh century. The slaughterer is Christianity – specifically the Crusaders who fought Islam in Palestine and elsewhere, murdering Jews on the way. The angel of death is the Ottoman Empire, who controlled Palestine until the First World War. The song concludes with an expression of faith that 'this too shall pass' and the Jewish people will return to its land. So it has been in our days.

Alternatively, it may be that the song was suggested by the statement of R. Judah bar Ilai in the Talmud (*Baba Batra* 10a):

> There are ten strong things in the world:
> Rock is strong, but iron breaks it.

Iron is strong, but fire melts it.
Fire is strong, but water extinguishes it.
Water is strong, but the clouds carry it.
The clouds are strong, but the wind drives them.
The wind is strong, but man withstands it.
Man is strong, but fear weakens him.
Fear is strong, but wine removes it.
Wine is strong, but sleep overcomes it.
Sleep is strong, but death stands over it.
What is stronger than death?
Acts of generosity (*tzedakah*), for it is written,
'*Tzedakah* delivers from death' (Proverbs 10:2).

More deeply, though, the song harks back to the beginning of creation and forward to the end of history. A *midrash* says that when God was about to create mankind, He consulted with the angels:

The ministering angels split into contending groups. Some said, 'Let him be created!' while others said, 'Let him not be created!' That is why it is written, 'Mercy and truth collided, righteousness and peace engaged in a clash' (Psalms 85:11).

Mercy said, 'Let him be created, for he will do merciful deeds.' Truth said, 'Let him not be created, for he will be full of falsehood.' Righteousness said, 'Let him be created, for he will do righteous deeds.'

Peace said, 'Let him not be created, for he will never cease quarrelling.' What did the Holy One, blessed be He, do? He took truth and threw it to the ground.

This remarkable *midrash* turns the fundamental problem of faith upside down. The question is not: given the nature of the world, how can God exist? but rather, given the nature of God, how can the world exist? How could God who creates in love bring into being a creature, man, who destroys in hate? How, having made the universe, could God create the one being capable of destroying it?

The *midrash* offers an answer: God took truth and threw it to the ground, saying, 'Let truth grow from the earth'. Human beings cannot stand exposure to too much truth. Reality is too awesome for us to see it steadily and whole. Therefore God proposes that man suffice with truth as it is on earth, not as it is in heaven. We see fragments of the Divine Presence, not more. Were we to see God face to face, we would cry, as did the Israelites at Sinai, 'But now, why should we die? This great fire will consume us, and we will die if we hear the voice of the Lord our God any longer. For what mortal man has ever heard the voice of the living God speaking out of fire as we have, and survived?' (Deuteronomy 5:25–26). We catch glimpses of truth, fugitive and fleeting insights and no more; but it suffices.

Thus God answered the protest of truth. But what of the claim of peace? Since Cain and Abel the human story has been one of conflict, sibling rivalry, war and bloodshed. Nor does it end. The Babylonians defeat the Assyrians, the Persians conquer the Babylonians, the Greeks overcome the Persians, and so it goes. Will there ever be a world of peace? The very silence of the *midrash* on this question suggests its own answer. The creation of man by God was an act of faith. An ancient rabbinic teaching interprets the phrase in Moses' final address, 'God of faith', to mean *God who had faith in the world He was about to create.* More than we have faith in God, God has faith in us – that one day we will learn the lesson of peace, that war never solved any conflict in the long run; that in victory the victor too is defeated; that in conquering others we diminish ourselves; that only in and through peace do we honour the image of God that is mankind.

Sir Henry Sumner Maine once wrote: 'War is as old as mankind, but peace is a modern invention.' In one respect he was wrong: the prophets of Israel were the first people in history, by many centuries, to conceive of peace as an ideal. No vision has echoed more eloquently than the words of Isaiah – today inscribed on a plaque opposite the United Nations building – 'They will beat their swords into ploughshares and their spears into pruning hooks. Nation will not take up sword against nation, nor will they train for war any more' (Isaiah 2:4). The vision of the prophets was of a world at peace, when, again in Isaiah's words:

> He will destroy on this mount the shroud
> That is drawn over the faces of all the peoples
> And the sheet that is spread
> Over all the nations.
> He will destroy death forever. (Isaiah 25:7–8)

So, having earlier expressed the *Jewish* hope, 'Next year in Jerusalem', we end the seder night with the *universal* hope that the angel of death will one day be defeated by the long-overdue realization that God is life; that worshipping God means sanctifying life; that God's greatest command is 'Choose life'; that we bring God into the world by making a blessing over life.

I find it almost unbearably moving that a people who knew so much suffering could summon the moral courage to end this evening of Jewish history on a supreme note of hope, and write it into the hearts of their children in the form of a nursery-rhyme, a song. For what we give our children on this night of nights is something more and greater than the bread of affliction and the taste of Jewish tears. It is a faith that in this world, with all its violence and cruelty, we can create moments of redemption, signals of transcendence, acts of transfiguring grace. No people has risked and suffered more for a more slender hope, but no hope has lifted a people higher and led it, time and again, to greatness. So we end the night with a prayer and a conviction. The prayer: 'God of life, help us win a victory over the forces of death.' And the conviction? That by refusing to accept the world that is, together we can start to make the world that ought to be.

The Chief Rabbi's
HAGGADAH

HEBREW AND ENGLISH TEXT WITH

NEW ESSAYS AND COMMENTARY BY

Jonathan Sacks

HarperCollins*Publishers*

To Michael and Penny
Beloved friends

HarperCollins*Publishers*
77–85 Fulham Palace Road, London W6 8JB
www.**fire**and**water**.com

First published in Great Britain in 2003 by HarperCollins*Publishers*

A catalogue record for this book is available from the British Library.

ISBN 0 00 714825 9

Designed by Michael Marks at The Custard Design Partnership

Printed in Great Britain by Creative Print & Design (Wales), Ebbw Vale, Gwent

Note on the text

The Haggadah, with an English translation by
Rabbi Shlomo Riskin, adapted and with a commentary
by Chief Rabbi Jonathan Sacks, begins at page *5*, with
some introductory comments on page *1* and following.

The Chief Rabbi's Essays on Passover are to be found at
the other end of the book, and are read from left to right
in the normal English fashion.

The Seder

The word seder means 'order', and it is central to the Jewish concept of freedom. We become God's 'partners in the work of creation' when we create order in society – an order that honours all persons as the image of God. If God's presence is to be found not just in rare moments of ecstasy, but in the daily transactions of society as a whole, then it must have a seder, a set of rules we all honour. Order turns individuals into a community and communities into a people. The seder night reflects the order that binds us to other Jews throughout the world and in previous generations.

At the same time, the seder leaves room for spontaneity. No two seder nights are the same. Ideally each family, each year, adds new insights as we reflect on our birth as a people and relate it to the present. 'The more we tell… the more we are to be praised.' Pesach is a fine example of the Jewish counterpoint between structure and spontaneity. We all tell the same story in the same words, but we each add something uniquely ours. The rules are the same, but the commentaries and interpretations are always different. That is how an ancient story stays young.

The Seder plate

In ancient times the participants used to recline on couches, and each had an individual table. Nowadays, though we still recline to drink the wine, eat the matzah, and tell the story, we group the ingredients of the seder on a single plate, often made and decorated specially for the occasion. Its elements are these:

1. **Matzah** – three matzot, representing the double portion of bread always eaten on Sabbaths and festivals, together with a third to represent the special duty of eating matzah tonight.

2. **Zeroa** – a roasted shankbone, recalling the paschal offering. The bone itself symbolises the 'outstretched arm' with which God rescued the Israelites.

3. **Betzah** – a roasted egg, reminding us of the *chagigah*, the other festive offering which was eaten on Pesach.

4. **Maror** – the bitter herbs, recalling the bitterness of slavery in Egypt. Nowadays this usually takes two forms. [A] In the time of the Mishnah, the food eaten as maror was usually lettuce (*chazeret*). Although this does not always taste bitter to our palates, lettuce begins by being sweet and ends by becoming bitter and hard. It thus epitomises the experience of the Israelites in Egypt. Usually Romain lettuce is used. [B] The other form, horseradish, was the form of bitter herbs most readily available in Eastern Europe. Some have the custom to place both on the seder plate, eating them both in combination, or using the lettuce for the first maror and the horseradish for the sandwich with matzah.

5. **Charoset** – a mixture of fruit and spices in which the maror is dipped. The custom of using charoset on Pesach dates back to Mishnaic times, but since it is a custom, not an obligation, we do not have a special blessing for it. There are two reasons for the charoset. It recalls the mortar with which the Israelites made bricks when they were slaves. But it also recalls the verse from the Song of Songs, 'Under the apple tree I awakened you,' which the sages applied to the love between God and Israel which led to redemption. Thus the custom has developed of making the charoset with the various fruits mentioned in the Song of Songs – apples, pomegranates, figs, nuts and dates – together with ground spices (cinnamon and ginger are the most common) which recall the grinding of straw in those days. Wine is added to the mixture until it has the consistency of mortar.

6. **Karpas** – the vegetable which we dip in the salt water at the beginning of the seder to arouse the interest of a child. The original karpas was probably celery, but other vegetables have been used by different communities at various times. Our custom is to use parsley.

7. **Salt water** – in which the karpas is dipped, recalling the tears of the Israelites in Egypt.

The Order

We owe to French Tosafist (sage of the school of Rashi, 12–13th centuries) Rabbi Shmuel of Falaise, the 15-word summary of the seder service:

1. **Kaddesh** – the recitation of Kiddush
2. **U'Rechatz** – washing before Karpas
3. **Karpas** – eating a vegetable dipped in salt water
4. **Yachatz** – breaking the middle matzah
5. **Maggid** – the narrative of the Exodus, set in motion by questions asked by a child
6. **Rachtzah** – washing the hands before the meal

7. **Motzie** – the blessing over food
8. **Matzah** – the special blessing over matzah
9. **Maror** – eating the bitter herbs
10. **Korech** – the sandwich of matzah and maror
11. **Shulchan Orekh** – the 'prepared table', the meal
12. **Tzafun** – the 'hidden' matzah or afikoman, the last food to be eaten
13. **Barekh** – Grace after the meal
14. **Hallel** – concluding Hallel along with other songs of praise
15. **Nirtzah** – final prayer that our seder be accepted by God, and become a prelude to future redemption.

These fifteen stages echo other 'fifteens' – the fifteen Psalms headed 'A Song of Degrees', the fifteen steps between the Women's Court and the Court of the Israelites on which, in Temple times, the Levites would stand and sing praises, and the fifteen occasions of God's kindness to the Jewish people recounted in the song *Dayenu*.

Pesach and the home

It is no coincidence that this, the oldest of Jewish rituals, takes place, as it did in Egypt, in the home. Judaism attaches immense significance to the family. The Book of Genesis is entirely devoted to families: Adam and Eve, Noah and his family, Abraham and Sarah, Isaac and Rebecca, Jacob, Rachel and Leah and their children. The family is the birthplace of a free society. It is where we learn the reciprocity on which the moral life depends. It is where, sharing our vulnerabilities, we discover strength. Through the bonds it creates, we learn *chessed*, the duty that flows from love. Above all it is where we learn *who we are*, where we came from and what our story is.

Significantly, in the only place where the Torah explains why Abraham was chosen to carry the promise of the covenant, the reason is given in terms of parenthood: 'For I have chosen him so that he will instruct his children and his household after him, that they may keep the way of the Lord, doing what is right and just' (Genesis 18:19). Abraham was chosen *in order to be a parent*. He was also chosen to be an educator. The two concepts, so different in many societies, including our own, are in Judaism inseparable.

Fatherhood and motherhood are two distinct phenomena, and Judaism attaches equal importance to both. A child derives its biological identity as part of the Jewish people from its mother. The Hebrew word for compassion, *rachamim*, derives from *rechem*, meaning 'a womb'. A mother, more than a father, is bound to a child through unconditional love.

Fatherhood, by contrast, is a social construct. It belongs to culture rather than nature. There are animals including primates, genetically close to human beings, in which fathers do not even recognise their children after a few months. Fatherhood, like fidelity, is not a constant across cultures. The supreme challenge of any civilization, said the anthropologist Margaret Mead, is to socialize males and persuade them to invest their energies in the home, the family and children.

This was one of Judaism's greatest achievements through the ages. The Hebrew word for male, *zakhar*, is closely related to the word for memory, *zakhor*. It is the task of fathers to hand on to their children the memories of the past. For we are related to the past not just biologically

but also culturally, through the stories we tell and the history we relate. That is what we do on Pesach. Thus Pesach, the festival of Jewish memory, is celebrated in the home, the birthplace of memory.

Families are a source of immense strength, but they can also be the source of narrowness, nepotism and indifference to the world outside. There is a potential conflict between the family and the wider concerns that are needed to build a society of justice and compassion. For that reason a Jewish home must always be open – to the hungry, the lonely, and visitors. Abraham and Sarah, waiting at their tent to provide food and shelter to passers-by, are an enduring symbol of this Jewish value. 'Greater is hospitality,' said the sages, 'than welcoming the Divine presence.' The Hebrew letter *beit*, which means 'house', is open at one side, to show that a Jewish house must always be open to the needy. Thus the seder night begins with an invitation, 'Let all who are hungry come and eat.' In fact, in all ages, Jews celebrating Pesach sought guests long before the meal began. The invitation, at this point, is simply to remind us that a free society only exists where families share their warmth with others.

The Haggadah

Pour the first cup of wine.
If the festival occurs on Friday night, recite the following:

קַדֵּשׁ

בלחש:_וַיְהִי־עֶרֶב_וַיְהִי־בֹקֶר

יוֹם הַשִּׁשִּׁי:_וַיְכֻלּוּ הַשָּׁמַיִם וְהָאָרֶץ וְכָל צְבָאָם:_וַיְכַל אֱלֹהִים בַּיּוֹם הַשְּׁבִיעִי מְלַאכְתּוֹ אֲשֶׁר עָשָׂה_וַיִּשְׁבֹּת בַּיּוֹם הַשְּׁבִיעִי מִכָּל מְלַאכְתּוֹ אֲשֶׁר עָשָׂה:_וַיְבָרֶךְ אֱלֹהִים אֶת־יוֹם הַשְּׁבִיעִי_וַיְקַדֵּשׁ אֹתוֹ כִּי בוֹ שָׁבַת מִכָּל־מְלַאכְתּוֹ אֲשֶׁר־בָּרָא אֱלֹהִים לַעֲשׂוֹת:

On Friday night, continue with the following, including all the words in parentheses. On weekday nights, begin here.

בָּרוּךְ: אַתָּה יהוה אֱלֹהֵינוּ מֶלֶךְ הָעוֹלָם בּוֹרֵא פְּרִי הַגָּפֶן: בָּרוּךְ אַתָּה יהוה אֱלֹהֵינוּ מֶלֶךְ הָעוֹלָם אֲשֶׁר בָּחַר־בָּנוּ מִכָּל־עָם וְרוֹמְמָנוּ מִכָּל־לָשׁוֹן וְקִדְּשָׁנוּ בְּמִצְוֹתָיו._וַתִּתֶּן־לָנוּ יהוה אֱלֹהֵינוּ בְּאַהֲבָה (שַׁבָּתוֹת לִמְנוּחָה וּ) מוֹעֲדִים לְשִׂמְחָה חַגִּים וּזְמַנִּים לְשָׂשׂוֹן אֶת יוֹם (הַשַּׁבָּת הַזֶּה וְאֶת־יוֹם) חַג הַמַּצּוֹת הַזֶּה זְמַן חֵרוּתֵנוּ (בְּאַהֲבָה) מִקְרָא קֹדֶשׁ זֵכֶר לִיצִיאַת מִצְרָיִם. כִּי בָנוּ בָחַרְתָּ וְאוֹתָנוּ קִדַּשְׁתָּ מִכָּל־הָעַמִּים (וְשַׁבָּת) וּמוֹעֲדֵי קָדְשֶׁךָ (בְּאַהֲבָה וּבְרָצוֹן) בְּשִׂמְחָה וּבְשָׂשׂוֹן הִנְחַלְתָּנוּ בָּרוּךְ אַתָּה יהוה מְקַדֵּשׁ (הַשַּׁבָּת וְ) יִשְׂרָאֵל וְהַזְּמַנִּים:

Kiddush

We begin the seder by the formal act of sanctifying the day. The *kiddush* tonight is the same as for other festivals. None the less *kiddush* as such has a particular connection with Pesach, since the command to establish the calendar was first given to the Israelites in Egypt prior to the exodus: 'This month shall mark for you the beginning of the months; it shall be the first of the months of the year for you' (Exodus 12:2). This was the first command given to Israel as a people.

R. Avraham Pam explained this in the following way: the difference between a slave and a free human being does not lie in how long or hard they work. Free people often work long hours doing arduous tasks. The difference lies in who controls time. A slave works until he or she is allowed to stop. A free person decides when to begin and when to end. Control over time is the essential difference between slavery and freedom. The determination of the calendar gave to the Israelites the power to decide when the New Moon occurred, and thus when the festivals occur. They were given authority over time. The first command to the Israelites was thus an essential prelude to freedom. It said: learn how to value time and make it holy. 'Teach us to number our days that we may get a heart of wisdom.'

See Essays on Passover "History and Memory" page 27

Pour the first cup of wine.
If the festival occurs on Friday night, recite the following:

Kaddesh

The sixth day! The heavens and earth were finished, and all that was in them. On the seventh day God had finished all the work He had made, and on the seventh day He rested from all the work He had made. God blessed the seventh day and made it holy, for it was then that He rested from all His work, which God, in creating, had made.

On Friday night, continue with the following, including all the words in parentheses. On weekday nights, begin here.

Blessed are you, O God our Lord, King of the world,

Creator of the fruit of the vine.

Blessed are you, O God our Lord, King of the world, who chose us from all nations and raised us among every language, by making us holy with His commandments. You gave us, O God our Lord, with love, (Sabbaths for rest,) festivals for gladness, holidays and seasons for joy; (this Sabbath day, and) this feast day of unleavened bread, the time of our freedom (with love), a holy convocation in memory of the Exodus from Egypt. For it is us You have chosen, and us You have made holy from all the nations, giving us as an inheritance your holy (Sabbath and) festivals with (love and favour,) gladness and joy. Blessed are You O God, Sanctifier of (the Sabbath,) Israel, and the seasons.

When Pesach falls on Shabbat

The two forms of holiness – Shabbat and festivals – are different. Shabbat represents *creation*. The festivals represent *redemption*. Shabbat is about the presence of God in nature. The festivals are about the presence of God in history. Accordingly Shabbat was declared holy by God Himself at the culmination of creation. God 'blessed the seventh day and declared it holy.' The festivals, by contrast, are sanctified by the Jewish people through their determination of the calendar – just as redemption takes place in history when we act in partnership with God. Thus on Shabbat we end the kiddush by saying *Mekadesh ha-Shabbat*, meaning that it is God who sanctifies Shabbat; but on festivals we say *Mekadesh Yisrael veha-zemanim*, meaning, 'God sanctifies Israel, and Israel in turn sanctifies time.' Shabbat is holiness 'from above to below'. The festivals are holiness 'from below to above'.

When Yom Tov falls on Shabbat, Shabbat takes priority. This is because the sanctity of Shabbat is of a higher order. Its prohibitions are more extensive and the penalties for breaking them are more severe. It also, though, exemplifies the general rule in Judaism that 'When a frequent obligation coincides with a rare one, the more frequent one takes precedence.' This is in itself an expression of Jewish values. In many faiths, a sense of holiness and spirituality belongs to moments that are rare, unusual, exceptional. In Judaism what is holy is the texture of everyday life itself. Judaism is not poetry but prose. It is the religious drama of daily deeds, words and relationships. God is not distant but in the here-and-now – if we create space in our hearts for His presence.

If the Seder falls on Saturday night, add the following:

בָּרוּךְ אַתָּה יהוה אֱלֹהֵינוּ מֶלֶךְ הָעוֹלָם בּוֹרֵא מְאוֹרֵי הָאֵשׁ:

בָּרוּךְ אַתָּה יהוה אֱלֹהֵינוּ מֶלֶךְ הָעוֹלָם הַמַּבְדִּיל בֵּין קֹדֶשׁ לְחוֹל
בֵּין אוֹר לְחֹשֶׁךְ בֵּין יִשְׂרָאֵל לָעַמִּים בֵּין יוֹם הַשְּׁבִיעִי לְשֵׁשֶׁת יְמֵי
הַמַּעֲשֶׂה. בֵּין קְדֻשַּׁת שַׁבָּת לִקְדֻשַּׁת יוֹם טוֹב הִבְדַּלְתָּ וְאֶת יוֹם
הַשְּׁבִיעִי מִשֵּׁשֶׁת יְמֵי הַמַּעֲשֶׂה קִדַּשְׁתָּ. הִבְדַּלְתָּ וְקִדַּשְׁתָּ אֶת עַמְּךָ
יִשְׂרָאֵל בִּקְדֻשָּׁתֶךָ. בָּרוּךְ אַתָּה יהוה הַמַּבְדִּיל בֵּין קֹדֶשׁ לְקֹדֶשׁ:

This blessing is always recited.

בָּרוּךְ אַתָּה יהוה אֱלֹהֵינוּ מֶלֶךְ הָעוֹלָם שֶׁהֶחֱיָנוּ
וְקִיְּמָנוּ וְהִגִּיעָנוּ לַזְּמַן הַזֶּה:

Drink the first cup of wine while leaning to the left.

וּרְחַץ

The officiant washes his hands

The usual blessing recited when washing the hands is not said.

כַּרְפַּס

Dip the celery into salt water and recite the following blessing before eating:

בָּרוּךְ אַתָּה יהוה אֱלֹהֵינוּ מֶלֶךְ
הָעוֹלָם בּוֹרֵא פְּרִי הָאֲדָמָה:

Who chose us from all nations and raised us among every language, by making us holy with His commandments

Chosenness is not a privilege but a responsibility. Jews are different not because of what we are but because of what we are called on to be: not because of the hardware but the software of the Jewish people. God chose us not because of any innate superiority but in order to 'make us holy with His commandments'. When we are true to that vocation, we bring blessing not just to ourselves but to the world.

Washing

In the time of the Mishnah, many people were careful to wash their hands before eating moist foods. Nowadays the custom is not widely observed except on seder night, when it is done for the *karpas*, which is dipped in liquid. To signal the difference between this washing, which is customary, and the washing before eating bread, which is obligatory, no blessing is said.

If the Seder falls on Saturday night, add the following:

Blessed are You, O God our Lord, King of the world, Creator of the lights of the fire.

Blessed are You, O God our Lord, King of the world, who divides between holy and profane, between light and darkness, between Israel and the nations, and between the seventh day and the six working days. You distinguished the holiness of the Sabbath from the holiness of a festival, and You sanctified and separated the seventh day from the six days of work. You have sanctified Your people Israel with Your own holiness. Blessed are You O God, who distinguishes between holy and holy.

This blessing is always recited.

Blessed are you O God our Lord, King of the World, who has granted us life, kept us, and let us reach this season.

Drink the first cup of wine while leaning to the left.

U'Rechatz The officiant washes his hands

The usual blessing recited when washing the hands is not said.

Karpas The Celery

Dip the celery into salt water and recite the following blessing before eating:

Blessed are You, O God our Lord, King of the world, Creator of the fruit of the earth.

Karpas

Dipping *karpas* in salt water or vinegar is one of the things we do on the seder night to arouse the curiosity of children so that they will ask, 'Why is this night different?' It is one of the two acts referred to in the question, 'On all other nights we do not dip even once, but tonight we dip twice.' The second, just before the meal, is the dipping of *maror* in *charoset*.

There is symbolic significance in these two acts. The Exodus began and ended with acts of dipping. It began when Joseph's brothers sold him into slavery. They dipped his robe in the blood of a slaughtered goat (Genesis 37:31) and brought it to Jacob, to persuade him that Joseph had been attacked and killed by a wild animal. The sale of Joseph into slavery in Egypt was the beginning of the long process through which the entire family of Jacob travelled to Egypt and eventually became slaves.

The exile ended with the Israelites taking bunches of hyssop, dipping it in the blood of the paschal offering, and daubing it on the door-frames of their houses (Exodus 12:22). God 'passed over' these houses during the final plague, after which they went free.

The two dippings recall these events. The *karpas*, itself sweet, is dipped in salt and becomes sour. The *maror*, itself bitter, is dipped in the sweet *charoset* and has some of the bitterness removed. These two acts remind us that freedom, which is sweet, becomes sour when we use it to mistreat others. Slavery, which is bitter, is sweetened when collective suffering becomes human solidarity and thus a prelude to freedom.

יַחַץ

Take the middle matzah, break it in two.
The larger of the two pieces is put away (until after the meal) for the Afikoman.
Replace the small piece between the two matzahs.

מַגִּיד

Raise the seder tray, uncover the matzah and begin reciting the Haggadah.

הָא לַחְמָא עַנְיָא דִּי אֲכָלוּ אַבְהָתָנָא
בְּאַרְעָא דְמִצְרָיִם. כָּל דִּכְפִין יֵיתֵי
וְיֵכֻל. כָּל דִּצְרִיךְ יֵיתֵי וְיִפְסַח. הָשַׁתָּא הָכָא
לְשָׁנָה הַבָּאָה בְּאַרְעָא דְיִשְׂרָאֵל. הָשַׁתָּא עַבְדֵי
לְשָׁנָה הַבָּאָה בְּנֵי חוֹרִין:

Yachatz: Break the middle matzah

Of the three *matzot*, the upper and lower represent the *lechem mishneh*, the double portion of mannah that fell before Sabbaths and festivals in the wilderness so that the Israelites would not have to gather food on the holy day itself. The third – the middle *matzah* – represents the special duty to eat unleavened bread on Pesach.

There are two reasons why we break it in half. The first is that it is described as 'the bread of affliction' or, as the sages interpreted it, 'the bread of a poor person'. One who is so poor that he does not know where his next meal is coming from does not eat all his food at once. He divides it into two, saving half for later.

The second is that, with the destruction of the Temple, *matzah* takes the place of the paschal offering. Just as the paschal offering was eaten at the end of the meal – so as to be experienced as holy food, not just food eaten to satisfy hunger – so we reserve half of the *matzah* (the *afikoman*) to be eaten at the end of the meal. The custom that children hide the *afikoman* is part of the spirit of the seder service, which contains many elements designed to attract and sustain the interest of a child.

However, there is also a third significance to breaking the middle *matzah*. *Matzah* represents two apparently contradictory ideas. At the beginning of the seder we describe it as 'the bread of affliction which our ancestors ate in the land of Egypt'. Ibn Ezra explains that slaves were given unleavened bread because, being hard, it takes longer to digest. It removes hunger for longer than ordinary bread. Later in the seder, we describe it as the bread which the Israelites ate as they were leaving Egypt, in too much of a hurry to allow the dough to rise. We divide the *matzah*, therefore, to show that it has two symbolisms, not one. Now, at the beginning of the seder, it is the bread of affliction. Later, once we have relived the exodus, it becomes the bread of freedom. The difference between freedom and slavery does not lie in the quality of bread we eat, but the state of mind in which we eat it.

Maggid: Narration

This is the beginning of the seder narrative, known as *Maggid*, from the word *Haggadah*, 'to relate, recount, declare, proclaim'. The story of the Exodus is known as *Haggadah* because of the verse, 'And you shall tell (*vehigadta*) your son on that day saying, "I do this because of what the Lord did for me when I came out of Egypt"' (Exodus 13:8). However, the word haggadah derives from a verb that also means 'to bind, join, connect'. The story of the Exodus is more than a recounting (*sippur*) of things that happened long ago. It binds the present to the past and future. It connects one generation to the next. It joins us to our children. Jewish continuity means that each successive generation commits itself to continuing the story. Our past lives on in us.

Yachatz Divide the Matzah

Take the middle matzah, break it in two.
The larger of the two pieces is put away (until after the meal) for the Afikoman.
Replace the small piece between the two matzahs.

Maggid Tell the Passover Story

Raise the seder tray, uncover the matzah and begin reciting the Haggadah.

This is the bread of affliction that our fathers ate in the land of Egypt.

Let all who are hungry, come and eat.

Let all who are needy, come and celebrate Passover.

This year we are here – next year, may we be in the Land of Israel.

This year we are slaves – next year, may we be free.

This is the bread of affliction

This is a strange invitation: 'This is the bread of affliction which our ancestors ate in the land of Egypt. Let all that are hungry come and eat.' What hospitality is it to offer the hungry the taste of suffering? In fact, though, this is a profound insight into the nature of slavery and freedom. As noted above, *matzah* represents two things: it is the food of slaves, and also the bread eaten by the Israelites as they left Egypt in liberty. What transforms the bread of affliction into the bread of freedom is *the willingness to share it with others*.

Primo Levi was a survivor of Auschwitz. In his book, *If This Is a Man*, he describes his experiences there. According to Levi, the worst time of all was when the Nazis left in January 1945, fearing the Russian advance. All prisoners who could walk were taken on the brutal 'death marches'. The only people left in the camp were those who were too ill to move. For ten days they were left alone with only scraps of food and fuel. Levi describes how he worked to light a fire and bring some warmth to his fellow prisoners, many of them dying. He then writes:

'When the broken window was repaired and the stove began to spread its heat, something seemed to relax in everyone, and at that moment Towarowski (a Franco-Pole of twenty-three, typhus) proposed to the others that each of them offer a slice of bread to us three who had been working. And so it was agreed.

'Only a day before a similar event would have been inconceivable. The law of the Lager said: "eat your own bread, and if you can, that of your neighbour," and left no room for gratitude. It really meant that the law of the Lager was dead.

'It was the first human gesture that occurred among us. I believe that that moment can be dated as the beginning of the change by which we who had not died slowly changed from *Haftlinge* [prisoners] to men again.'

Sharing food is the first act through which slaves become free human beings. One who fears tomorrow does not offer his bread to others. But one who is willing to divide his food with a stranger has already shown himself capable of fellowship and faith, the two things from which hope is born. That is why we begin the seder by inviting others to join us. Bread shared is no longer the bread of affliction. Reaching out to others, giving help to the needy and companionship to those who are alone, we bring freedom into the world, and with freedom, God.

This year we are here – next year, may we be in the Land of Israel.

At the very moment that we gather to remember the past, we speak about the future. The seder brings together the three dimensions of time. Before the meal we tell the story of redemption in the past. During the meal we experience it in the present. After the meal, as we conclude Hallel and say 'Next year in Jerusalem', we look forward to redemption in the future.

Fill the second cup of wine.
The youngest present then asks:

מַה נִּשְׁתַּנָּה הַלַּיְלָה הַזֶּה מִכָּל־הַלֵּילוֹת.
שֶׁבְּכָל הַלֵּילוֹת אָנוּ אוֹכְלִין חָמֵץ וּמַצָּה הַלַּיְלָה הַזֶּה כֻּלּוֹ מַצָּה.
שֶׁבְּכָל הַלֵּילוֹת אָנוּ אוֹכְלִין שְׁאָר יְרָקוֹת
הַלַּיְלָה הַזֶּה מָרוֹר. שֶׁבְּכָל הַלֵּילוֹת אֵין אָנוּ
מַטְבִּילִין אֲפִילוּ פַּעַם אֶחָת הַלַּיְלָה הַזֶּה שְׁתֵּי
פְעָמִים. שֶׁבְּכָל הַלֵּילוֹת אָנוּ אוֹכְלִין בֵּין יוֹשְׁבִין
וּבֵין מְסֻבִּין הַלַּיְלָה הַזֶּה כֻּלָּנוּ מְסֻבִּין:

What is distinctive about Jewish time is that we experience the present not as an isolated moment, but as a link in a chain connecting past and future. The very fact that they had been liberated in days of Moses gave our ancestors confidence that they would be liberated again. The Jewish people would return to the land of Israel. Here we see one of the most profound instincts of the Jewish mind: *memory is the guardian of hope.* Those who forget the past become prisoners of the present. Those who remember the past have faith in the future. We can face it without fear, because we have been there before.

This year we are slaves – next year, may we be free.

There are two words for freedom in Hebrew, *chofesh* and *cherut*. *Chofesh* is 'freedom from'. *Cherut* is 'freedom to'. *Chofesh* is what a slave acquires when released from slavery. He or she is free from being subject to someone else's will. But this kind of liberty is not enough to create a free society. A world in which everyone is free to do what they like begins in anarchy and ends in tyranny. That is why *chofesh* is only the beginning of freedom, not its ultimate destination. *Cherut* is collective freedom, a society in which my freedom respects yours. A free society is always a moral achievement. It rests on self-restraint and regard for others. The ultimate aim of the Torah is to fashion a society on the foundations of justice and compassion, both of which depend on recognising the sovereignty of God and the integrity of creation. Thus we say, 'Next year may we be *bnei chorin*,' invoking *cherut* not *chofesh*. It means, 'May we be free in a way that honours the freedom of all.'

What makes this night different?

The Torah speaks of children asking questions on Pesach. 'And when your children ask you, "What does this ceremony mean to you?" then tell them...' From this, tradition inferred that the story of the exodus from Egypt must be told, wherever possible, in response to the questions asked by a child.

The Torah has two words for inheritance, *yerushah* and *nachalah*, and they represent the two different ways in which a heritage is passed on across the generations. The word *nachalah* comes from the root *nachal*, which also means 'a river'. It represents an inheritance that is merely handed down, without any work on the part of the recipient, as water flows in a river. *Yerushah*, by contrast, means active inheritance. R. Samson Raphael Hirsch pointed out that *lareshet*, the verbal form of *yerushah*, sometimes means 'to conquer' or 'to capture'. It means actively taking hold of what one has been promised. An inheritance for which one has worked is always more secure than one for which one has not. That is why Judaism encourages children to ask questions. When a child asks, it has already begun the work of preparing to receive. Torah is a *yerushah*, not a *nachalah*. It needs work on behalf of the child if it is to be passed on across the generations.

Fill the second cup of wine.

The youngest present then asks:

The Four Questions

What makes this night different from all other nights?

On all nights we eat bread or matzah, but this night only matzah.

On all nights we eat other greens, but on this night a bitter vegetable.

On all nights we do not dip even once, but on this night (we must dip) two times (celery in the vinegar or salt water, and the bitter herb in charoseth).

On other nights we drink sitting or leaning, but on this night we all lean.

What makes this night different?

The history of *Mah nishtanah* is fascinating. The text itself goes back some two thousand years. It is recorded in the Mishnah and was almost certainly the form of words used in Second Temple times. Everything else about it, though, was different. It was said not before the meal but afterwards. It was said, not by the child but by the parent. And it was not a set of questions but a set of statements. How so?

In Temple times the meal was eaten first. The sanctity of the moment was palpable. Families had travelled from all parts of Israel to bring their sacrifice to the Temple and eat their meal in the precincts of Jerusalem. The questions of the child arose naturally from acts done that night that were done at no other point in the year. If the child was too young to ask, the father would prompt him by saying, *Mah nishtanah halaylah hazeh*, meaning not 'Why is this night different?' but 'See how different this night is from all other nights.' He would then enumerate the differences, encouraging the child to ask, 'Why?'

One of the most remarkable achievements of the sages was to preserve the continuity of Jewish life through a series of tragedies – the destruction of the Temple, the end of the Pesach sacrifice, and the loss of the entire atmosphere of collective celebration in Jerusalem. The narrative was moved from after the meal to before it, so that words would do the work of place: the Jewish people no longer had Jerusalem, but we still had the story. And instead of children asking spontaneously, each in their own words (the 'four children' of the Haggadah), the *mah nishtanah* became a standard formula that every child could learn. Old words took on a new function. A ritual once celebrated in the vicinity of the Temple became a ceremony that could be observed throughout the world without losing its original character. Everywhere that Jews gathered to celebrate Pesach became a fragment of Jerusalem. The city, the land and the sacrificial order lay in ruins, but the words remained.

One of the things achieved by turning *mah nishtanah* into a standard formula was that now there was no division of children into the wise, the wicked, the simple, and the child unable to ask. In a beautiful and deeply characteristic gesture, custom ordained that every child should ask in the same way, using the same words, so as not to put any child to shame. All Jewish children are precious and we do not make distinctions between them.

What makes this night different?

The four questions correspond to the 'four children' of the Haggadah. The wise child turns immediately to the central symbol of Pesach, the matzah. His question is profound. Matzah is the 'bread of affliction' but Pesach is the 'festival of freedom'. Why then do we eat only matzah? The 'wicked child' asks about the *maror* because, being bitter towards Judaism he tastes only the bitterness, not the sweetness, of Jewish life. The simple child asks about the dipping, the act done precisely to provoke a question on the part of a child. The one who does not know how to ask, asks why people are reclining. His attention is not on the seder service at all but on the people gathered round the table.

Uncover the matzahs, and say:

עֲבָדִים הָיִינוּ לְפַרְעֹה בְּמִצְרָיִם.

וַיּוֹצִיאֵנוּ יהוה אֱלֹהֵינוּ
מִשָּׁם בְּיָד חֲזָקָה וּבִזְרוֹעַ נְטוּיָה. וְאִלּוּ לֹא הוֹצִיא הַקָּדוֹשׁ
בָּרוּךְ הוּא אֶת אֲבוֹתֵינוּ מִמִּצְרָיִם. הֲרֵי אָנוּ וּבָנֵינוּ וּבְנֵי בָנֵינוּ.
מְשֻׁעְבָּדִים הָיִינוּ לְפַרְעֹה בְּמִצְרָיִם. וַאֲפִילוּ כֻּלָּנוּ חֲכָמִים.
כֻּלָּנוּ נְבוֹנִים. כֻּלָּנוּ זְקֵנִים. כֻּלָּנוּ יוֹדְעִים אֶת הַתּוֹרָה.
מִצְוָה עָלֵינוּ לְסַפֵּר בִּיצִיאַת מִצְרָיִם.
וְכָל הַמַּרְבֶּה לְסַפֵּר בִּיצִיאַת מִצְרָיִם הֲרֵי זֶה מְשֻׁבָּח:

We were slaves to Pharaoh in Egypt

The Mishnah states as a general rule that in telling the story of the exodus we must 'Begin with the shame and end with the praise.' A Jewish story begins in sadness and ends in joy.

What, specifically, does this mean on Pesach? The Talmud records two views, those of Rav and Shmuel, two sages of the third century. According to Shmuel it means saying, 'We were slaves to Pharaoh in Egypt and the Lord our God brought us out.' According to Rav it means saying, 'Originally our ancestors worshipped idols, but God brought us close to Him.' Out of respect for these two views, we say them both, beginning with the answer according to Shmuel.

The two opinions reflect different approaches to the Exodus. According to Shmuel the central fact is physical redemption. Our ancestors were slaves who were liberated by God. According to Rav the essential theme is spiritual redemption. Our ancestors were idolators who found, and were found by, God.

There is a difference, too, in their approach to history. Shmuel focuses on the immediate event of Egypt, slavery and redemption. Rav places the event in a wider context – the whole history of the Jewish people from Abraham to Joshua and the conquest of the land. For Rav, Pesach is part of a larger drama, from founding father to the birth of a nation in its own land.

Maimonides draws a third distinction. There are two elements to the seder service: there is the story we tell our children, and the story we tell ourselves. Shmuel focuses on the story as told to a child. Rav speaks of the story as an adult reflection. Children can understand the drama of slavery and freedom together with the many miracles that were involved. It takes an adult to understand the journey from polytheism to monotheism, from myth to faith.

Slavery and freedom

In the Kovno ghetto in the early 1940s an extraordinary scene took place one morning in the makeshift synagogue. The Jews in the ghetto had begun to realise the fate that lay in store for them. They knew that none of them would escape, that the work camps to which they would be transported were in fact factories of death. And at the morning service, the leader of prayer, an old and pious Jew, could finally say the words no longer. He had come to the blessing in which we thank God for not having made us slaves. He turned to the congregation and said: 'I cannot say this prayer. How can I thank God for my freedom when I am now a prisoner facing death? Only a madman could say this prayer now.'

Some members of the congregation turned to the rabbi for advice. Could a Jew in the Kovno ghetto pronounce the blessing thanking God for not having made him a slave? The rabbi replied very simply. 'Heaven forbid that we should abolish the blessing now. Our enemies wish to make us their slaves. But though they control our bodies they do not own our souls. By making this blessing we show that even here we still see ourselves as free men, temporarily in captivity, awaiting God's redemption.'

The hardest question for faith today is: Where was God at Auschwitz? Where was God when His faithful

Uncover the matzahs, and say:

The Answer

We were slaves to Pharaoh in Egypt,

and God our Lord took us out of there with a strong hand and an outstretched arm.

If God had not taken our fathers out of Egypt, then even we,
our children and our children's children would still be slaves in Egypt.

Even if we are all wise and understanding, all elders, expert in the Torah,
we are still obliged to speak of the Exodus from Egypt.
Whoever discusses the Exodus at length should be praised.

---

servants were being turned to ashes and dying as martyrs in their millions? Where was redemption when the Jews of Europe were gassed and burned and God was silent? That question haunts us on the night of Passover, because on this night we remember that slavery in Egypt was not the only, or even the worst, chapter of Jewish suffering. There have been Pharaohs in every generation. And not only Jews have been their victims. There are peoples today who live under the threat of genocide. If God redeems – not in heaven but here on earth – where is His redemption?

The greatest prophets asked this question and received no answer. None the less there is a fragment of an answer, and it was given by the rabbi in the Kovno ghetto. God has chosen only one dwelling place in this finite, physical universe and that is the human heart. Whenever we banish God from the human heart, tragic things happen. When rulers set themselves in place of God, they begin by taking other people's freedom and end by taking other people's lives. There is a direct line from tyranny to idolatry to bloodshed. Our greatest defence is the knowledge that above all earthly powers is the supreme king of kings, God Himself, who has endowed all human beings with His image. No absolute ruler has ever succeeded in extinguishing that spark from the souls of a people, which expresses itself in a passion for freedom. That is why all tyrannies have failed and will always fail.

Where was God in the Kovno ghetto? In the hearts of those who, though they were prisoners in the valley of the shadow of death, insisted on pronouncing a blessing as free human beings. Their story has no simple happy ending, but they left us an immortal legacy: the knowledge that the human spirit cannot be killed, and that therefore freedom will always win the final battle.

If God had not taken our fathers out of Egypt

One of the rules of telling the story on Pesach is that each person must see himself or herself as if they had personally left Egypt. History becomes memory. The past becomes the present. At this stage, therefore, we speak of the continuing consequences of the past. Had the exodus not happened and the Israelites stayed in Egypt, none of the subsequent events of Jewish history would have occurred. What and where we are now is the result of what happened then.

Even if we are all wise

There is a fundamental difference between knowing and telling the story. We do not tell the narrative of the exodus to know what happened in the past. We do so because each telling engraves that event more thoroughly in the memory, and because each year adds its own insights and interpretations. Judaism is a constant dialogue between past and present, and since the present always changes, there is always a new juxtaposition, a new facet of the story. The sages said, 'There is no house of study without *chiddush*, some new interpretation.' The story of Pesach never grows old, because the struggle for freedom never ends, and therefore each generation adds its own commentary to the old-new story.

מַעֲשֶׂה בְּרַבִּי אֱלִיעֶזֶר וְרַבִּי יְהוֹשֻעַ וְרַבִּי
אֶלְעָזָר בֶּן־עֲזַרְיָה וְרַבִּי עֲקִיבָא וְרַבִּי טַרְפוֹן שֶׁהָיוּ
מְסֻבִּין בִּבְנֵי־בְרַק וְהָיוּ מְסַפְּרִים בִּיצִיאַת מִצְרַיִם
כָּל־אוֹתוֹ הַלַּיְלָה עַד שֶׁבָּאוּ תַלְמִידֵיהֶם וְאָמְרוּ לָהֶם.
רַבּוֹתֵינוּ הִגִּיעַ זְמַן קְרִיאַת שְׁמַע שֶׁל שַׁחֲרִית.
אָמַר רַבִּי אֶלְעָזָר בֶּן־עֲזַרְיָה. הֲרֵי אֲנִי כְּבֶן
שִׁבְעִים שָׁנָה. וְלֹא זָכִיתִי שֶׁתֵּאָמֵר יְצִיאַת מִצְרַיִם
בַּלֵּילוֹת. עַד שֶׁדְּרָשָׁהּ בֶּן זוֹמָא. שֶׁנֶּאֱמַר לְמַעַן תִּזְכֹּר
אֶת יוֹם צֵאתְךָ מֵאֶרֶץ מִצְרַיִם כֹּל יְמֵי חַיֶּיךָ. יְמֵי חַיֶּיךָ
הַיָּמִים. כֹּל יְמֵי חַיֶּיךָ הַלֵּילוֹת. וַחֲכָמִים אוֹמְרִים. יְמֵי
חַיֶּיךָ הָעוֹלָם הַזֶּה. כֹּל יְמֵי חַיֶּיךָ לְהָבִיא לִימוֹת הַמָּשִׁיחַ:

בָּרוּךְ הַמָּקוֹם. בָּרוּךְ הוּא. בָּרוּךְ
שֶׁנָּתַן תּוֹרָה לְעַמּוֹ יִשְׂרָאֵל. בָּרוּךְ הוּא.

כְּנֶגֶד אַרְבָּעָה בָנִים דִּבְּרָה תוֹרָה. אֶחָד חָכָם.
וְאֶחָד רָשָׁע. וְאֶחָד תָּם. וְאֶחָד שֶׁאֵינוֹ יוֹדֵעַ לִשְׁאוֹל:

Rabbi Elazar, son of Azariah, said

See Essays on Passover "The Sages at Bnei Brak" page 85
See Essays on Passover "Ben Zoma and the Sages" page 121

The four children

This famous passage is based on the fact that the Torah speaks in four separate places about the dialogue between parents and children:

1 'And when your children say, "What does this service mean to you?" you shall say, "It is the Passover sacrifice to the Lord, because He passed over the houses of the Israelites in Egypt when He smote the Egyptians, but saved our houses."' (Exodus 12:25–26)
2. 'And you shall tell your son on that day, "It is because of what the Lord did for me when I went free from Egypt."' (Exodus 13:8)
3. 'And when, in time to come, your son asks you, saying, "What is this?" you shall say to him, "It was with a mighty hand that the Lord brought us out from Egypt, the house of bondage."' (Exodus 13:14)
4. 'When, in time to come, your children ask you, "What mean the testimonies, statutes and judgements that the Lord our God has commanded you?" you shall say to your children, "We were slaves to

It happened that Rabbi Eliezer, Rabbi Yehoshua, Rabbi Elazar ben Azariah, Rabbi Akiva and Rabbi Tarfon were reclining (at a Seder) in Bnei Berak. They were discussing the Exodus all that night, until their students came and told them,

"Masters! It is time for the morning prayer Sh'ma!"

Rabbi Elazar ben Azariah, said: I am like seventy years old, but I had not been able to show that the Exodus must be recited at night until Ben Zoma explained it. It is said, "That you may remember the day you left Egypt all the days of your life" (Deuteronomy 16:3). "The days of your life" [alone] would indicate the days; "all the days of your life" [also] indicates the night. The [other] sages said that "the days of your life" [alone] indicates our present world. "All the days of your life" [also] includes the age of the Messiah.

Blessed is the Ever-present! Blessed is He!
Blessed is He who gave the Torah to His people Israel!
Blessed is He!

The Four Children

The Torah speaks of four children:
One is wise, one wicked, one simple, and one does not know how to ask.

Pharaoh in Egypt and the Lord freed us from Egypt with a mighty hand."' (Deuteronomy 6:20–21) Rather than seeing them as restatements of the same idea, the sages detected, in the different ways the verses are phrased, four distinctive personalities – thus, four kinds of children.

The four children

It may be that the 'four children' are not different people but successive stages in the development of a child. We begin by being unable to ask. We accept the world as given. The next stage in intellectual growth is curiosity (the 'simple' son). We ask questions with no ulterior motive. We simply want to learn. This is often followed by a period of testing and challenging the values we have received (the 'wicked' or adolescent son). The Hebrew word for adolescent, *na'ar*, also means 'to shake off'. The teenage years are ones where we develop our own identity by putting received values to the test. This can sometimes lead to rebellion as a form of self-exploration. The culmination of cognitive growth is 'wisdom', the point at which we have both internalised the values of our heritage and are sufficiently mature to see their objective merits. Although the Haggadah uses the word 'wise', rabbinic tradition preferred the phrase *talmid chakham*, a 'wise disciple'. Wisdom, in Judaism, is not a state, but a process of constant learning. That is why it lies as much in the questions one asks as in the answers. Every answer is itself the prelude to a deeper question, and thus there is constant growth as we move to new levels of understanding.

חָכָם מַה הוּא אוֹמֵר. מָה הָעֵדוֹת וְהַחֻקִּים
וְהַמִּשְׁפָּטִים אֲשֶׁר צִוָּה יהוה אֱלֹהֵינוּ אֶתְכֶם. וְאַף
אַתָּה אֱמָר־לוֹ כְּהִלְכוֹת הַפֶּסַח. אֵין מַפְטִירִין אַחַר
הַפֶּסַח אֲפִיקוֹמָן:

רָשָׁע מַה הוּא אוֹמֵר. מָה הָעֲבוֹדָה הַזֹּאת
לָכֶם. לָכֶם וְלֹא לוֹ. וּלְפִי שֶׁהוֹצִיא אֶת־עַצְמוֹ מִן
הַכְּלָל כָּפַר בְּעִקָּר. וְאַף אַתָּה הַקְהֵה אֶת־שִׁנָּיו וֶאֱמָר
לוֹ בַּעֲבוּר זֶה עָשָׂה יהוה לִי בְּצֵאתִי מִמִּצְרָיִם. לִי
וְלֹא לוֹ. אִלּוּ הָיָה שָׁם לֹא הָיָה נִגְאָל:

The four children

The four children are a vignette of the Jewish people. One asks because he wants to hear the answer. A second asks because he does *not* want to hear the answer. A third asks because he does not understand. The fourth does not ask because he doesn't understand that he doesn't understand. Ours has never been a monolithic people.

Yet there is a message of hope in this family portrait. Though they disagree, they sit around the same table, telling the same story. Though they differ, they stay together. They are part of a single family. Even the rebel is there, although part of him does not want to be. This too is who we are.

The Jewish people is an extended family. We argue, we differ, there are times when we are deeply divided. Yet we are part of the same story. We share the same memories. At difficult times we can count on one another. We feel one another's pain. Out of this multiplicity of voices comes something none of us could achieve alone. Sitting next to the wise child, the rebel is not fated to remain a rebel. Sitting next to the rebel, the wise child may share his wisdom rather than keep it to himself. The one who cannot ask will in time learn how. The simple child will learn complexity. The wise child will learn simplicity. Each draws strength from the others, as we draw strength from belonging to a people.

The wise child

The three other children appear in the book of Exodus, at the time of the going out of Egypt itself. The question of the wise son appears in the book of Deuteronomy, forty years later. Historical understanding takes time. In the midst of events we are too close to see their significance, even to ask the right questions. As a Hassidic sage said: 'It took one day to take the Israelites out of Egypt. It took forty years to take Egypt out of the Israelites.'

The wise child, what does he say? [He asks],

"What are the testimonies, statutes and laws that God our Lord has commanded you?" (Deuteronomy 6:20).

Then you shall tell him [all] the laws of Passover [up to], "we do not taste anything after the Passover Afikoman."

The wicked child, what does he say? [He asks,]

"What is this service to you?" (Exodus 12:26). "To you – but not to me!" Since he dissociates himself from the group, he denies a basic principle [of faith]. You should also give him a blunt answer and say, "Because of this, God did [things] for me, when I left Egypt" (Exodus 13:8): "for me – but not for you! If you had been there, you would not have been saved!"

The wise child

The wise child shows his wisdom by distinguishing the three different kinds of commandment, understanding that Judaism is a complex system in which not every law has the same purpose.

Edot, testimonies, are commands like those of Shabbat and the festivals that remind us of the presence of God in nature and history.

Chukkim, statutes, are commands like the prohibition of milk and meat, which have no obvious reason. Some Jewish thinkers believed that *chukkim* were commands without a reason. Saadia Gaon said that they were commanded to confer on us a reward for pure obedience. Maimonides, in *The Guide for the Perplexed*, argued that each of the *chukkim* had a reason, though it became clear only after long investigation. Nachmanides and Rabbi Samson Raphael Hirsch held that *chukkim* were ecological commands, rules respecting the integrity of nature and the distinctness of different species and forms of life.

Mishpatim are laws of social justice. Biblical Hebrew has two words for justice, *tzedek* and *mishpat*. *Mishpat* refers to the principles of the rule of law, impartiality and retributive justice ('measure for measure'). *Tzedek* refers to equity and distributive justice. The word *tzedakah* does not mean, as it is usually translated, 'charity'. Instead it means justice in this broader sense. It comes from the idea, fundamental to Judaism, that what we possess we do not ultimately own. We hold it in trust from God, and one of the conditions of that trust is that we share part of what we have with others in need.

One way of expressing the difference between the three types of command is that through *edot* we fulfil our duty to the past, through *mishpatim* our duty to others, and through *chukkim* to the natural world.

An alternative: though each essentially involves action, in the case of *mishpatim* it is the act itself that is the purpose of the command. It creates justice. In *edot*, the point of the action is the belief or attitude to which it gives rise. On Shabbat we focus on creation, on Pesach on redemption, on Shavuot on revelation. In the case of *chukkim* the ultimate purpose is to shape character, train dispositions and emotions, and create 'habits of the heart'.

תָּ**ם** מַה הוּא אוֹמֵר. מַה זֹּאת. וְאָמַרְתָּ אֵלָיו
בְּחֹזֶק יָד הוֹצִיאָנוּ יהוה מִמִּצְרַיִם מִבֵּית־עֲבָדִים.

וְשֶׁאֵינוֹ יוֹדֵעַ לִשְׁאוֹל אַתְּ פְּתַח לוֹ. שֶׁנֶּאֱמַר
וְהִגַּדְתָּ לְבִנְךָ בַּיּוֹם הַהוּא לֵאמֹר בַּעֲבוּר זֶה עָשָׂה
יהוה לִי בְּצֵאתִי מִמִּצְרָיִם:

יָכוֹל מֵרֹאשׁ חֹדֶשׁ. תַּלְמוּד לוֹמַר בַּיּוֹם הַהוּא.
אִי בַּיּוֹם הַהוּא יָכוֹל מִבְּעוֹד יוֹם. תַּלְמוּד לוֹמַר
בַּעֲבוּר זֶה. בַּעֲבוּר זֶה לֹא אָמַרְתִּי אֶלָּא בְּשָׁעָה שֶׁיֵּשׁ
מַצָּה וּמָרוֹר מֻנָּחִים לְפָנֶיךָ:

The wicked child

There are many explanations given by the commentators as to why this particular question should be seen as a sign of rebellion. The simplest answer is that, whereas other children are spoken of as *asking*, in this case the verse speaks of children *saying*. This is a child who does not seek an answer; he seeks only to make a statement.

Another possibility is his use of the word *avodah* 'service'. The Torah uses the same word *avodah* to describe *both* slavery to Pharaoh *and* service to God. The wicked child is in effect asking: what advantage did our people gain by leaving Egypt? They merely exchanged one *avodah* for another. Then they were servants to Pharaoh, now they have become servants to God. But in both cases they had a master; in neither case were they free. The rebellious child understands freedom to mean having no master at all. He has not yet understood that freedom is not the ability to do what you like; it is the ability to do what you ought. A society in which 'everyone did what was right in their own eyes' (Judges 21:25) does not have freedom, but anarchy. Without the sovereignty of God and law (the Torah and its commands), the strong rule the weak, and the powerful take advantage of the powerless. The difference between serving Pharaoh and serving God makes all the difference in the world: between injustice and justice, slavery and freedom, a society where people are used as means and one where they are respected as ends in themselves.

Since he dissociates himself from the group, he denies a basic principle

What principle? The answer is that though the rebellious child denies none of the thirteen principles of faith enumerated by Moses Maimonides, he does deny something else. Maimonides explains (*Hilkhot Teshuvah* 3:11): 'One who separates himself from the community, even if he does not commit a transgression but only holds aloof from the congregation of Israel, does not fulfil religious precepts in common with his people, shows himself indifferent when they are in distress, does not observe their fasts, but goes his own way as if he were one of the nations and did not belong to the Jewish people – such a person has no share in the world to come.'

The simple child, what does he say? [He merely asks], "What is this?" You shall say to him, "With a strong hand God took us out of Egypt, from the house of slaves" (Exodus 13:14).

As for the one who does not know how to ask, you must explain for him, as it is written, "You shall tell your child on that day, 'Because of this, God did [things] for me when I left Egypt'" (Exodus 13:8).

One might think that he should begin on the first of the month. The Torah therefore continues, "on that day." If the Torah had only said, "on that day," one might think that [the Seder is begun] during the day. The Torah therefore stresses, "because of this." One cannot say ["this"] unless matzah and the bitter herb are lying before you.

The mere fact that an individual fails to identify with the collective fate of the Jewish people – even though he observes the commandments – is a denial of one of the principles of Judaism, namely that ours is a *collective* faith. Martin Buber was wrong when he called his great work on faith *I and Thou*. In Judaism the primary relationship is *We and Thou*. Despite its insistence on individual responsibility ('If I am not for myself, who will be?'), Judaism is equally insistent on collective responsibility ('And if I am only for myself, what am I?'). Long before Moses encountered God, he 'went out to his own people and watched them at their hard labour.' This was the birth of his active identity as a Jew. Though many Jews in the modern age found it difficult to believe, they identified with the Jewish people, fought its cause, and gave it their support. *Belonging is the first step to believing.* What makes the wicked son wicked, according to the Haggadah, is not that he fails to believe, but that he fails to identify with the people of whom he is a part.

As for the one who does not know how to ask, you must open for him

What is the significance of the phrase, 'You shall open for him'? It is said that the Rebbe Menahem Mendel of Kotzk once asked his disciples, 'Where does God live?' The disciples were perplexed. 'What does the Rebbe mean: Where does God live? Where does God not live? Surely we have been taught that no place is devoid of His presence? He fills the heavens and the earth.' The Rebbe replied, 'You have not understood. God lives *where we let Him in*.'

On another occasion he asked, 'Why does it say in the Shema: "And these words shall be on your heart"? Why "on" and not "in"?' He answered: 'The heart is not always open. Therefore the Torah says, Lay these words *on* your heart, so that when the time comes that your heart opens, they will be there, ready to fall in.' In Judaism, spirituality means openness. To one who is open, God is closer than we are to ourselves. To one who is closed, He is further away than the most distant galaxies. The task of education is to teach a child to be open – to the voice of God and the miracle of existence. A question, asked with sincerity, is an opening in the soul.

מִתְּחִלָּה עוֹבְדֵי עֲבוֹדָה זָרָה הָיוּ אֲבוֹתֵינוּ.
וְעַכְשָׁו קֵרְבָנוּ הַמָּקוֹם לַעֲבוֹדָתוֹ. שֶׁנֶּאֱמַר וַיֹּאמֶר
יְהוֹשֻׁעַ אֶל־כָּל־הָעָם כֹּה־אָמַר יהוה אֱלֹהֵי יִשְׂרָאֵל
בְּעֵבֶר הַנָּהָר יָשְׁבוּ אֲבוֹתֵיכֶם מֵעוֹלָם תֶּרַח אֲבִי
אַבְרָהָם וַאֲבִי נָחוֹר וַיַּעַבְדוּ אֱלֹהִים אֲחֵרִים: וָאֶקַּח
אֶת־אֲבִיכֶם אֶת־אַבְרָהָם מֵעֵבֶר הַנָּהָר וָאוֹלֵךְ אוֹתוֹ
בְּכָל־אֶרֶץ כְּנָעַן וָאַרְבֶּה אֶת־זַרְעוֹ וָאֶתֶּן לוֹ אֶת־יִצְחָק:
וָאֶתֵּן לְיִצְחָק אֶת־יַעֲקֹב וְאֶת־עֵשָׂו וָאֶתֵּן
לְעֵשָׂו אֶת־הַר שֵׂעִיר לָרֶשֶׁת אוֹתוֹ וְיַעֲקֹב וּבָנָיו יָרְדוּ מִצְרָיִם:
בָּרוּךְ שׁוֹמֵר הַבְטָחָתוֹ לְיִשְׂרָאֵל בָּרוּךְ הוּא.
שֶׁהַקָּדוֹשׁ בָּרוּךְ הוּא חִשַּׁב אֶת הַקֵּץ לַעֲשׂוֹת כְּמָה
שֶׁאָמַר לְאַבְרָהָם אָבִינוּ בִּבְרִית בֵּין הַבְּתָרִים.
שֶׁנֶּאֱמַר וַיֹּאמֶר לְאַבְרָם יָדֹעַ תֵּדַע כִּי־גֵר יִהְיֶה זַרְעֲךָ
בְּאֶרֶץ לֹא לָהֶם וַעֲבָדוּם וְעִנּוּ אֹתָם אַרְבַּע מֵאוֹת שָׁנָה.
וְגַם אֶת־הַגּוֹי אֲשֶׁר יַעֲבֹדוּ דָּן אָנֹכִי וְאַחֲרֵי כֵן
יֵצְאוּ בִּרְכֻשׁ גָּדוֹל:

Cover the matzah, raise the cup of wine and say:

וְהִיא שֶׁעָמְדָה לַאֲבוֹתֵינוּ וְלָנוּ:
שֶׁלֹּא אֶחָד בִּלְבָד עָמַד עָלֵינוּ לְכַלּוֹתֵנוּ.
אֶלָּא שֶׁבְּכָל דּוֹר וָדוֹר עוֹמְדִים עָלֵינוּ
לְכַלּוֹתֵנוּ. וְהַקָּדוֹשׁ בָּרוּךְ הוּא מַצִּילֵנוּ מִיָּדָם:

At first our fathers served idols. But now God has brought us close [to Him that we may] serve Him [alone]. It is thus written, "Joshua said to the people: Thus said God, the Lord of Israel, 'Your fathers had always lived on the other side of the [Euphrates] River. [They included] Terach, father of Abraham and Nachor, and they served other gods (Joshua 24:2).

"'I took your father Abraham from across the river, and led him through the whole land of Canaan. I increased his family and gave him Isaac. To Isaac I gave Jacob and Esau, and to Esau I gave Mount Seir to keep. Jacob and his children went down to Egypt'" (Joshua 24:3,4).

Blessed is He who keeps His promise to Israel, blessed be He! God had calculated that the end would come just as He had told Abraham [in the Promise] between the Halves. It is written, "[God] said to Abram, 'Know that your children will be strangers in a land that is not theirs. [The people of that land] will make them slaves and be cruel to them for four hundred years. But then I will judge the nation whom they will serve, and after that they will leave with great wealth'" (Genesis 15:13 –14).

Cover the matzah, raise the cup of wine and say

It is this [promise] that has stood by our fathers and by us! For it was not one man alone who stood up against us, but in every generation they stand up against us to destroy us – and the Holy Blessed One saves us from their hand!

One might think that he should begin on the first of the month

Just as in Egypt, so now, the preparation for Pesach begins well in advance of the day itself. One might have thought that the story could be told from the moment preparations begin. The Torah, however, establishes a fundamental rule about how to pass your values on to the next generation: *tell the story while you are doing the deed*, when 'Pesach, matzah and maror are in front of you.' Values are caught, not taught. They are communicated by what we do more than by what we say. That is why the story of the Exodus must be told at the time we re-enact it. Living it ourselves is the best way of ensuring that it will live on in the imagination of a child.

Replace the cup and uncover the matzah:

צֵא וּלְמַד. מַה בִּקֵּשׁ לָבָן הָאֲרַמִּי
לַעֲשׂוֹת לְיַעֲקֹב אָבִינוּ. שֶׁפַּרְעֹה
לֹא גָזַר אֶלָּא עַל הַזְּכָרִים וְלָבָן בִּקֵּשׁ לַעֲקוֹר אֶת
הַכֹּל. שֶׁנֶּאֱמַר: אֲרַמִּי אֹבֵד אָבִי וַיֵּרֶד מִצְרַיְמָה
וַיָּגָר שָׁם בִּמְתֵי מְעָט וַיְהִי שָׁם לְגוֹי גָּדוֹל עָצוּם וָרָב:

וַיֵּרֶד מִצְרַיְמָה. אָנוּס עַל פִּי הַדִּבּוּר:
וַיָּגָר שָׁם. מְלַמֵּד שֶׁלֹּא יָרַד יַעֲקֹב אָבִינוּ
לְהִשְׁתַּקֵּעַ בְּמִצְרַיִם אֶלָּא לָגוּר שָׁם. שֶׁנֶּאֱמַר וַיֹּאמְרוּ
אֶל פַּרְעֹה לָגוּר בָּאָרֶץ בָּאנוּ כִּי אֵין מִרְעֶה לַצֹּאן
אֲשֶׁר לַעֲבָדֶיךָ כִּי־כָבֵד הָרָעָב בְּאֶרֶץ כְּנָעַן וְעַתָּה יֵשְׁבוּ
נָא עֲבָדֶיךָ בְּאֶרֶץ גֹּשֶׁן:

Go and learn

We now come to the exposition of the four verses (Deuteronomy 26:5–8) which, according to the Mishnah, constitute the core of the Haggadah. These were originally part of the 'confession' made when bringing first fruits to Jerusalem, usually on the festival of Shavuot. Most scholars take the view that this text was chosen because it would have been well known to most Jews in Temple times and subsequently, before texts of the Haggadah, written or printed, were freely available.

Another reason is that the confession was preceded by the words, 'I declare (*higadti*) today…' The verb is from the same root as the word *Haggadah*, and thus tradition may have seen in this coincidence of terminology a suggestion that it was this passage that should be recited on the night of Pesach, when we are commanded to 'declare' to our children (*Vehigadta levincha*).

The four verses summarise the main events of the exile and exodus. To each phrase is added a passage of midrash, rabbinic commentary, either clarifying the meaning or connecting it to other biblical passages.

Go and learn what Laban the Aramean wanted to do to our father Jacob

As commentators have noted, this is a strange passage with which to begin the exposition. The plain sense of the words *Arami oved avi* is 'My father was a wandering Aramean' (meaning Abraham, according to Rashbam; or Jacob, according to Ibn Ezra and Sforno). The interpretation of the Haggadah – 'An Aramean tried to destroy my father' – is not the plain sense. Then there is no clear evidence in the Torah that Laban did try to 'destroy' Jacob. He pursued him, and God appeared to him at night telling him to do Jacob no harm, but we are not told what his intentions were. Most significantly, the interpretation seems to cut across the whole theme of the Haggadah, which is about slavery in Egypt. It is strange indeed to begin by saying that what Pharaoh did was bad, but Laban was worse. However, Rabbi Z. H. Ferber offered the following explanation.

The sun and the wind were once arguing as to which was stronger. The sun said, 'I am stronger, because I give light and warmth to the whole world.' The wind said, 'I am stronger, because nothing can stand in my way.' Just then a farmer began ploughing his field. The sun said to the wind, 'Let us settle the matter once and for all. Let us see which of us can remove the jacket from the man. That will prove which is the stronger.'

Replace the cup and uncover the matzah:

Go and learn what Laban the Aramean wanted to do to our father Jacob.

Pharaoh only wanted to kill the young boys, but Laban wanted to uproot the whole [Jewish nation, by killing Jacob]. Thus it is written, "An Aramean [wanted to] destroy my father. But he went down to Egypt, and lived there as a stranger, few in number. There he became a nation, great, mighty, and many" (Deuteronomy 26:5).

"But he went down to Egypt" – forced by [God's] word.

"And lived there as a stranger" – This teaches that [Jacob] did not go to settle in Egypt, but only to remain there a short time. It is thus written, "They said to Pharaoh, 'We have come to live in your land a while, for there is nothing [even] for our sheep to eat, so great is the hunger in the land of Canaan. Now, if you please, let [us] your servants live in the land of Goshen'" (Genesis 47:4).

The wind accepted the challenge and began to blow. But the harder it blew, the more tightly the farmer clung on to his jacket, until the wind gave up, exhausted. Then the sun began to shine. As soon as the farmer felt its heat, he took his jacket off. Warmth is more powerful than the wind.

So it was in Israel. Pharaoh and his people afflicted the Israelites, but 'The more they were oppressed, the more they multiplied and spread' (Exodus 1:12). Laban did not afflict Jacob. To the contrary, while he was with Laban, Jacob grew rich. The danger was that he would remain with Laban and forget who he was. So it has been throughout Jewish history. The more Jews suffered, the more they prayed, studied and kept the commands. The paradox is that the danger to Jewish continuity has been not slavery and suffering, but affluence and freedom.

So Moses warned at the end of his life: 'Be careful that you do not forget the Lord your God... Otherwise, when you eat and are satisfied, when you build fine houses and settle down, and when your herds and flocks grow large and your silver and gold increase and all you have is multiplied, then your heart will become proud and you will forget the Lord your God who brought you out of Egypt, out of the land of slavery' (Deuteronomy 8:11–14).

Interpreted this way the passage contains a powerful message: 'Do not think that the story of Pesach ends with the exodus. It only begins there. It is one thing to believe in God when you need His help. It is another when you have already received it. Affluence, no less than slavery, can make us forget who we are and why.'

But he went down... forced by [God's] word

Jacob, having heard that his son Joseph was still alive, prepared to travel to Egypt to see him. He then received a vision of God at night, telling him: 'Do not be afraid to go down to Egypt, for I will make you into a great nation there' (Genesis 46:3). We are not told what fear Jacob had that led to this Divine reassurance, but the text implies that Jacob already had a presentiment of the slavery and suffering his descendants would ultimately face as a result of this journey. He went, 'compelled by the word of God'. Thus the prophecy granted to Abraham two generations earlier, that his children would become strangers in a foreign land, began to be fulfilled.

   See Essays on Passover "The Unasked Question" page 129

בִּמְתֵי מְעָט. כְּמָה שֶׁנֶּאֱמַר בְּשִׁבְעִים נֶפֶשׁ יָרְדוּ

אֲבֹתֶיךָ מִצְרָיְמָה וְעַתָּה שָׂמְךָ יהוה אֱלֹהֶיךָ כְּכוֹכְבֵי הַשָּׁמַיִם לָרֹב:

וַיְהִי שָׁם לְגוֹי. מְלַמֵּד שֶׁהָיוּ יִשְׂרָאֵל מְצֻיָּנִים שָׁם:

גָּדוֹל עָצוּם. כְּמָה שֶׁנֶּאֱמַר וּבְנֵי יִשְׂרָאֵל פָּרוּ

וַיִּשְׁרְצוּ_וַיִּרְבּוּ_וַיַּעַצְמוּ בִּמְאֹד מְאֹד_וַתִּמָּלֵא הָאָרֶץ אֹתָם:

וָרָב. כְּמָה שֶׁנֶּאֱמַר רְבָבָה כְּצֶמַח הַשָּׂדֶה נְתַתִּיךְ

וַתִּרְבִּי_וַתִּגְדְּלִי_וַתָּבֹאִי בַּעֲדִי עֲדָיִים שָׁדַיִם נָכֹנוּ

וּשְׂעָרֵךְ צִמֵּחַ וְאַתְּ עֵרֹם וְעֶרְיָה: וָאֶעֱבֹר עָלַיִךְ

וָאֶרְאֵךְ מִתְבּוֹסֶסֶת בְּדָמָיִךְ וָאֹמַר לָךְ בְּדָמַיִךְ חֲיִי

וָאֹמַר לָךְ בְּדָמַיִךְ חֲיִי:

This teaches that [Jacob] did not go to settle

Jacob's dying request was to be buried in what would later become the land of Israel. So too Joseph, at the end of his life, gathered his family and told them, 'I am about to die. But God will surely come to your aid and take you up out of this land to the land He promised in oath to Abraham, Isaac and Jacob.' His last recorded words were: 'God will surely come to your aid, and then you must carry my bones up from this place' (Genesis 50:25). This charge was eventually carried out by Moses himself.

Wherever Jews were scattered, they saw their condition as *galut*, 'exile', rather than mere dispersion, *tefutzot*. There were places like Germany where they had lived for a thousand years. There were others, like Babylon, which had a continuous Jewish settlement for two-and-a-half thousand years. Yet Jews saw themselves, and were seen by others, as being *here* but belonging *elsewhere*. This did not mean, as their critics claimed, that they had dual loyalties. Few groups were as loyal to their societies and non-Jewish rulers as were the Jews. They made significant contributions to the nations where they lived, and whenever they had the opportunity to do so, added vastly to the arts, sciences, medicine and the economy.

Since the days of Jeremiah they remembered his instruction to 'Seek the peace and prosperity of the city to which I have carried you into exile. Pray to the Lord for it, for in its peace you will find peace' (Jeremiah 29:7). But they knew that, at some date in the future, the Jewish people would return home. They never mistook the immediate for the ultimate. It was this more than anything else that preserved Jewish identity as a distinctive people, and sustained hope during the long centuries of exile and expulsion. It preserved Jews against the internal decay that has beset every other civilization. Forgetfulness of the past, heedlessness of the long term future and a loss of moral purpose in the pursuit of the here-and-now, has been the beginning of the decline of other cultures. The sense of *galut*, 'exile', was the Jewish immune-system. It meant that the past and future were as real as the present. This saved Jews from the ravages of time.

Few in number

The rapid population growth of the Israelites in Egypt was mirrored in modern times. By the end of the eighteenth century, it has been estimated that the total world Jewish population was no more than 1.5 million. By the outbreak of the Second World War it was close to 18 million.

Jews, though, have never measured their strength in numerical terms. The American writer Milton Himmelfarb wrote: 'The number of Jews in the world is smaller than a small statistical error in the Chinese census. Yet we remain bigger than our numbers. Big things seem to happen around us and to us.'

The Torah indicates (Exodus 30:12) that it is dangerous to count Jews. Instead, in biblical times, they were

"Few in number" – as it is written, "With seventy souls your father went down to Egypt. Now God your Lord has made you as many as the stars of the sky" (Deuteronomy 10:22).

"There he became a nation" – This teaches that the Israelites were distinctive there.

"Great, mighty" – as it is written, "The children of Israel were fertile and had large families. They became very, very great in number and might, and the land became filled with them" (Exodus 1:7).

"And many" – as it is written, "I made you as many as the plants of the field. You became many and grew, and became mature. Your breasts were full, your hair was grown, but you were naked and bare" (Ezekiel 16:7).

---

each to donate a half-shekel to the maintenance of the sanctuary, and by counting up the donations one could calculate the total population. The lesson is this. Nations usually undertake censuses to know their strength, military or economic. If the Jewish people ever believed that strength lay in numbers, they would be in danger of despair. The Jewish people is small. It always has been. Moses said, 'The Lord did not set His affection on you and choose you because you were more numerous than other peoples, for you are the fewest of all peoples' (Deuteronomy 7:7). Instead the Torah tells us not to count Jews but to *count their contributions*. And our contributions, to the world and to one another, have been vast.

There he became a nation

The Vilna Gaon explains that the word *goi*, 'nation', is related to the word *geviyah*, 'a body'. A group of individuals becomes a nation when it becomes like a single body. Rabbi Shimon bar Yochai taught, 'Israel is like one body with a single soul. When one is injured, all feel the pain.'

The late R. Joseph Soloveitchik, in his essay *Kol Dodi Dofek*, spoke of the two covenants that bind Jews to one another: *brit goral*, the 'covenant of fate', and *brit ye'ud*, the 'covenant of destiny'. The first arises out of shared suffering in the past, the second out of a collective vision of the future. In Egypt the Israelites entered into the 'covenant of fate'. They were united by suffering. A midrash states: 'In Egypt the Israelites gathered to dwell as a group, all of them becoming as one, and they covenanted to act with loving-kindness toward one another' (*Tanna dvei Eliyahu*). That is how they first became a nation.

This teaches that the Israelites were distinctive there

They did not assimilate. According to the sages, the Israelites preserved their identity in four ways: they did not change their names, their language, or their customs, and they did not betray one another.

The Hebrew word for distinctive, *metsuyan*, is derived from the same word as Zion. In modern Hebrew it means 'excellent'. It signifies something that stands out from its surroundings. The word *tsiyun* means a 'signpost'. The prophet Jeremiah told the Jews of his generation who were going into exile that they should set up signposts (*tsiyyunim*) so that they would not forget the way back to Israel. The sages interpreted this to mean that they should not abandon Judaism. 'Even though I exile you from the land, remain distinctive (*metsuyyanim*) by your performance of the commands.'

Zion is not just a place. It is a way of life. Jews are called to moral excellence, to have the courage to stand out from their surroundings, to be different and to be a signpost in the wilderness from whom others get their bearing and sense of direction. Zionism is not only a matter of *where* we live, but also *how* we live.

וַיָּרֵעוּ אֹתָנוּ הַמִּצְרִים _וַיְעַנּוּנוּ_וַיִּתְּנוּ עָלֵינוּ עֲבֹדָה קָשָׁה:

_וַיָּרֵעוּ אֹתָנוּ הַמִּצְרִים. כְּמָה שֶׁנֶּאֱמַר הָבָה
נִתְחַכְּמָה לוֹ פֶּן יִרְבֶּה וְהָיָה כִּי תִקְרֶאנָה מִלְחָמָה
וְנוֹסַף _גַּם הוּא עַל שֹׂנְאֵינוּ וְנִלְחַם בָּנוּ וְעָלָה מִן הָאָרֶץ:

_וַיְעַנּוּנוּ. כְּמָה שֶׁנֶּאֱמַר _וַיָּשִׂימוּ עָלָיו שָׂרֵי מִסִּים
לְמַעַן עַנֹּתוֹ בְּסִבְלֹתָם _וַיִּבֶן עָרֵי מִסְכְּנוֹת לְפַרְעֹה אֶת
פִּתֹם וְאֶת רַעַמְסֵס:

_וַיִּתְּנוּ עָלֵינוּ עֲבֹדָה קָשָׁה. כְּמָה שֶׁנֶּאֱמַר _וַיַּעֲבִדוּ
מִצְרַיִם אֶת בְּנֵי־יִשְׂרָאֵל בְּפָרֶךְ:

_וַנִּצְעַק אֶל יהוה אֱלֹהֵי אֲבֹתֵינוּ _וַיִּשְׁמַע יהוה
אֶת־קֹלֵנוּ _וַיַּרְא אֶת־עָנְיֵנוּ וְאֶת עֲמָלֵנוּ וְאֶת־לַחֲצֵנוּ:
_וַנִּצְעַק אֶל־יהוה אֱלֹהֵי אֲבֹתֵינוּ. כְּמָה שֶׁנֶּאֱמַר
_וַיְהִי בַיָּמִים הָרַבִּים הָהֵם _וַיָּמָת מֶלֶךְ מִצְרַיִם _וַיֵּאָנְחוּ
בְנֵי־יִשְׂרָאֵל מִן־הָעֲבֹדָה _וַיִּזְעָקוּ _וַתַּעַל שַׁוְעָתָם אֶל־
הָאֱלֹהִים מִן־הָעֲבֹדָה:

Judaism is the great counter-voice in the conversation of mankind. To be a Jew is to be willing to think and act differently, to swim against the tide. It is to be *part* of society but also *apart* from it, to live not only in the 'now' but with the wisdom of the past and a vision of the future. Matthew Arnold once wrote: 'As long as the world lasts, all who want to make progress in righteousness will come to Israel for inspiration, as to the people who have had the sense for righteousness most glowing and strongest.'

This teaches that the Israelites were distinctive there

'It is told of Baron Nathaniel Rothschild that, after winning his battle of many years to have the disabilities to members of the Jewish faith removed from the House of Lords, he slipped away from the hierarchy of Britain congratulating him on the achievement and was to be found prostrate in prayer in a small synagogue in the Whitechapel ghetto of East London, his lips murmuring, "Would that this freedom shall not mean the diminution of our faith"' (Yaacov Herzog, *A People that Dwells Alone*).

The Egyptians ill – treated us, as it is said, 'Come let us act wisely against them'

It is likely that the Haggadah interprets the verb as 'befriended us' (from *re'a*, 'neighbour') rather than 'ill treated us' (from *ra*, 'evil'). According to the midrash, the 'wise dealing' of Pharaoh consisted in inflicting slavery slowly and by degrees, so that the Israelites would become accustomed to it rather than try to flee. First Pharaoh issued a proclamation calling on all Egyptians and Israelites to work on his construction projects for pay. Pharaoh himself joined them. After a month, the Egyptians gradually withdrew, leaving the Israelites working alone. Then they stopped paying their wages. By then the Israelites had become slaves and the Egyptians their taskmasters. Gradualism later became part of the Nazi programme of genocide.

"The Egyptians ill-treated us.
They made us suffer and gave us hard work." (Deuteronomy 26:6).

"The Egyptians were bad to us" – as it is written, "Come let us act wisely against them. Otherwise, they may become so many that if there is a war, they will join our enemies, fight against us, and leave the land" (Exodus 1:10).

"They made us suffer" – as it is written, "They appointed slave drivers over them to make them suffer with hard work, and they built storage cities for Pharaoh, Pithom and Ramses" (Exodus 1:11).

"And gave us hard work" – as it is written, "The Egyptians compelled the children of Israel to work with rigour" (Exodus 1:13).

"We cried out to God, Lord of our fathers. God heard our voice, and He saw our suffering, our labour and our oppression" (Deuteronomy 26:7).

"We cried out to God, Lord of our fathers" – as it is written, "During that long period, the king of Egypt died. The children of Israel groaned because of the hard work, and they cried out. Their moaning from the labour came up before God" (Exodus 2:23).

"The Egyptians compelled the children of Israel to work with rigour"

The sages defined 'rigour' as 'work that has no time-limit', as, for example, ordering someone to dig the ground 'until I return'. There are two aspects of slavery, physical and psychological, and Jewish law recognised that the psychological effects can sometimes be worse than the physical exhaustion of back-breaking labour. 'Rigour' is work designed to crush the spirit of slaves by depriving them of the freedom to make decisions and subjecting them to someone else's will. In Judaism, what is essential to our humanity is our will – our ability to make free choices, and thereby choose the good though it is difficult, over the bad though it is attractive. What is morally unacceptable about slavery, therefore, is its deliberate attempt to destroy the independent will of the slave.

"We cried out to God, Lord of our fathers"

Sometimes the deepest truths are told through jokes. The story is told of a highly assimilated Jewish couple in the nineteenth century. They had joined the aristocracy and become a Count and Countess. The Countess was expecting a child. Labour began and the nurses arrived. Meanwhile the count remained in his study, playing cards with a friend. Cries began to come from the bedroom. 'Mon Dieu, Mon Dieu.' 'Should you not go up to your wife?' said the friend, 'She is giving birth.' The Count replied, 'Now is not the time.' Louder cries were heard, 'My God, My God.' The friend looked up at the Count, who shrugged his shoulders and said, 'Now is not the time.' Then a third cry was heard. 'Gevalt!' The Count rose. 'Now is the time.'

When we cry, the masks slip away until eventually we reach the core of who we are. The proof text cited here (Exodus 2:23) uses three verbs: 'The Israelites groaned (vaye'anchu) in their slavery and cried out (vayiz'aku), and their cry for help (shav'atam) because of their slavery went up to God.' Initially their cries were

---

וַיִּשְׁמַע יְהוָה אֶת־קֹלֵנוּ. כְּמָה שֶׁנֶּאֱמַר וַיִּשְׁמַע
אֱלֹהִים אֶת־נַאֲקָתָם וַיִּזְכֹּר אֱלֹהִים אֶת־בְּרִיתוֹ אֶת־
אַבְרָהָם אֶת־יִצְחָק וְאֶת־יַעֲקֹב:

וַיַּרְא אֶת־עָנְיֵנוּ. זוֹ פְּרִישׁוּת דֶּרֶךְ אֶרֶץ. כְּמָה
שֶׁנֶּאֱמַר וַיַּרְא אֱלֹהִים אֶת־בְּנֵי יִשְׂרָאֵל וַיֵּדַע אֱלֹהִים:

וְאֶת־עֲמָלֵנוּ. אֵלוּ הַבָּנִים. כְּמָה שֶׁנֶּאֱמַר כָּל־
הַבֵּן הַיִּלּוֹד הַיְאֹרָה תַּשְׁלִיכֻהוּ וְכָל־הַבַּת תְּחַיּוּן:

וְאֶת־לַחֲצֵנוּ. זֶה הַדְּחַק. כְּמָה שֶׁנֶּאֱמַר וְגַם־
רָאִיתִי אֶת־הַלַּחַץ אֲשֶׁר מִצְרַיִם לֹחֲצִים אֹתָם:

וַיּוֹצִאֵנוּ יְהוָה מִמִּצְרַיִם בְּיָד חֲזָקָה וּבִזְרֹעַ
נְטוּיָה וּבְמֹרָא גָּדֹל וּבְאֹתוֹת וּבְמֹפְתִים:

mere complaints. Then they became anguish. Finally they turned to God. It was then that God knew the time had come.

Another explanation: When Pharaoh's daughter was bathing in the Nile and saw the ark containing Moses, we read 'She opened it and saw the baby (yeled) and behold the youth (na'ar) was crying.' The verse begins by calling Moses a baby and ends by calling him a youth. Rashi explains that 'he cried in an adult way'. On this, Rabbi Meir Shapiro of Lublin commented: 'There are two ways of crying. A child cries when it is in pain. An adult cries when it sees someone else in pain.' Already the princess felt in Moses a sensitivity to the suffering of others. 'And we cried' speaks of collective tears. When the Israelites moved beyond their own pain and cried on behalf of their fellows, God in return responded to their cry.

God heard

In the Torah the word Shema means more than 'to hear'. It means 'to listen, pay attention, and act accordingly'. This explains an unusual feature of biblical Hebrew, namely that it has no word that means 'to obey'. The word used by the Torah is Shema, which means 'to listen attentively to and act accordingly'. Judaism does not demand blind obedience. To the contrary, it asks us, as far as possible, to understand the reasons for the commandments, even though their full wisdom will always be beyond our understanding. Obedience in Judaism is a form of active listening. Pre-modern English used the word 'hearken' to convey this, but there is now no word in common usage that has this precise sense. 'God heard' means 'He attended to the cries of the Israelites and set it in the context of the promise He had given the patriarchs that He would bring their children safely out of slavery and back to the land of Israel. He therefore knew that He must act.'

"God heard our voice" – as it is

written, "God heard their groaning, and God remembered His
promise to Abraham, Isaac and Jacob" (Exodus 2:24).

"And He saw our suffering" – This is the separation of husband
and wife, as it is said, "God saw the children of Israel, and God knew"
(Exodus 2:25).

"Our labour" – these are the children, as it is written, "Every boy that
is born, you shall throw into the river, but every daughter you shall let
live" (Exodus 1:22).

"And our oppression" – This is the pressure, as it is written,
"I also see the pressure to which Egypt is subjecting them" (Exodus 3:9).

"God brought us out of Egypt with a strong hand and an outstretched arm,
with great fear, signs and wonders" (Deuteronomy 26:8).

"And He saw our suffering" – This is the separation of husband and wife

In the previous verse, 'suffering' was interpreted to mean the burden of hard labour. Here, therefore, another kind of suffering must be referred to. We are commanded on Yom Kippur to 'afflict ourselves', and the sages interpreted this to mean, among other things, that sexual relations are forbidden on this day (*Yoma* 77a). The Talmud derives this from Laban's warning to Jacob not to 'afflict my daughters' (Genesis 31:50), meaning, 'Do not deprive them of their conjugal rights.'

The Egyptians, fearing the population increase of the Israelites, tried to separate man and wife. One way they did this was to make the men work and sleep in the fields, while the women remained in the cities.

Rabbinic tradition gives a moving account of how the Israelite women frustrated this plan. 'R. Shimon bar Halafta said: What did the women do? They would go to bring water from the Nile. God arranged that, along with the water, they would catch fish. Some they cooked. Others they sold, and with the money bought wine. Then they went out to the fields and gave food and drink to their husbands. The women would then take out their bronze mirrors and make themselves attractive. Thus family life continued, and the Israelites multiplied and grew. Later, when the Israelites were in the desert and God commanded Moses to make the Tabernacle, some brought gifts of gold, others of silver. The women said, 'What do we have to contribute?' They brought their bronze mirrors. At first Moses was angry and refused to accept them. But God said to him, 'Moses, do you despise this gift? Because of these mirrors all these multitudes were born in Egypt. Take them and make them into the bronze basin with which the priests will purify themselves' (*Tanhuma, Pekudei*).

וַיּוֹצִאֵנוּ יהוה מִמִּצְרַיִם. לֹא עַל־יְדֵי מַלְאָךְ
וְלֹא עַל־יְדֵי שָׂרָף וְלֹא עַל־יְדֵי שָׁלִיחַ. אֶלָּא הַקָּדוֹשׁ
בָּרוּךְ הוּא בִּכְבוֹדוֹ וּבְעַצְמוֹ. שֶׁנֶּאֱמַר:

וְעָבַרְתִּי בְאֶרֶץ־מִצְרַיִם בַּלַּיְלָה הַזֶּה וְהִכֵּיתִי
כָל־בְּכוֹר בְּאֶרֶץ מִצְרַיִם מֵאָדָם וְעַד בְּהֵמָה
וּבְכָל אֱלֹהֵי מִצְרַיִם אֶעֱשֶׂה שְׁפָטִים אֲנִי יהוה:

וְעָבַרְתִּי בְאֶרֶץ־מִצְרַיִם בַּלַּיְלָה הַזֶּה. אֲנִי וְלֹא מַלְאָךְ.
וְהִכֵּיתִי כָל־בְּכוֹר בְּאֶרֶץ־מִצְרַיִם. אֲנִי וְלֹא שָׂרָף.
וּבְכָל־אֱלֹהֵי מִצְרַיִם אֶעֱשֶׂה שְׁפָטִים. אֲנִי וְלֹא הַשָּׁלִיחַ.
אֲנִי יהוה. אֲנִי הוּא וְלֹא אַחֵר.

"God saw the children of Israel, and God knew"

The verb 'to know' in Hebrew means something quite different from its meaning in Greek and subsequent Western thought. Knowledge, for the Greeks, was a form of cognition, a detached appraisal of facts. In the Torah, knowledge is a form of moral relationship, a commitment. Thus Adam 'knew' his wife – meaning he joined himself to her, physically, emotionally and morally. God says about Abraham, 'I have known him', meaning, 'I have chosen him, set my love on him, made a covenant with him.' In the Torah, knowledge is not simply an intellectual attribute. It also has consequences for emotion and action. In this case 'and God knew' means that He not only saw the suffering of the Israelites. He was pained by it, and determined to act to redeem them.

"Our labour" – These are the children

The sages are here echoing the verse from the Book of Job (5:7): 'Man is born to labour (le-amal).' This evocation adds to our sense of pathos at the plight of the male children condemned to death. The Book of Job is a meditation on the suffering of the innocent. The sages, echoing it here, were reflecting on the still greater innocence of the children condemned by Egypt to death. This reverberates even more strongly after the Holocaust, during which one-and-a-half million Jewish children were murdered.

"And our oppression" – This is the pressure

The sages are translating biblical Hebrew (lachatz) into rabbinic Hebrew (dechak).

Not by an angel, not by an archangel, and not by a messenger

The Haggadah is striking for its almost complete omission of any reference to Moses and his part in the redemption. The emphasis throughout is on the saving acts of God.

"God brought us out of Egypt" – not by an angel, not by an archangel, and not by a messenger. It was God alone, in His glory, and by Himself. Thus it is written,

"On that night I will pass through the land of Egypt, and I will strike down all the first-born of Egypt, man and beast. I will judge all the gods of Egypt. I am God" (Exodus 12:12).

"On that night I will pass through the land of Egypt" – I, not an angel!
"And I will strike down all the first-born in Egypt" – I, not an archangel!
"I will judge all the gods of Egypt" – I, not a messenger!
"I am God" – I and none other!

To understand this we have to remember the world-view of ancient Egypt. The pharaohs were regarded as incarnate gods, usually the god of the sun. The Torah was the first document in history to insist on the complete separation between God, nature, and mankind. God is absolutely transcendent. He cannot be identified either with a phenomenon of nature or with a human being, however exalted. This apparently infinite distance nonetheless creates a new possibility of communication. God speaks to mankind. Mankind speaks to God. Between them lies the bond of language.

In the world of myth there was no need for revelation. The gods constantly revealed themselves, in the rising and setting sun, the rain that fell, the wind that blew. In Judaism, revelation is both necessary and possible, and takes place not through a show of power but through the communication of meaning, namely words, promises, commands and prayers. Language becomes invested with holiness. In Torah, God speaks to us. In prayer, we speak to God. Because God is God, man can become man. Because He is absolutely transcendent, He leaves space for free human action, whose highest form is to become 'a partner with the Holy One, blessed be He, in the work of creation'. This was an utterly new form of religious consciousness, and remains only incompletely understood today.

The drama of the plagues is a twofold confrontation. At one level, it is a battle between Pharaoh and Moses, two human beings. At another it is a contest between the man-who-believes-he-is-a-god and God Himself. The Egyptians worshipped nature – the combination of sun and the river waters that made the Nile delta at that time one of the most fertile places on earth. Each of the first nine plagues is designed to show both the Israelites and the Egyptians that nature is not the ultimate reality. It can be a blessing; it can also be a curse. One by one the familiar features of the Egyptian ecology are overturned – to teach the Egyptians that one cannot worship nature at the cost of subjugating man.

It was essential for both the Israelites and the Egyptians to understand that this was not the work of man, but of God. Hence the emphasis throughout the seder on the intervention of God Himself, as if to say Moses was not a Jewish equivalent of pharaoh, a man-god, a doer of mighty deeds with the forces of nature at his command. The active agent throughout the redemption process was God Himself.

בְּיָד חֲזָקָה. זוֹ הַדֶּבֶר. כְּמָה שֶׁנֶּאֱמַר הִנֵּה
יַד יְהוָה הוֹיָה בְּמִקְנְךָ אֲשֶׁר בַּשָּׂדֶה בַּסּוּסִים בַּחֲמוֹרִים
בַּגְּמַלִּים בַּבָּקָר וּבַצֹּאן דֶּבֶר כָּבֵד מְאֹד:

וּבִזְרֹעַ נְטוּיָה. זוֹ הַחֶרֶב. כְּמָה שֶׁנֶּאֱמַר וְחַרְבּוֹ
שְׁלוּפָה בְּיָדוֹ נְטוּיָה עַל־יְרוּשָׁלָיִם:

וּבְמֹרָא גָּדֹל. זוֹ גִּלּוּי שְׁכִינָה. כְּמָה שֶׁנֶּאֱמַר אוֹ
הֲנִסָּה אֱלֹהִים לָבוֹא לָקַחַת לוֹ גוֹי מִקֶּרֶב גּוֹי בְּמַסֹּת
בְּאֹתֹת וּבְמוֹפְתִים וּבְמִלְחָמָה וּבְיָד חֲזָקָה וּבִזְרוֹעַ
נְטוּיָה וּבְמוֹרָאִים גְּדֹלִים כְּכֹל אֲשֶׁר־עָשָׂה לָכֶם יְהוָה
אֱלֹהֵיכֶם בְּמִצְרַיִם לְעֵינֶיךָ:

וּבְאֹתוֹת. זֶה הַמַּטֶּה. כְּמָה שֶׁנֶּאֱמַר וְאֶת־
הַמַּטֶּה הַזֶּה תִּקַּח בְּיָדֶךָ אֲשֶׁר תַּעֲשֶׂה בּוֹ אֶת־הָאֹתֹת:

וּבְמֹפְתִים זֶה הַדָּם. כְּמָה שֶׁנֶּאֱמַר וְנָתַתִּי
מוֹפְתִים בַּשָּׁמַיִם וּבָאָרֶץ.

The Plagues

The account of the ten plagues is the nearest the Hebrew Bible comes to Greek tragedy. Pharaoh's hubris leads to nemesis. By repeatedly refusing to let the Israelites go, he brings disaster on himself and his country. It is one of the great confrontations – between the quasi-divine leader of the greatest empire of the ancient world, and the God who intervenes on behalf of a helpless group of slaves.

At their first encounter, Pharaoh dismisses Moses with contempt. 'Who is the Lord that I should obey Him and let Israel go? I do not know the Lord and I will not let Israel go.' At this point, Pharaoh's reaction is understandable. Within his worldview, the God of Moses is no more than a tribal deity, whose powerlessness is shown by the fact that his people are slaves. As the plagues gather momentum, and the awesome power of God begins to be seen, Pharaoh's obstinacy rises to tragic proportions. During the first five plagues he 'hardens his heart'. Thereafter God is spoken of as 'hardening his heart', meaning that by now Pharaoh has become a prisoner of his own pride. It is not only the Israelites who are slaves. Pharaoh too has become a slave to his moral blindness. By the eighth plague Pharaoh's own advisers are begging him to relent: 'Do you not yet realise that Egypt is ruined?' However, having closed his ears to Moses' pleas, by now Pharaoh can no longer hear the anguish of his own people.

The plagues themselves occupy the borderline, so common to the Torah, between the natural and the supernatural. Commentators have been divided between those who emphasise their miraculous character and others who have sought to provide a scientific account of the disasters in terms of a series of chain reactions to an initial ecological disaster, possibly the appearance of algae in the Nile which turned the water red and caused the fish to die. Which view speaks more compellingly to us will depend on whether we understand by the word 'miracle' – a suspension of the laws of nature, or an event which occurs within nature but by happening when and to whom it does, reveals a providential pattern in history.

"With a strong hand" – This is the plague, as it is

written, "Behold, God's hand will be against your livestock in the field, against the horses, donkeys, camels, cattle and sheep – a very serious plague" (Exodus 9:3).

"And an outstretched arm" – This is the sword, as it is written, "His sword was drawn in his hand, outstretched over Jerusalem" (I Chronicles 21:16).

"With great fear" – This is the revelation of the Divine Presence, as it is written, "Has any god ever tried to take for himself one nation out from another nation, with trials, signs, wonders, and war, with a strong hand and an outstretched arm, and with great fearsome acts, like all that God your Lord did for you in Egypt, before your very eyes?" (Deuteronomy 4:34).

"Signs" – This is the staff. It is written, "Take this staff in your hands, and with it perform the signs" (Exodus 4:17).

"And wonders" – This is the blood, as it is written, "I will display wonders in heaven and earth.

The Torah is deliberately ambiguous about this, as about so many other things, which is why it communicates at so many levels. Certainly the plagues themselves are events of a kind not unknown in that part of the world. What is more significant – a fact emphasised by the Torah – is that, as signs of God, they speak the language of the Egyptians. The Egyptians worshipped nature, and now nature was turning against them. The message the plagues conveyed was twofold. If nature was a force, it was in turn controlled by a higher force, and this higher power was a moral one. Nowhere is this more vividly in evidence than in the first plague. The Egyptians had drowned Israelite children in the Nile, and now its waters were turning red. We catch an echo here of God's words to Cain after the first recorded murder: 'Your brother's blood cries out to me from the ground.'

No less important is the Torah's use of irony as a way of mocking human pretensions whenever people think that they can defy God. So the Egyptian magicians replicate the first two plagues, blood and frogs, apparently mindless of the fact that they are making things worse, not better. The plague that defeats them is lice. This is a sardonic comment on the monumental scale of Egyptian architecture. The Egyptians believed that the gods were to be found in things that are big. God shows them His presence in something so small as to be almost invisible (compare T. S. Eliot's 'I will show you fear in a handful of dust'). The irony recurs in the division of the Red Sea, where Pharaoh's greatest military asset, the chariots, prove to be his undoing, as their wheels sink into the mud. The key to the plagues – as in God's covenant with Noah – is the principle of reciprocity: As you do, so shall you be done to. Those who harm others will themselves be harmed. Nations that begin by depriving others of their liberty, in the end destroy themselves. Historically, this was so. Egypt never again recovered the greatness it had had in the earlier part of Ramses II's rule.

The plagues as 'judgements against Egypt's gods'

Several times in the Torah, God is spoken of as executing judgement against the gods of Egypt. The ninth plague, darkness, seems to break the sequence of the previous eight, which until then have grown steadily more severe. A period of darkness seems no more than a discomfort. Its significance lies in the fact that Ra or Re, the sun god, was the greatest in the pantheon of Egyptian deities. The ninth plague, which blotted out the light of the sun, may have been directed not against the people but their object of worship. This is probably also the significance of the first, the turning of the Nile into blood. The river, too, was worshipped by the Egyptians, in the form of Hapi, the Nile god. A similar motif may also be present in the second plague. The Egyptians knew of a frog goddess, Heqt, who was thought to assist women in childbirth. The overrunning of Egypt by frogs may have been interpreted by them as a sign of judgement against the slaughter of newborn Israelite children. The Torah does not dwell in any detail on these symbolisms because they were directed at the Egyptians. It is they, rather than the Israelites, who would have understood their message.

Spill three drops of wine

דָּם וָאֵשׁ וְתִמְרוֹת עָשָׁן:

דָּבָר אַחֵר. בְּיָד חֲזָקָה שְׁתַּיִם. וּבִזְרֹעַ נְטוּיָה שְׁתַּיִם.

וּבְמֹרָא גָּדֹל שְׁתַּיִם. וּבְאֹתוֹת שְׁתַּיִם.

וּבְמֹפְתִים שְׁתַּיִם: אֵלּוּ עֶשֶׂר מַכּוֹת שֶׁהֵבִיא הַקָּדוֹשׁ

בָּרוּךְ הוּא עַל־הַמִּצְרִים בְּמִצְרַיִם וְאֵלּוּ הֵן:

At the mention of each plague, spill a drop of wine.

דָּם. צְפַרְדֵּעַ. כִּנִּים. עָרוֹב.
דֶּבֶר. שְׁחִין. בָּרָד. אַרְבֶּה. חֹשֶׁךְ.
מַכַּת בְּכוֹרוֹת.

רַבִּי יְהוּדָה הָיָה נוֹתֵן בָּהֶם סִמָּנִים:
דְּצַ"ךְ עֲדַ"שׁ בְּאַחַ"ב:

Rabbi Yehudah used to express them with an abbreviation

Rabbi Judah groups the plagues into threes because, with the exception of the last, they occurred in a three-fold pattern. The first three were performed by Aaron, the second three by Moses, and the third three by Moses 'stretching out his hand'. In each group, the first was preceded by a warning 'in the morning', the second by a warning whose time is not specified, and the third came without warning.

Spilling wine

Our custom is to spill a drop of wine at the words, 'Blood', 'Fire', and 'Pillars of smoke'; at the mention of each of the plagues; and at the three words of R. Judah's mnemonic. Many explanations have been offered. The most beautiful is that of Avudraham, who interprets it in accordance with the verse in Proverbs (24:17), 'Do not rejoice when your enemy falls.' Even as we give thanks for the miracle of the plagues, as a result of which our ancestors gained their freedom, we also shed a symbolic tear for those who suffered. According to some commentators, that is why the Torah does not mention the word *simchah*, 'rejoicing,' in connection with Pesach, unlike the other festivals. A talmudic passage (*Megillah* 10b) states that when the waters of the sea returned and trapped the pursuing Egyptian army, the angels wished to sing a song of

Spill three drops of wine.

Blood
and fire
and pillars of smoke" (Joel 3:3).

Another explanation is this:
"A strong hand" – makes two plagues,
"An outstretched arm" – another two,
"Great fear" – two more,
"Signs" – another two,
"And wonders" – the last two.

These are the Ten Plagues that God brought upon the Egyptians in Egypt.
And these are (The Ten Plagues):

At the mention of each plague, spill a drop of wine.

1. Blood
2. Frogs
3. Lice
4. Wild Beasts
5. Cattle Plague
6. Boils
7. Hail
8. Locusts
9. Darkness
10. Death of the First-born

Rabbi Yehudah used to express them with an abbreviation:

DeTzaKh ADaSh BeAChaB

praise. God silenced them with the words, 'My creatures are drowning in the sea, and you wish to sing a song?' God does not rejoice in the downfall of the wicked.

Moral maturity involves an ability to live with complex situations and emotions. We may be uplifted by an event because it represents the triumph of justice, while at the same time identifying with the suffering of the victims. One of the glories of Judaism is that it reflects the complexity of the moral life without retreating into scepticism or relativism. The heroes of the Torah are rarely without their faults, nor are the villains wholly without virtues. This does not prevent us from making moral judgements, any more than grey refutes the existence of black and white. But it should protect us against the kind of attitude that grew up among the sectarians of the Dead Sea Scrolls who divided humanity into the 'children of light' and the 'children of darkness'. Judaism forbids *Schadenfreude*, malicious joy in the discomfort of others. It was the first faith in history to teach the unity of mankind under the universal fatherhood of God. Tears, therefore, are a universal language, and sympathy should know no religious or national borders.

רַבִּי יוֹסֵי הַגְּלִילִי אוֹמֵר. מִנַּיִן אַתָּה אוֹמֵר
שֶׁלָּקוּ הַמִּצְרִים בְּמִצְרַיִם עֶשֶׂר מַכּוֹת וְעַל הַיָּם לָקוּ
חֲמִשִּׁים מַכּוֹת. בְּמִצְרַיִם מַה הוּא אוֹמֵר. וַיֹּאמְרוּ
הַחַרְטֻמִּם אֶל־פַּרְעֹה אֶצְבַּע אֱלֹהִים הוּא. וְעַל־הַיָּם
מַה הוּא אוֹמֵר. וַיַּרְא יִשְׂרָאֵל אֶת־הַיָּד הַגְּדֹלָה אֲשֶׁר
עָשָׂה יְהוָה בְּמִצְרַיִם וַיִּירְאוּ הָעָם אֶת־יְהוָה וַיַּאֲמִינוּ
בַּיהוָה וּבְמֹשֶׁה עַבְדּוֹ. כַּמָּה לָקוּ בָּאֶצְבַּע עֶשֶׂר מַכּוֹת.
אֱמֹר מֵעַתָּה בְּמִצְרַיִם לָקוּ עֶשֶׂר מַכּוֹת וְעַל־הַיָּם לָקוּ
חֲמִשִּׁים מַכּוֹת:

רַבִּי אֱלִיעֶזֶר אוֹמֵר. מִנַּיִן שֶׁכָּל מַכָּה וּמַכָּה
שֶׁהֵבִיא הַקָּדוֹשׁ בָּרוּךְ הוּא עַל הַמִּצְרִים בְּמִצְרַיִם
הָיְתָה שֶׁל אַרְבַּע מַכּוֹת. שֶׁנֶּאֱמַר יְשַׁלַּח־בָּם חֲרוֹן
אַפּוֹ עֶבְרָה וָזַעַם וְצָרָה מִשְׁלַחַת מַלְאֲכֵי רָעִים.
עֶבְרָה אַחַת. וָזַעַם שְׁתַּיִם. וְצָרָה שָׁלֹשׁ. מִשְׁלַחַת
מַלְאֲכֵי רָעִים אַרְבַּע. אֱמֹר מֵעַתָּה בְּמִצְרַיִם לָקוּ
אַרְבָּעִים מַכּוֹת וְעַל־הַיָּם לָקוּ מָאתַיִם מַכּוֹת:

רַבִּי עֲקִיבָא אוֹמֵר. מִנַּיִן שֶׁכָּל מַכָּה וּמַכָּה שֶׁהֵבִיא
הַקָּדוֹשׁ בָּרוּךְ הוּא עַל הַמִּצְרִים בְּמִצְרַיִם
הָיְתָה שֶׁל חָמֵשׁ מַכּוֹת שֶׁנֶּאֱמַר יְשַׁלַּח־בָּם חֲרוֹן אַפּוֹ
עֶבְרָה וָזַעַם וְצָרָה מִשְׁלַחַת מַלְאֲכֵי רָעִים. חֲרוֹן אַפּוֹ
אַחַת. עֶבְרָה שְׁתַּיִם. וָזַעַם שָׁלֹשׁ. וְצָרָה אַרְבַּע.
מִשְׁלַחַת מַלְאֲכֵי רָעִים חָמֵשׁ: אֱמֹר מֵעַתָּה בְּמִצְרַיִם
לָקוּ חֲמִשִּׁים מַכּוֹת וְעַל הַיָּם לָקוּ חֲמִשִּׁים וּמָאתַיִם מַכּוֹת:

Rabbi Yosi of the Galilee said

This dialogue, between R. Yosi, R. Eliezer and R. Akiva, was included here as an example of the kind of conversation that kept the sages up all night at Bnei Brak. Behind it is the serious point that the miracle at the Red Sea was greater than the Ten Plagues. It exemplified the principle of 'measure for measure' – the Egyptians had drowned Israelite children and now they too were drowned. It marked the decisive boundary between slavery and freedom. Once the Israelites had crossed the sea, they could not go back. They were no longer within territory commanded by Pharaoh. They had become 'God's people' in a way they could immediately sense. This is why we recite the 'Song at the Sea' every day, but only on Pesach do we recount the Ten Plagues.

Rabbi Yosi of the Galilee said: We can show that if the Egyptians were

struck with ten plagues in Egypt, then they were struck with fifty plagues at the Red Sea.

In Egypt we find the statement, "The magicians said to Pharaoh, 'It is God's finger'" (Exodus 8:15). At the Red Sea, it is written, "Israel saw the great hand that God had directed against Egypt. The people feared God and believed in God and in His servant Moses" (Exodus 14:31).

Now, if one finger brought ten plagues, [an entire hand would bring fifty]. From this we see that if there were ten plagues in Egypt, there were fifty at the Red Sea.

Rabbi Eliezer said: We can show that each plague God brought on the

Egyptians in Egypt was really made up of four plagues. [When the Psalms speak of the Ten Plagues] it says, "[God] sent against them His fierce anger, fury, rage and trouble, [and] a mission of evil angels" (Psalms 78:49).

"Fury" – makes one.

"Rage" – makes two.

"Trouble" – makes three.

"A mission of evil angels" – makes four.

From this we see that in Egypt they were struck with a total of forty plagues. Therefore, at the Red Sea, they were struck with two hundred plagues.

Rabbi Akiva said: We can [even] show that each plague that God brought

upon the Egyptians was made up of five different plagues. Take the same verse: "He sent against them His fierce anger, fury, rage, trouble, [and] a mission of evil angels."

"His fierce anger" – makes one.

"Fury" – makes two.

"Rage" – makes three.

"Trouble" – makes four.

"A mission of evil angels" – makes five.

From here we see that in Egypt they were struck with fifty plagues. Therefore, at the Red Sea, they were struck with 250 plagues.

The people believed in God and in His servant Moses

This incidental reference is the only mention of Moses on the seder night. Nothing more strikingly conveys the difference between Moses and Pharaoh, and the value-systems they represented. Pharaoh was the sun god made manifest. In Judaism no human being is a god or godlike, but everyone is in the image of God. The exodus was the prelude to a political-religious order in which we are equal citizens under the sovereignty of God and in which no one needs an intermediary – a god, priest or holy person – to approach God. Only under the sacred canopy of faith does an entire society, as opposed to rare individuals, achieve its full stature and freedom.

כַּמָּה מַעֲלוֹת טוֹבוֹת לַמָּקוֹם עָלֵינוּ

אִלּוּ הוֹצִיאָנוּ מִמִּצְרַיִם

וְלֹא־עָשָׂה בָהֶם שְׁפָטִים, דַּיֵּנוּ:

אִלּוּ עָשָׂה בָהֶם שְׁפָטִים

וְלֹא־עָשָׂה בֵאלֹהֵיהֶם, דַּיֵּנוּ:

אִלּוּ עָשָׂה בֵאלֹהֵיהֶם

וְלֹא־הָרַג אֶת־בְּכוֹרֵיהֶם, דַּיֵּנוּ:

אִלּוּ הָרַג אֶת־בְּכוֹרֵיהֶם

וְלֹא־נָתַן לָנוּ אֶת־מָמוֹנָם, דַּיֵּנוּ:

אִלּוּ נָתַן לָנוּ אֶת־מָמוֹנָם

וְלֹא־קָרַע לָנוּ אֶת־הַיָּם, דַּיֵּנוּ:

אִלּוּ קָרַע לָנוּ אֶת־הַיָּם

וְלֹא־הֶעֱבִירָנוּ בְתוֹכוֹ בֶּחָרָבָה, דַּיֵּנוּ:

אִלּוּ הֶעֱבִירָנוּ בְתוֹכוֹ בֶּחָרָבָה

וְלֹא־שִׁקַּע צָרֵינוּ בְּתוֹכוֹ, דַּיֵּנוּ:

אִלּוּ שִׁקַּע צָרֵינוּ בְּתוֹכוֹ

וְלֹא־סִפֵּק צָרְכֵּנוּ בַּמִּדְבָּר אַרְבָּעִים שָׁנָה, דַּיֵּנוּ:

It would have been enough

This series of praises, with the refrain *Dayenu*, enumerates the kindnesses of God to His people on the long journey from slavery to freedom. The number fifteen – the acts the poem enumerates – has a deep association with thanksgiving, reminding us of the fifteen Psalms which bear the title *Shir Hama'alot*, 'A Song of Degrees', and the fifteen steps in the Temple on which the Levites stood as they sang to God.

The word *day*, meaning 'enough', echoes the phrase from Malachi (3:10), recited as part of the haftarah for the Shabbat before Pesach, 'I will pour you out a blessing *ad bli day*' which the sages translated as 'until your lips are exhausted through saying, Enough.'

This song is a *tikkun*, a making-right, for the ingratitude of the Israelites in the wilderness. At almost every stage of the way they complained: about the water, the food, the difficulties of the journey, the challenge of conquering the land. It is as if the poet were saying: Where they complained, let us give thanks. Each stage was a miracle. Each would have been enough to convince us that there is a providence at work in our fate.

As Hegel points out, slavery gives rise to a culture of *ressentiment*, a generalised discontent; and the Israelites were newly released slaves. One of the signs of freedom is the capacity for gratitude. Only a free person can thank with a full heart.

If He had not given us their treasure

Before the Israelites left Egypt they were commanded to ask of their neighbours silver and gold and other precious objects. The morality of this has long been a source of perplexity. The key to understanding it lies in the later law to which it gave rise. When you let a slave go free, commands the Torah, 'you shall not let him go empty-handed. Supply him liberally from your flock, your threshing-floor and your wine-press. Give to

How many good things has God done for us!

If He had brought us out from Egypt,   And had not judged against them,

    It would have been enough (Dayenu).

If He had judged against them,   And not destroyed their idols,

    It would have been enough (Dayenu).

If He had destroyed their idols,   And not killed their first-born,

    It would have been enough (Dayenu).

If He had killed their first-born,   And not given us their treasure,

    It would have been enough (Dayenu).

If He had given us their treasure,   And not split the Red Sea,

    It would have been enough (Dayenu).

If He had split the Red Sea,   And not brought us through it dry,

    It would have been enough (Dayenu).

If He had brought us through it dry,   And not drowned our foes in it,

    It would have been enough (Dayenu).

If He had drowned our foes in it,   And not helped us forty years in the desert,

    It would have been enough (Dayenu).

---

him as the Lord your God has blessed you. Remember that you were slaves in Egypt and the Lord your God redeemed you. That is why I give you this command today' (Deuteronomy 15:13–15).

Slavery is an insult to the human condition and it leaves a legacy of bitterness which itself prevents an ex-slave from being fully free of the past. Freedom involves more than just releasing a slave. It means furnishing him or her with the means to begin an independent life. It also involves tangible recognition of the work he or she did while a slave. Without this a slave continues to resent his former owner. With it, they can face one another in mutual dignity and respect. Payment is restitution in the deepest sense of the word, not only financial but also psychological.

Benno Jacob (quoted in Chief Rabbi Hertz's commentary to the Torah) suggests that the phrase 'and you shall despoil the Egyptians' (Exodus 3:22) is a mistranslation. The verb *venitzaltem* means not 'you shall despoil' but 'you shall save' – meaning, 'You shall *save the reputation* of the Egyptians and their standing in your eyes.' The Torah did not want the Israelites to harbour ill-will toward the Egyptians. Indeed it forbids resentment: 'You shall not despise an Egyptian, for you were a stranger in his land' (Deuteronomy 23:8). Only when justice has been done – when a slave receives compensation for his or her slavery – can one let go of the past and shape a new society without lingering animosities.

If He had given us the Sabbath

Shabbat is the ultimate expression of a free society, the antithesis of slavery in Egypt. On this day, all relationships of dominance and subordination are suspended. We may not work, nor command others to work, 'so that your man-servant and maid-servant may rest as you do.' At many times in history, people have dreamed of an ideal world. The name given to such visions is 'utopia', meaning 'no place', because at no time

אִלּוּ סִפֵּק צָרְכֵּנוּ בַּמִּדְבָּר אַרְבָּעִים שָׁנָה
וְלֹא־הֶאֱכִילָנוּ אֶת־הַמָּן, דַּיֵּנוּ:

אִלּוּ הֶאֱכִילָנוּ אֶת־הַמָּן
וְלֹא־נָתַן לָנוּ אֶת־הַשַּׁבָּת, דַּיֵּנוּ:

אִלּוּ נָתַן לָנוּ אֶת־הַשַּׁבָּת
וְלֹא־קֵרְבָנוּ לִפְנֵי הַר־סִינַי, דַּיֵּנוּ:

אִלּוּ קֵרְבָנוּ לִפְנֵי הַר־סִינַי
וְלֹא־נָתַן לָנוּ אֶת־הַתּוֹרָה, דַּיֵּנוּ:

אִלּוּ נָתַן לָנוּ אֶת־הַתּוֹרָה
וְלֹא־הִכְנִיסָנוּ לְאֶרֶץ יִשְׂרָאֵל, דַּיֵּנוּ:

אִלּוּ הִכְנִיסָנוּ לְאֶרֶץ יִשְׂרָאֵל
וְלֹא־בָנָה לָנוּ אֶת בֵּית הַבְּחִירָה, דַּיֵּנוּ:

עַל אַחַת כַּמָּה וְכַמָּה טוֹבָה כְפוּלָה וּמְכֻפֶּלֶת לַמָּקוֹם עָלֵינוּ. שֶׁהוֹצִיאָנוּ מִמִּצְרַיִם. וְעָשָׂה בָהֶם שְׁפָטִים. וְעָשָׂה בֵאלֹהֵיהֶם. וְהָרַג אֶת־בְּכוֹרֵיהֶם. וְנָתַן לָנוּ אֶת־מָמוֹנָם. וְקָרַע לָנוּ אֶת־הַיָּם. וְהֶעֱבִירָנוּ בְתוֹכוֹ בֶּחָרָבָה. וְשִׁקַּע צָרֵינוּ בְּתוֹכוֹ. וְסִפֵּק צָרְכֵּנוּ בַּמִּדְבָּר אַרְבָּעִים שָׁנָה. וְהֶאֱכִילָנוּ אֶת הַמָּן. וְנָתַן לָנוּ אֶת הַשַּׁבָּת. וְקֵרְבָנוּ לִפְנֵי הַר־סִינַי. וְנָתַן לָנוּ אֶת־הַתּוֹרָה. וְהִכְנִיסָנוּ לְאֶרֶץ יִשְׂרָאֵל. וּבָנָה לָנוּ אֶת בֵּית הַבְּחִירָה לְכַפֵּר עַל־כָּל־עֲוֹנוֹתֵינוּ:

or place have these dreams been realised on a society-wide basis. Shabbat is the sole successful utopian experiment in history. It is based on the simple idea that utopia (in Judaism, the messianic age) is not solely in the future. It is something we can experience in the midst of time, one day in seven. Shabbat became the weekly rehearsal of an ideal world, one not yet reached but still lived as a goal, of a world at peace with itself, recognising the createdness, and thus the integrity, of all people and all forms of life. If Egypt meant slavery, Shabbat is collective freedom, a 'foretaste of the world to come'.

If He had brought us to Mount Sinai and not given us the Torah

Maimonides writes (*Hilkhot Yesodei ha-Torah* 8:1) that the Israelites did not believe in Moses because of the miracles he performed. Miracles always leave open the possibility of scepticism: perhaps it was magic, illusion, chance or luck. Even when the Israelites 'believed in God and in Moses His servant' at the Red Sea, their belief was only temporary. What persuaded them of the truth of Moses and his prophecy was the revelation of God on Mount Sinai – the only occasion in history in which God appeared, not to a prophet or holy person but to an entire people. Thus, had God appeared at Sinai, even without giving us the Torah, it would still have established Jewish faith in the existence of God and His involvement in history on the basis of the direct experience of an entire nation, not the testimony of a prophet.

If He had helped us forty years in the desert,   And not fed us the Manna,

   It would have been enough (Dayenu).

If He had fed us the Manna,   And not given us the Sabbath,

   It would have been enough (Dayenu).

If He had given us the Sabbath,   And not brought us to Mount Sinai,

   It would have been enough (Dayenu).

If He had brought us to Mount Sinai,   And not given us the Torah,

   It would have been enough (Dayenu).

If He had given us the Torah,   And not brought us to the land of Israel,

   It would have been enough (Dayenu).

If He had brought us to the land of Israel,   And not built for us the Holy Temple,

   It would have been enough (Dayenu).

Therefore, how much good, doubled and re-doubled, has God done for us!

He brought us out of Egypt,   Judged against them,

Destroyed their idols,   Killed their first-born,

Gave us their treasure,   Split the Red Sea,

Brought us through it dry,   Drowned our foes in it,

Helped us forty years in the desert,   Fed us the Manna,

Gave us the Sabbath,   Brought us to Mount Sinai,

Gave us the Torah,   Brought us to the land of Israel,

And built for us the Holy Temple, to atone for all our sins.

If He had not built for us the Holy Temple

The Bible makes a connection between the exodus and the Temple. The building of the Temple by Solomon, begun 'in the four hundred and eightieth year after the Israelites had come out of Egypt' is the only event in the history of Israel to be dated by reference to the Exodus. In the Song the Israelites sang as they crossed the Red Sea they ended by looking forward to the building of the Temple:

> You will bring them and plant them in Your own mountain,
> The place You have made to dwell in, O Lord,
> The sanctuary, O Lord, which Your hands established.

The building of the Temple was thus the final act in the drama begun by the Exodus, and brought it to closure. The Temple was the symbol of the presence of God among a people who had established themselves as a sovereign power in their own land. It was the spiritual centre of national life.

רַבָּן גַּמְלִיאֵל הָיָה אוֹמֵר. כָּל שֶׁלֹא־אָמַר
שְׁלֹשָׁה דְבָרִים אֵלּוּ בַּפֶּסַח
לֹא־יָצָא יְדֵי חוֹבָתוֹ. וְאֵלּוּ הֵן

פֶּסַח   מַצָּה   וּמָרוֹר:

פֶּסַח שֶׁהָיוּ אֲבוֹתֵינוּ אוֹכְלִים בִּזְמַן שֶׁבֵּית הַמִּקְדָּשׁ
הָיָה קַיָּם עַל־שׁוּם מָה עַל־שׁוּם שֶׁפָּסַח הַקָּדוֹשׁ
בָּרוּךְ הוּא עַל בָּתֵּי אֲבוֹתֵינוּ בְּמִצְרָיִם. שֶׁנֶּאֱמַר וַאֲמַרְתֶּם
זֶבַח־פֶּסַח הוּא לַיהוה אֲשֶׁר פָּסַח עַל־בָּתֵּי בְנֵי־יִשְׂרָאֵל
בְּמִצְרַיִם בְּנָגְפּוֹ אֶת־מִצְרַיִם וְאֶת־בָּתֵּינוּ הִצִּיל וַיִּקֹד
הָעָם וַיִּשְׁתַּחֲווּ:

Raise the matzah and say:

מַצָּה זוֹ שֶׁאָנוּ אוֹכְלִים עַל שׁוּם מָה. עַל שׁוּם שֶׁלֹא
הִסְפִּיק בְּצֵקָם שֶׁל אֲבוֹתֵינוּ לְהַחֲמִיץ עַד שֶׁנִּגְלָה
עֲלֵיהֶם מֶלֶךְ מַלְכֵי הַמְּלָכִים הַקָּדוֹשׁ בָּרוּךְ הוּא
וּגְאָלָם. שֶׁנֶּאֱמַר וַיֹּאפוּ אֶת־הַבָּצֵק אֲשֶׁר הוֹצִיאוּ
מִמִּצְרַיִם עֻגֹת מַצּוֹת כִּי לֹא חָמֵץ כִּי גֹרְשׁוּ מִמִּצְרַיִם
וְלֹא יָכְלוּ לְהִתְמַהְמֵהַּ וְגַם־צֵדָה לֹא־עָשׂוּ לָהֶם:

Rabban Gamliel used to say: Whoever does not discuss three things

This is a requirement peculiar to Pesach. Normally commands are fulfilled by performing the requisite act with the intention of observing the commandment. To fulfil the duty of *sukkah*, for example, we do not have to tell the story of the wandering of the Israelites in the desert. However in the case of Pesach two commands coincide: the first, to eat the festive meal; the second, to tell the story. Rabban Gamliel argues that the two are connected. The story explains the food; the food allows us to relive the story.

The Torah states: 'When you enter the land that the Lord your God will give you as He promised, observe this ceremony. And when your children ask you, "What does this ceremony mean to you?" then tell them, "It is a Passover sacrifice to the Lord, who passed over the houses of the Israelites in Egypt and spread our homes when He struck down the Egyptians."' (Exodus 12:25–27). Thus from the very outset a connection was drawn between eating, asking and explaining, and it is this on which Rabban Gamliel bases his view that all three elements of the Passover meal must be explained.

The Passover lamb, matzah and the bitter herbs

The Passover lamb symbolises freedom. The bitter herbs represents slavery. Matzah combines both. It was the bread the Israelites ate in Egypt as slaves. It was also the bread they left when leaving Egypt as free people.

Why do the symbols of freedom precede the bitter herbs of slavery? Surely slavery preceded freedom? The Hassidic masters answered: only to a free human being does slavery taste bitter. Had the Israelites forgotten freedom they would have grown used to slavery. 'The worst exile is to forget that you are in exile.'

Rabban Gamliel used to say: Whoever does not discuss three things on Passover has not kept [the Seder] properly.

They are:

The Passover Lamb,   the Matzah,   and the Bitter Herbs.

Our fathers ate the Passover Lamb long ago when the Holy Temple (in Jerusalem) stood. What was the reason for it? It was because God passed over our fathers' houses in Egypt. It is thus written, "You shall say, 'It is the Passover offering to God, because He passed over the houses of the children of Israel in Egypt. He struck the Egyptians with a plague, but he spared our houses and the people kneeled and bowed down'" (Exodus 12:27).

Raise the matzah and say:

We eat this matzah, but what is the reason for it? It is because the dough prepared by our fathers did not have time to rise before God revealed Himself to them and immediately delivered them. Thus it is written, "They baked the dough that they had brought out of Egypt into matzah cakes, because it did not rise. They had been driven out of Egypt, and could not delay; they had also not prepared any other food" (Exodus 21:39).

The Passover Lamb

Unlike the other two foods, we do not lift, or point at, the roasted bone on the seder plate in case this gesture should be interpreted as dedicating it as a sacrifice. Even after the destruction of the Temple it was not unknown for individuals in Israel and outside to eat meat prepared to resemble the paschal lamb. The sages took exception to this, and we are therefore careful to avoid any act that might look as if we were bestowing special status on the object symbolising the paschal offering.

Matzah

In the Torah the festival that we call *Pesach* is consistently described as *Chag ha-Matzot*, the festival of unleavened bread (*Chag ha-Pesach*, in the Torah, is confined to the fourteenth of Nisan, the day prior to the seder, when the paschal sacrifice was brought). R. Levi Yitzhak of Berdichev gave a beautiful explanation for this dual terminology. The name *Pesach* signifies the greatness of God who 'passed over' the houses of the Israelites. The name *Chag ha-Matzot* suggests the greatness of the Israelites, that they were willing to follow God into the desert without any provisions. In the Torah God calls the festival *Chag ha-Matzot* in praise of Israel. The Jewish people, though, called the festival *Pesach* to sing the praise of God.

Matzah

In the German concentration camp of Bergen-Belsen in 1944, the Jewish prisoners did not have matzah. The rabbis in the camp gave permission for them to eat bread, since without it they would certainly die. They composed the following benediction:

'Our father in Heaven, behold it is evident and known to You that it is our desire to do Your will and to celebrate the festival of Passover by eating matzah and by observing the prohibition of leavened food. But our heart is pained that the enslavement prevents us and we are in danger of our lives. Behold we are prepared and ready to fulfil Your comandment: 'And you shall live by them – and not die by them.' We pray to You that You may keep us alive and preserve us and redeem us speedily so that we may observe Your statutes and do Your will and serve You with a perfect heart. Amen.'

Raise the bitter herbs and say:

מָרוֹר זֶה שֶׁאָנוּ אוֹכְלִים עַל־שׁוּם מָה. עַל שׁוּם
שֶׁמֵּרְרוּ הַמִּצְרִים אֶת־חַיֵּי אֲבוֹתֵינוּ בְּמִצְרָיִם. שֶׁנֶּאֱמַר
וַיְמָרֲרוּ אֶת חַיֵּיהֶם בַּעֲבֹדָה קָשָׁה בְּחֹמֶר וּבִלְבֵנִים וּבְכָל
עֲבֹדָה בַּשָּׂדֶה אֵת כָּל־עֲבֹדָתָם אֲשֶׁר עָבְדוּ בָהֶם בְּפָרֶךְ:

בְּכָל דּוֹר וָדוֹר חַיָּב אָדָם לִרְאוֹת אֶת־עַצְמוֹ כְּאִלּוּ הוּא
יָצָא מִמִּצְרָיִם. שֶׁנֶּאֱמַר וְהִגַּדְתָּ לְבִנְךָ בַּיּוֹם הַהוּא לֵאמֹר
בַּעֲבוּר זֶה עָשָׂה יהוה לִי בְּצֵאתִי מִמִּצְרָיִם. לֹא אֶת־
אֲבוֹתֵינוּ בִּלְבָד גָּאַל הַקָּדוֹשׁ בָּרוּךְ הוּא אֶלָּא אַף אֹתָנוּ גָּאַל
עִמָּהֶם שֶׁנֶּאֱמַר וְאוֹתָנוּ הוֹצִיא מִשָּׁם לְמַעַן הָבִיא אֹתָנוּ
לָתֶת לָנוּ אֶת הָאָרֶץ אֲשֶׁר נִשְׁבַּע לַאֲבֹתֵינוּ:

Cover the matzah, raise the cup of wine and say:

לְפִיכָךְ אֲנַחְנוּ חַיָּבִים לְהוֹדוֹת לְהַלֵּל לְשַׁבֵּחַ לְפָאֵר
לְרוֹמֵם לְהַדֵּר לְבָרֵךְ לְעַלֵּה וּלְקַלֵּס לְמִי
שֶׁעָשָׂה לַאֲבוֹתֵינוּ וְלָנוּ אֶת־כָּל הַנִּסִּים
הָאֵלֶּה הוֹצִיאָנוּ מֵעַבְדוּת לְחֵרוּת מִיָּגוֹן לְשִׂמְחָה
וּמֵאֵבֶל לְיוֹם טוֹב וּמֵאֲפֵלָה לְאוֹר גָּדוֹל וּמִשִּׁעְבּוּד
לִגְאֻלָּה וְנֹאמַר לְפָנָיו שִׁירָה חֲדָשָׁה הַלְלוּיָהּ:

Matzah... because they could not delay

The Hebrew terminology echoes the description of Lot who 'delayed' when told to escape from Sodom. God brought it about that the Israelites were 'driven out' by the Egyptians. Had they delayed, they might never have left. Slaves, as Rousseau and Marx said, get used to their chains.

Bitter Herbs

A Jew was sent to Siberia by the Communist government for illegally maintaining a network of Jewish education during the years when Judaism was suppressed. When he finally obtained his freedom he told his friends, 'It was difficult to keep Pesach in the labour camp. One year we had no matzot. Another year we had no wine. But of bitter herbs, we were never short.' This was told to me by his son.

In every generation

Most texts of the Haggadah reproduce the language of the Mishnah: 'In every generation each individual should *see* (*lir'ot*) himself as if he had personally left Egypt.' Maimonides, however, writes that each individual should *show* (*lehar'ot*) himself as if he had left. This is because Maimonides holds that there are two separate commands of reciting the Haggadah: (1) to tell ourselves the story, (2) to tell our children the story. Seeing is part of the first mitzvah, showing is part of the second. For us to feel the full impact of the drama, we have to internalise it. For us to show it to others, we have to externalise it by, for example, reclining as we

---

See Essays on Passover "The First Pesach" page 125

Raise the bitter herbs and say:

We eat this bitter herb, but what is the reason for it?

It is because the Egyptians made our fathers' lives bitter in Egypt.
It is thus written, "They made their lives bitter with hard work, with
mortar and bricks, and all kinds of work in the field. All the work
they made them do was backbreaking" (Exodus 1:14).

In every generation one must look upon himself as if he had
personally left Egypt. It is thus written, "You shall tell your child on
that day, 'Because of this, God did [things] for me when I left Egypt'"
(Exodus 13:8).

For not only did God save our fathers from Egypt, but He also saved
us with them. Thus it is written (in the answer that we give our
children on Passover), "It was ourselves that He brought out of there,
so that He might lead us, and give us the land that He swore to our
fathers" (Deuteronomy 6:23).

Cover the matzah, raise the cup of wine and say:

It is therefore our duty to thank, praise, be grateful, glorify, exalt,
acclaim, and sing out to the One who did all these miracles for our
fathers and for us. He led us from slavery to freedom, from bondage
to redemption, from misery to joy, and from mourning to a holiday,
and from deep darkness to great light. Let us therefore sing before
Him: Halleluyah – Praise God!

---

drink the wine. In general, Judaism reverses the usual order of emotion and action. In other cultures, feeling
leads to doing. In Judaism, doing leads to feeling. We are commanded to act in certain ways in order
eventually to feel in certain ways. Thus, *showing* our freedom to others is one of the best ways of coming to
see it ourselves.

It is therefore our duty to thank

This is one of the transitional moments of the Haggadah, when we move from story to song, from
prose to poetry, from recitation (*Maggid*) to praise (*Hallel*). We have told the story of the Exodus. Now, like the
Israelites 3,300 years ago, we sing a song of praise. We lift the cup at this point, fulfilling the words of the
Psalm, 'I will lift the cup of salvation and call on the name of God' (Psalm 116:13).

Song plays a vital part in Judaism. At the end of his life Moses gave the Israelites the last of the
commands – that in every generation we should write a new Sefer Torah. On that occasion he used an
unusual word. He called the Torah a 'song' (Deuteronomy 31:19). Words are the language of the mind. Music
is the language of the soul. Whenever speech is invested with deep emotion it aspires to the condition of
song. Thus we do not say our prayers; we sing them. We do not read the Torah; we chant it. We do not study
Talmud; we intone it. Each kind of text, and each period of the Jewish year, has its own melody. Thus Moses
was saying: to transmit Torah across the generations as a living faith, it must be, not just a code of law, but
also the song of the Jewish people.

Replace the cup of wine and uncover the matzah

הַלְלוּיָהּ הַלְלוּ עַבְדֵי יהוה הַלְלוּ אֶת־שֵׁם יהוה:
יְהִי שֵׁם יהוה מְבֹרָךְ מֵעַתָּה וְעַד־עוֹלָם:
מִמִּזְרַח שֶׁמֶשׁ עַד־מְבוֹאוֹ מְהֻלָּל שֵׁם יהוה: רָם עַל־
כָּל־גּוֹיִם יהוה. עַל הַשָּׁמַיִם כְּבוֹדוֹ: מִי כַּיהוה אֱלֹהֵינוּ.
הַמַּגְבִּיהִי לָשָׁבֶת. הַמַּשְׁפִּילִי לִרְאוֹת בַּשָּׁמַיִם וּבָאָרֶץ:
מְקִימִי מֵעָפָר דָּל. מֵאַשְׁפֹּת יָרִים אֶבְיוֹן: לְהוֹשִׁיבִי
עִם־נְדִיבִים. עִם נְדִיבֵי עַמּוֹ: מוֹשִׁיבִי עֲקֶרֶת הַבַּיִת
אֵם־הַבָּנִים שְׂמֵחָה הַלְלוּיָהּ:

בְּצֵאת יִשְׂרָאֵל מִמִּצְרָיִם בֵּית יַעֲקֹב מֵעַם לֹעֵז:
הָיְתָה יְהוּדָה לְקָדְשׁוֹ יִשְׂרָאֵל מַמְשְׁלוֹתָיו:
הַיָּם רָאָה וַיָּנֹס. הַיַּרְדֵּן יִסֹּב לְאָחוֹר: הֶהָרִים רָקְדוּ
כְאֵילִים. גְּבָעוֹת כִּבְנֵי צֹאן: מַה לְּךָ הַיָּם כִּי תָנוּס.
הַיַּרְדֵּן תִּסֹּב לְאָחוֹר: הֶהָרִים תִּרְקְדוּ כְאֵילִים.
גְּבָעוֹת כִּבְנֵי צֹאן: מִלִּפְנֵי אָדוֹן חוּלִי אָרֶץ. מִלִּפְנֵי
אֱלוֹהַּ יַעֲקֹב: הַהֹפְכִי הַצּוּר אֲגַם־מָיִם. חַלָּמִישׁ לְמַעְיְנוֹ־מָיִם:

Hallel

Hallel (Psalms 113–118) is the great song of deliverance which, according to the Talmud, was sung at all the great triumphs of Jewish history. In our day we have added two new occasions when we say it: on *Yom ha-Atzma'ut,* Israel's Independence Day, and *Yom Yerushalayim,* Jerusalem Day.

The late Rabbi Joseph Soloveitchik asked an interesting question about the recitation of Hallel at the seder table. The Talmud states that we do not say Hallel on Purim because 'the reading of the Megillah is equivalent to saying Hallel'. Why then do we not apply the same reasoning to seder night? We have recited the Haggadah, the counterpart of the Megillah on Purim. Surely, then, the recital of Hallel is superfluous.

The answer I would give is that there are two different commands to say Hallel (this is the view of the *Maggid Mishneh* and the *Netziv*). The first is at the time of a miracle. The second is as a form of remembrance on the anniversary of the miracle. Thus at the time of Hanukkah, the Maccabees said Hallel at the moment of victory. The next year they established it as an annual obligation. The two forms of Hallel arise from different psychological states. The first is expressive, the second evocative. The first gives voice to an emotion we already feel. The second creates that emotion by an act of memory, recalling an event that occurred in the past.

Telling the story of a miracle, as we do on Purim, is equivalent to the second form of Hallel. It is an act of memory. On Pesach, however, we do not merely tell the story. We relive it. We eat the bread of affliction and the bitter herbs. We taste the wine of freedom. We recline as free people. 'In every generation a person should see himself as if he personally left Egypt.' The Hallel we say on the seder night is therefore of the first kind, not the second. It arises out of the emotions we feel having lived through the event again. It is a 'new song'. This kind of Hallel is not cancelled by telling the story.

Replace the cup of wine and uncover the matzah

Halleluyah – praise God!

Let God's servants praise, let them praise God's name;

May God's name be praised now and forever!

From when the sun rises until it sets, let God's name be praised.

God is high above all nations, His glory is above the heavens.

Who is like God our Lord, enthroned on high,

Looking down upon the heavens and the earth?

He raises the poor from the dust, and the beggar from the waste heap,

Giving them a place among princes, among the princes of His people.

He makes the woman in a childless house a joyful mother of children:

Halleluyah – praise God!

When Israel went out from Egypt,

Jacob's family from a people of foreign tongue,

Judah became His holy one, Israel His own kingdom.

The sea looked and fled, the Jordan turned back;

The mountains danced like rams, the hills like lambs.

Why, O Sea, do you flee, O Jordan, why do you turn back?

O Mountains, why do you dance like rams, and the hills, why like lambs?

Before the Master, who formed the earth!

Before the God of Jacob!

He turns the rock into a pool of water, bedrock into a flowing spring!

Let God's servants praise

The sages commented, 'and not the servants of Pharaoh'. The transition from being an *eved* (slave/servant) owned by a human being to being an *eved* to God is not a move from one form of servitude to another. It is the move from slavery to freedom. Only under the sovereignty of God can we be free in such a way that our freedom does not injure the freedom of others.

From when the sun rises until it sets, let God's name be praised.

The prophet Malachi (1:11) says in the name of God: 'From where the sun rises to where it sets, My name is honoured among the nations.' The God of Israel is the God of all humanity.

God is high above all nations... He raises the poor from the dust

Rabbi Yochanan said: 'Wherever you find God's greatness, there you find His humility.' The greatness of God lies in His concern for the poor, the weak, the marginal and the disenfranchised. Moral as opposed to physical power is shown in the regard we have for the powerless.

   "He raises the poor from the dust" commentary continues on page 52

Raise the cup of wine and say:

בָּרוּךְ אַתָּה יהוה אֱלֹהֵינוּ מֶלֶךְ הָעוֹלָם אֲשֶׁר גְּאָלָנוּ
וְגָאַל אֶת אֲבוֹתֵינוּ מִמִּצְרַיִם וְהִגִּיעָנוּ הַלַּיְלָה הַזֶּה
לֶאֱכָל בּוֹ מַצָּה וּמָרוֹר. כֵּן יהוה אֱלֹהֵינוּ וֵאלֹהֵי אֲבוֹתֵינוּ
יַגִּיעֵנוּ לְמוֹעֲדִים וְלִרְגָלִים אֲחֵרִים הַבָּאִים לִקְרָאתֵנוּ
לְשָׁלוֹם שְׂמֵחִים בְּבִנְיַן עִירֶךָ וְשָׂשִׂים בַּעֲבוֹדָתֶךָ וְנֹאכַל
שָׁם מִן הַזְּבָחִים וּמִן הַפְּסָחִים

On Motzei Shabbat add the words in brackets:

(מִן הַפְּסָחִים וּמִן הַזְּבָחִים) אֲשֶׁר יַגִּיעַ דָּמָם עַל
קִיר מִזְבַּחֲךָ לְרָצוֹן וְנוֹדֶה לְךָ שִׁיר חָדָשׁ עַל גְּאֻלָּתֵנוּ
וְעַל פְּדוּת נַפְשֵׁנוּ . בָּרוּךְ אַתָּה יהוה גָּאַל יִשְׂרָאֵל:

Raise the cup and say:

בָּרוּךְ אַתָּה יהוה אֱלֹהֵינוּ מֶלֶךְ הָעוֹלָם בּוֹרֵא פְּרִי הַגָּפֶן:

Drink the second cup, while leaning to the left.

He raises the poor from the dust...

These lines echo Hannah's prayer at the birth of her child, Samuel:

> She who was barren has borne seven children,
> But she who has had many sons pines away...
> The Lord sends poverty and wealth;
> He humbles and exalts.
> He raises the poor from the dust
> And lifts the needy from the ash-heap;
> He seats them with princes
> And has them inherit a throne of honour.

In Judaism, religion is not 'the opium of the people', the defence of the established order. It is a constant call for the established order to be tested against the template of justice and compassion. In Judaism there is no 'divine right of kings'. The greatest ruler, if evil, is brought low. The lowliest human being, if righteous, is raised high.

See Essays on Passover page 59, page 67 & page 75   The Haggadah

Raise the cup of wine and say:

Blessed are You, O God our Lord,

King of the world, who freed us and our fathers from Egypt, and brought us

here this night to eat matzah and bitter herbs. So, O God our Lord and Lord

of our fathers, may You bring us to [celebrate] other holidays and festivals in

peace, rejoicing in the building of Your city, and happy in serving You. There

may we be able to eat of the offerings and Passover Lambs

On Motzei Shabbat add the words in brackets:

(of the Passover Lambs and offerings) whose blood is placed

on the side of Your altar for acceptance.

May we thank You with a new song for our freedom, and for saving our

lives. Blessed are You O God who freed Israel.

Raise the cup and say:

Blessed are you, O God, our Lord, King of the world, Creator of the fruit of the vine.

Drink the second cup, while leaning to the left.

When Israel went out from Egypt

'One of the finest lyrics in literature. Nowhere do we find a more exquisite picture of the liberation from
Egypt, or a more poetic representation of the birth of Israel. In inimitably vivid manner, it sketches the three
most wonderful events in Israel's history: the Exodus, the Revelation, and Israel's sustenance in the wilderness'
(J. H. Hertz).

On this magnificent climax, we bring the first part of the seder to a close. We have told the story, sung
the song and made our people's past live again.

The hands are washed

רָחְצָה

בָּרוּךְ אַתָּה יהוה אֱלֹהֵינוּ מֶלֶךְ הָעוֹלָם אֲשֶׁר קִדְּשָׁנוּ
בְּמִצְוֹתָיו וְצִוָּנוּ עַל נְטִילַת יָדָיִם:

The hands are then wiped completely dry.

מוֹצִיא מַצָּה

Take all three matzahs in hand and say:

בָּרוּךְ אַתָּה יהוה אֱלֹהֵינוּ מֶלֶךְ הָעוֹלָם הַמּוֹצִיא
לֶחֶם מִן הָאָרֶץ:

Release the bottom matzah and say:

בָּרוּךְ אַתָּה יהוה אֱלֹהֵינוּ מֶלֶךְ הָעוֹלָם אֲשֶׁר קִדְּשָׁנוּ
בְּמִצְוֹתָיו וְצִוָּנוּ עַל אֲכִילַת מַצָּה:

Break a piece of the upper and middle matzah, eat of it while leaning to the left.

Blessed are You

This, a blessing over the past and a prayer for the future, was composed by two great scholars of the Mishnaic age. The first part was written by Rabbi Tarfon, the second by Rabbi Akiva. Rabbi Akiva was the guardian of hope at one of the darkest times of Jewish history. The Talmud (*Makkot* 24b) tells of an occasion when he and other sages were walking on Mount Scopus when they saw a fox walking through the Holy of Holies amid the ruins of the Temple. The others wept, but Rabbi Akiva comforted them, saying, Since the prophecies of destruction have come true, the prophecies of consolation will also come true. The day will come when, in Zechariah's words, 'Once again men and women of a ripe old age will sit in the streets of Jerusalem... and the city streets will be filled with boys and girls playing there' (Zechariah 8:4). It took nearly two thousand years, but it has happened in our lifetime. It was Akiva's hope – expressed here in the vision of 'days that are coming to meet us in peace' – that sustained the Jewish people in exile.

The hands are washed

Rachtzah Wash

Wash hands for matzah and recite:

Blessed are You, O God our Lord, King of the world, who made us holy with His commandments and instructed us regarding the washing of hands.

The hands are then wiped completely dry.

Motzie Matzah Bless and Eat Matzah

Take all three matzahs in hand and say:

Blessed are you, O God our Lord, King of the world,

who brings bread out of the earth.

Release the bottom matzah and say:

Blessed are You, O God our Lord, King of the world, who made us holy with His commandments and instructed us to eat matzah.

Break a piece of the upper and middle matzah, eat of it while leaning to the left.

Eating the matzah

We make two blessings over the *matzah*. The first, *hamotzi*, is over the bread as such. It is one of the *birkot hanehenin*, blessings we make over eating and drinking. The second, *asher kidshanu*, is a different kind of blessing, one of the *birkot ha-mitzvot*, the blessings we make over commanded acts.

For the first blessing, all the matzot should be raised. For the second, where we draw attention to the broken middle matzah which is unique to the seder, we put down the bottom matzah and make the blessing only over the top and middle matzot.

A portion of both the top and middle matzot is distributed to everyone around the table. Each should eat an 'olive's bulk' – approximately two-thirds of the normal size of a machine-made matzah. Since the amount distributed from the top and middle matzot will not be sufficient, each should complete the minimum quantity by eating from other matzah on the table.

The Ashkenazi custom is not to put salt on the matzah. The Maharal explains that this is because of our special love for the taste of matzah on the seder night. We do not diminish its impact by adding any other taste. One should recline while eating the matzah, since this is one of the primary expressions of freedom tonight.

מָרוֹר

Take some bitter herb, dip into haroseth and say:

בָּרוּךְ אַתָּה יהוה אֱלֹהֵינוּ מֶלֶךְ הָעוֹלָם אֲשֶׁר קִדְּשָׁנוּ
בְּמִצְוֹתָיו וְצִוָּנוּ עַל אֲכִילַת מָרוֹר:

כּוֹרֵךְ:

Break two pieces of the bottom matzah, put bitter herbs between them and say while leaning to the left:

זֵכֶר לְמִקְדָּשׁ כְּהֵלֵּל . כֵּן עָשָׂה הִלֵּל בִּזְמַן שֶׁבֵּית
הַמִּקְדָּשׁ הָיָה קַיָּם . הָיָה כּוֹרֵךְ (פֶּסַח) מַצָּה וּמָרוֹר
וְאוֹכֵל בְּיַחַד . לְקַיֵּם מַה שֶׁנֶּאֱמַר
עַל־מַצּוֹת וּמְרֹרִים יֹאכְלֻהוּ:

שֻׁלְחָן עוֹרֵךְ

The meal is eaten

Bitter Herbs

The *maror* is dipped in *charoset* and the blessing over the mitzvah, *al achilat maror* is made. The reason we do not make a further blessing, *bore pri ha-adamah*, is that we have already made it for the *karpas*.

There are differing customs as to which vegetables are to be used for maror. In the time of the Mishnah, lettuce (*chazeret*) was most commonly used. In northern and eastern parts of Europe, where this was difficult to obtain, the custom developed to use horseradish (*chrein*). Nowadays many use both, choosing Romaine lettuce at this point where maror is eaten on its own, and horseradish for the 'Hillel sandwich'. An olive-size bulk (1.1 fluid ounces) should be eaten. We do not recline for the maror, since it is a symbol not of freedom but of slavery.

Maror The Bitter Herb

Take some bitter herb, dip into haroseth and say:

Blessed are You, O God our Lord, King of the world, who made us holy
with His commandments, and instructed us to eat the bitter herbs.

Korekh Combine Matzah and Bitter Herbs

Break two pieces of the bottom matzah, put bitter herbs between them and say while leaning to the left:

In memory of the Temple, according to Hillel. This is what Hillel would
do long ago when the Temple stood: He would make a sandwich of the
Passover Lamb, matzah, and bitter herbs and eat them all together. This
was to keep what the Torah says, "They shall eat [the Passover Lamb]
together with matzah and bitter herbs" (Exodus 12:8).

Shulchan Orech The Meal is Served

The meal is eaten

Korekh

The bottom matzah is now taken. Each participant takes two pieces and between them places maror
which has been dipped in *charoset*. No blessing is made, since we have already made the blessings over the
matzah and maror separately.

It appears that there was a difference of opinion between Hillel and his contemporaries as to whether the
matzah and maror should be eaten separately or together. The view that they should be eaten separately
holds that these are distinctive commands, neither of which should diminish or detract from the other. Matzah
symbolises freedom; maror represents slavery. They have different tastes. They are opposite experiences. They
do not belong together.

Hillel, however, thought otherwise, and out of respect for his opinion we do as he did as well. Hillel was
guided by his understanding of the biblical verse that one should eat the Paschal offering 'with matzot and
bitter herbs', suggesting that all three be eaten together. Perhaps, too, he was reminding us of the Jewish
experience of history. Within the bitterness of slavery there was also the hope and promise of freedom. Within
freedom, we are also commanded each year never to forget the taste of slavery, so that we should not take
liberty for granted, nor forget those who are still afflicted.

צָפוּן

After the meal, the Afikoman which was put aside at the commencement of the seder is distributed.

Eat the Afikoman while leaning to the left.

בָּרֵךְ

Fill the third cup of wine and say the Grace after the Meal.

שִׁיר הַמַּעֲלוֹת בְּשׁוּב יהוה אֶת שִׁיבַת צִיּוֹן הָיִינוּ
כְּחֹלְמִים: אָז יִמָּלֵא שְׂחוֹק פִּינוּ וּלְשׁוֹנֵנוּ רִנָּה אָז יֹאמְרוּ
בַגּוֹיִם הִגְדִּיל יהוה לַעֲשׂוֹת עִם אֵלֶּה: הִגְדִּיל יהוה לַעֲשׂוֹת
עִמָּנוּ הָיִינוּ שְׂמֵחִים: שׁוּבָה יהוה אֶת שְׁבִיתֵנוּ
כַּאֲפִיקִים בַּנֶּגֶב: הַזֹּרְעִים בְּדִמְעָה בְּרִנָּה יִקְצֹרוּ: הָלוֹךְ
יֵלֵךְ וּבָכֹה נֹשֵׂא מֶשֶׁךְ הַזָּרַע בֹּא־יָבֹא בְרִנָּה נֹשֵׂא אֲלֻמֹּתָיו:

תְּהִלַּת יהוה יְדַבֶּר פִּי וִיבָרֵךְ כָּל־בָּשָׂר שֵׁם קָדְשׁוֹ לְעוֹלָם וָעֶד.
וַאֲנַחְנוּ נְבָרֵךְ יָהּ מֵעַתָּה וְעַד עוֹלָם הַלְלוּיָהּ.
הוֹדוּ לַיהוה כִּי־טוֹב כִּי לְעוֹלָם חַסְדּוֹ
מִי יְמַלֵּל גְּבוּרוֹת יהוה יַשְׁמִיעַ כָּל־תְּהִלָּתוֹ

Tzafun – the Afikoman

At the end of the meal we eat the other half of the broken matzah. This symbolises the paschal offering, which in Temple times was eaten at the end of the meal. It should be eaten before midnight.

Tradition has given the name *afikoman* to this matzah. It derives from the Mishnah – cited in answer to the 'wise' son – that we do not conclude with anything after the *afikoman*. Most scholars conjecture that the origin of the word is the Greek *epikomon*, which meant a drinking party. The Greeks would often end a festive meal by visiting friends and engaging in a night of drinking and conversation. Plato describes such an event in *The Symposium*. The sages ruled that such social activities were forbidden on Pesach. One should finish the evening with the taste of holy food in one's mouth. Hence the last part of the matzah became the Jewish *afikoman*, a sign of the difference between Jewish and Greek culture, between holiness and hedonism. It is no coincidence that whereas Greek culture rapidly disintegrated after the days of Alexander the Great, Judaism sustained its spiritual and moral energies throughout the many crises of its history.

Tzafun The Afikoman

After the meal, the Afikoman which was put aside at the commencement of the seder is distributed.

Eat the Afikoman while leaning to the left.

Barekh Grace after the Meal

Fill the third cup of wine and say the Grace after the Meal.

A Pilgrim Song

When the Eternal brought the exiles back to Zion, we were as in a dream.

Our mouths were filled with laughter, our tongues with songs of joy.

The nations said: "The Eternal has done great things for them."

Yes, the Eternal did great things for us, and we rejoiced.

Restore our fortune, O Eternal, as streams, once dry, flow again.

They that sow in tears shall reap in joy.

Though the planter may weep as he carries seed to the field,

He will yet return with joy, bearing sheaves of grain.

My mouth shall speak the praise of the Lord,

And all creatures shall bless His holy name for ever and ever.

But we will bless the Lord now and for ever more, Halleluyah!

Give thanks to the Lord, for He is good; for His love is never ending.

Who can express the mighty acts of God or make all His praise to be heard.

Grace after the Meal

Grace after meals is one of the elements of Jewish liturgy already specified in the Bible. It is commanded in the verse, 'When you have eaten and are satisfied, praise the Lord your God for the good land He has given you' (Deuteronomy 8:10). Eating is a biological function. That is why Judaism – with its emphasis on sanctifying the physical – is particularly concerned to turn the act of eating into a moment of spiritual affirmation.

It is said that Abraham and Sarah first drew people into the service of the one God by extending them hospitality. After their guests had eaten, they would turn to thank their hosts. Abraham would reply, 'Thank not us but God who provides food for all.' 'How shall we thank God?' 'Say: Blessed is the Lord who is blessed. Blessed be He who gives bread and food to all that lives.' This is more than a beautiful tradition. It is a basic theme of Judaism. It is in the physical that we find the spiritual. God made the world; therefore it is in the world that we find God.

The commentators ask why it is that the Grace after meals is a biblical command, whereas the grace *before* meals is only a rabbinic injunction. Their answer is that to thank God when we are hungry is natural. To thank him when we are sated is more difficult. It is precisely when we are most likely to forget that we need reminding – that what we have, we have from God, creator and sustainer of all.

If three men or more are present, the Grace is preceded by the following introductory phrases.

When ten or more are present, the words in parenthesis are added:

Host:

רַבּוֹתַי נְבָרֵךְ:

Company:

יְהִי שֵׁם יהוה מְבֹרָךְ מֵעַתָּה וְעַד עוֹלָם:

Host repeats the preceding sentence and continues:

בִּרְשׁוּת מָרָנָן וְרַבָּנָן וְרַבּוֹתַי נְבָרֵךְ
(אֱלֹהֵינוּ) שֶׁאָכַלְנוּ מִשֶּׁלּוֹ וּבְטוּבוֹ חָיִינוּ:

Company:

בָּרוּךְ (אֱלֹהֵינוּ) שֶׁאָכַלְנוּ מִשֶּׁלּוֹ וּבְטוּבוֹ חָיִינוּ:

Host repeats the preceding sentence and continues:

בָּרוּךְ הוּא וּבָרוּךְ שְׁמוֹ:

If less than three men are present, the Grace begins here.

בָּרוּךְ אַתָּה יהוה אֱלֹהֵינוּ מֶלֶךְ הָעוֹלָם הַזָּן אֶת הָעוֹלָם
כֻּלּוֹ בְּטוּבוֹ בְּחֵן בְּחֶסֶד וּבְרַחֲמִים הוּא נֹתֵן לֶחֶם לְכָל־
בָּשָׂר כִּי לְעוֹלָם חַסְדּוֹ. וּבְטוּבוֹ הַגָּדוֹל תָּמִיד לֹא חָסַר לָנוּ
וְאַל יֶחְסַר לָנוּ מָזוֹן לְעוֹלָם וָעֶד. בַּעֲבוּר שְׁמוֹ הַגָּדוֹל כִּי
הוּא אֵל זָן וּמְפַרְנֵס לַכֹּל וּמֵטִיב לַכֹּל וּמֵכִין מָזוֹן
לְכָל־בְּרִיּוֹתָיו אֲשֶׁר בָּרָא. בָּרוּךְ אַתָּה יהוה הַזָּן אֶת־הַכֹּל:

Grace after the Meal

The first three blessings – the original form of the Grace – represent three concentric circles of holiness.
The first blessing is for the world, the second for the land of Israel, the third for Jerusalem, home of the Divine
presence. In the first we thank God for providing sustenance for all humanity. In the second we thank Him for
His special providence over the land of Israel. In the third we acknowledge His presence in the holy city of
Jerusalem, the one place from which, according to the sages, the Divine presence was never exiled.

The order of these blessings represents the threefold nature of Jewish identity. First, we are citizens of the

If three men or more are present, the Grace is preceded by the following introductory phrases.
When ten or more are present, the words in parenthesis are added:

Host:

Let us say grace.

Company:

May the name of the Eternal be blessed from now and for evermore.

Host repeats the preceding sentence and continues:

With the permission of all present, let us praise Him (our God) whose food we have eaten and in whose goodness we live.

Company:

Blessed be He, (our God) whose food we have eaten, and in whose goodness we live.

Host repeats the preceding sentence and continues:

Blessed be He and blessed be His name.

If less than three men are present, the Grace begins here.

Blessed are You, Eternal, our God, Ruler of the universe, who sustains the whole universe in His goodness, with grace, loving-kindness and mercy. He gives food to all, for His mercy endures forever. In His great goodness, food has never failed us, and may it never fail us, for His great name's sake. It is He who provides for all, sustains all, and is good to all, preparing food for all His creatures that He has created. Blessed are You, Eternal, who provides food for all.

world, descendants of Noah and heirs to his covenant with God. We are part of the collective project of mankind. Secondly, we are Jews, faithful to our people, engaged – as our ancestors were since the days of Abraham and Sarah – in the long journey to the land of Israel. Whether we live there or in the Diaspora we pray for it and share in its crises and achievements. Thirdly, there is a part of us that belongs to Jerusalem. When the Temple was destroyed, said the sages, a fragment of its stones entered the hearts of the Jewish people. It remained and still remains the focus of the Jewish imagination, the home of future redemption. As we say the three blessings, therefore, we journey inward from the universal to the particular elements of Jewish identity.

נוֹדֶה לְּךָ יהוה אֱלֹהֵינוּ עַל שֶׁהִנְחַלְתָּ לַאֲבוֹתֵינוּ אֶרֶץ
חֶמְדָּה טוֹבָה וּרְחָבָה: וְעַל שֶׁהוֹצֵאתָנוּ יהוה אֱלֹהֵינוּ
מֵאֶרֶץ מִצְרַיִם וּפְדִיתָנוּ מִבֵּית עֲבָדִים וְעַל בְּרִיתְךָ שֶׁחָתַמְתָּ
בִּבְשָׂרֵנוּ וְעַל תּוֹרָתְךָ שֶׁלִּמַּדְתָּנוּ וְעַל חֻקֶּיךָ שֶׁהוֹדַעְתָּנוּ
וְעַל חַיִּים חֵן וָחֶסֶד שֶׁחוֹנַנְתָּנוּ וְעַל אֲכִילַת מָזוֹן שָׁאַתָּה זָן
וּמְפַרְנֵס אוֹתָנוּ תָּמִיד בְּכָל־יוֹם וּבְכָל עֵת וּבְכָל שָׁעָה:

וְעַל הַכֹּל יהוה אֱלֹהֵינוּ אֲנַחְנוּ מוֹדִים לָךְ וּמְבָרְכִים
אוֹתָךְ יִתְבָּרַךְ שִׁמְךָ בְּפִי כָּל־חַי תָּמִיד לְעוֹלָם וָעֶד.
כַּכָּתוּב וְאָכַלְתָּ וְשָׂבָעְתָּ וּבֵרַכְתָּ אֶת־יהוה אֱלֹהֶיךָ
עַל־הָאָרֶץ הַטֹּבָה אֲשֶׁר נָתַן־לָךְ. בָּרוּךְ אַתָּה יהוה
עַל הָאָרֶץ וְעַל הַמָּזוֹן:

רַחֶם נָא יהוה אֱלֹהֵינוּ עַל יִשְׂרָאֵל עַמֶּךָ וְעַל יְרוּשָׁלַיִם עִירֶךָ
וְעַל צִיּוֹן מִשְׁכַּן כְּבוֹדֶךָ וְעַל מַלְכוּת בֵּית דָּוִד מְשִׁיחֶךָ
וְעַל הַבַּיִת הַגָּדוֹל וְהַקָּדוֹשׁ שֶׁנִּקְרָא שִׁמְךָ עָלָיו. אֱלֹהֵינוּ
אָבִינוּ רְעֵנוּ זוּנֵנוּ פַּרְנְסֵנוּ וְכַלְכְּלֵנוּ וְהַרְוִיחֵנוּ
וְהַרְוַח־לָנוּ יהוה אֱלֹהֵינוּ מְהֵרָה מִכָּל צָרוֹתֵינוּ.
וְנָא אַל־תַּצְרִיכֵנוּ יהוה אֱלֹהֵינוּ לֹא לִידֵי מַתְּנַת בָּשָׂר וָדָם
וְלֹא לִידֵי הַלְוָאָתָם כִּי אִם לְיָדְךָ הַמְּלֵאָה הַפְּתוּחָה
הַקְּדוֹשָׁה וְהָרְחָבָה שֶׁלֹּא נֵבוֹשׁ וְלֹא נִכָּלֵם לְעוֹלָם וָעֶד:

The following paragraph is added on the Sabbath:

(רְצֵה וְהַחֲלִיצֵנוּ יהוה אֱלֹהֵינוּ בְּמִצְוֹתֶיךָ וּבְמִצְוַת יוֹם
הַשְּׁבִיעִי הַשַּׁבָּת הַגָּדוֹל וְהַקָּדוֹשׁ הַזֶּה כִּי יוֹם זֶה גָּדוֹל
וְקָדוֹשׁ הוּא לְפָנֶיךָ לִשְׁבָּת־בּוֹ וְלָנוּחַ בּוֹ בְּאַהֲבָה
כְּמִצְוַת רְצוֹנֶךָ וּבִרְצוֹנְךָ הָנִיחַ לָנוּ יהוה אֱלֹהֵינוּ שֶׁלֹּא תְהֵא
צָרָה וְיָגוֹן וַאֲנָחָה בְּיוֹם מְנוּחָתֵנוּ וְהַרְאֵנוּ יהוה אֱלֹהֵינוּ
בְּנֶחָמַת צִיּוֹן עִירֶךָ וּבְבִנְיַן יְרוּשָׁלַיִם עִיר קָדְשֶׁךָ כִּי
אַתָּה הוּא בַּעַל הַיְשׁוּעוֹת וּבַעַל הַנֶּחָמוֹת:)

We thank You, Eternal our God, for the desirable, good and spacious land which You gave to our fathers; for bringing us out from the Land of Egypt, O Eternal our God; and for redeeming us from the house of bondage; for Your covenant sealed in our flesh; for Your Torah that You taught us; for Your laws which You made known to us; for the life of grace and loving-kindness which You have graciously bestowed on us; and for the food with which You nourish and sustain us at all times, daily, at every season and every hour.

For all these blessings, Eternal, our God, we thank You and bless You. May Your name be blessed in the mouths of all the living at all times and for ever! Thus do we fulfill Your command: "You shall eat and be satisfied, and you shall bless the Eternal your God for the good land that He gave you." Blessed are You, Eternal, for the land and for our sustenance.

Eternal our God, have mercy on Israel Your people, on Jerusalem Your city, and Zion the dwelling place of Your glory, on the royal house of David Your anointed, and on the great and holy Temple called by Your name. Our God, Father and Shepherd: sustain us, support us and provide for all our needs. Eternal our God, speedily relieve us from all our troubles. Eternal our God, may we never be in need of the gifts or loans of other people, but only of Your full, open, holy and generous hand, so that we never face humiliation or shame.

The following paragraph is added on the Sabbath:
Eternal our God, by Your grace, strengthen us in Your commandments, especially the observance of the seventh day, this great and holy Sabbath. For it is a great and holy day given by You, in love, for rest and serenity. May it be Your will, Eternal our God, to grant us such repose that there shall be no sorrow, trouble or sighing on our day of rest. And, Eternal our God, may we see Zion Your city comforted and Jerusalem Your holy city rebuilt, for You are the God of salvation and consolation.

Have mercy... on Jerusalem, Your city

Whenever we mention Jerusalem in our prayers, we associate it with the word *rachamim*, mercy. The concept of mercy or compassion in Judaism is not abstract. The word *rachamim* comes from the word *rechem*, meaning a womb. The deepest and most unconditional love in creation is that of a mother for her child. Throughout nature, mothers are willing to risk their lives to protect their offspring. That and more is the nature of God's love for His children: 'Can a mother forget the baby at her breast? Can she lack compassion for the child she has borne? Though they may forget, I will not forget you' (Isaiah 49:15). Jerusalem is the womb, the matrix, of God's connection with the Jewish people. It was there that He first tested Abraham's love, in the binding of Isaac. It was there that He built His home in the form of the Temple. Thus it is the home of God's mercy, the birthplace of the covenant, the one place on earth where the presence of God – creator of the universe – is most tangible.

אֱלֹהֵינוּ וֵאלֹהֵי אֲבוֹתֵינוּ יַעֲלֶה וְיָבֹא וְיַגִּיעַ וְיֵרָאֶה וְיֵרָצֶה
וְיִשָּׁמַע וְיִפָּקֵד וְיִזָּכֵר זִכְרוֹנֵנוּ וּפִקְדוֹנֵנוּ וְזִכְרוֹן
אֲבוֹתֵינוּ וְזִכְרוֹן מָשִׁיחַ בֶּן דָּוִד עַבְדֶּךָ וְזִכְרוֹן יְרוּשָׁלַיִם
עִיר קָדְשֶׁךָ וְזִכְרוֹן כָּל עַמְּךָ בֵּית יִשְׂרָאֵל לְפָנֶיךָ
לִפְלֵיטָה לְטוֹבָה לְחֵן וּלְחֶסֶד וּלְרַחֲמִים לְחַיִּים וּלְשָׁלוֹם
בְּיוֹם חַג הַמַּצּוֹת הַזֶּה. זָכְרֵנוּ יְהוָה אֱלֹהֵינוּ בּוֹ לְטוֹבָה
וּפָקְדֵנוּ בוֹ לִבְרָכָה וְהוֹשִׁיעֵנוּ בוֹ לְחַיִּים (טוֹבִים) וּבִדְבַר
יְשׁוּעָה וְרַחֲמִים חוּס וְחָנֵּנוּ וְרַחֵם עָלֵינוּ וְהוֹשִׁיעֵנוּ כִּי
אֵלֶיךָ עֵינֵינוּ כִּי אֵל מֶלֶךְ חַנּוּן וְרַחוּם אָתָּה:

וּבְנֵה יְרוּשָׁלַיִם עִיר הַקֹּדֶשׁ בִּמְהֵרָה בְיָמֵינוּ.
בָּרוּךְ אַתָּה יְהוָה בּוֹנֵה בְרַחֲמָיו יְרוּשָׁלָיִם. אָמֵן:

בָּרוּךְ אַתָּה יְהוָה אֱלֹהֵינוּ מֶלֶךְ הָעוֹלָם הָאֵל אָבִינוּ מַלְכֵּנוּ
אַדִּירֵנוּ בּוֹרְאֵנוּ גּוֹאֲלֵנוּ יוֹצְרֵנוּ קְדוֹשֵׁנוּ קְדוֹשׁ יַעֲקֹב
רוֹעֵנוּ רוֹעֵה יִשְׂרָאֵל הַמֶּלֶךְ הַטּוֹב וְהַמֵּטִיב לַכֹּל שֶׁבְּכָל
יוֹם וָיוֹם הוּא הֵטִיב הוּא מֵטִיב הוּא יֵטִיב לָנוּ. הוּא
גְמָלָנוּ הוּא גוֹמְלֵנוּ הוּא יִגְמְלֵנוּ לָעַד לְחֵן וּלְחֶסֶד
וּלְרַחֲמִים וּלְרֶוַח הַצָּלָה וְהַצְלָחָה בְּרָכָה וִישׁוּעָה נֶחָמָה
פַּרְנָסָה וְכַלְכָּלָה וְרַחֲמִים וְחַיִּים וְשָׁלוֹם וְכָל טוֹב וּמִכָּל
טוּב לְעוֹלָם אַל יְחַסְּרֵנוּ:

הָרַחֲמָן הוּא יִמְלוֹךְ עָלֵינוּ לְעוֹלָם וָעֶד.
הָרַחֲמָן הוּא יִתְבָּרַךְ בַּשָּׁמַיִם וּבָאָרֶץ.
הָרַחֲמָן הוּא יִשְׁתַּבַּח לְדוֹר דּוֹרִים וְיִתְפָּאַר בָּנוּ לָעַד
וּלְנֵצַח נְצָחִים וְיִתְהַדַּר בָּנוּ לָעַד וּלְעוֹלְמֵי עוֹלָמִים.
הָרַחֲמָן הוּא יְפַרְנְסֵנוּ בְּכָבוֹד.
הָרַחֲמָן הוּא יִשְׁבּוֹר עֻלֵּנוּ מֵעַל צַוָּארֵנוּ
וְהוּא יוֹלִיכֵנוּ קוֹמְמִיּוּת לְאַרְצֵנוּ.
הָרַחֲמָן הוּא יִשְׁלַח לָנוּ בְּרָכָה מְרֻבָּה
בַּבַּיִת הַזֶּה וְעַל שֻׁלְחָן זֶה שֶׁאָכַלְנוּ עָלָיו.

Our God and God of our fathers, on this day of the Festival of Unleavened Bread,

may there come before You the remembrance of us and our fathers, of Jerusalem Your holy

city, of the Messiah the son of David Your servant, and of all Your people, the house of Israel.

May these come before You, and in tenderness, grace and mercy may they be heard and

accepted with favour by You, for life and peace, deliverance and happiness, blessing and good.

In accordance with Your word of salvation and mercy, have mercy on us and save us.

Our eyes are lifted towards You, for You are a gracious and merciful God and King.

Rebuild Jerusalem the holy city soon in our days! Blessed are You, Eternal,

Who will rebuild Jerusalem in His mercy. Amen.

Blessed are You, Eternal our God, Ruler of the universe, God our Father, our King, our

Mighty One, our Creator, our Redeemer, our Maker, our Holy One, the Holy One of Jacob;

our Shepherd and Shepherd of Israel, the good King who does good to all.

Even as He has daily done good to us, so may He continue to do good to us forever.

Even as He has dealt bountifully with us, so may He ever bestow upon us with boundless

grace, loving-kindness and mercy, help, prosperity, blessing, salvation, consolation, sustenance

and support, in life and peace and all that is good.

May the All-merciful rule over us for ever.

May the All-merciful be blessed in heaven and on earth.

May the All-merciful be praised for all generations and honoured among us for all eternity.

May the All-merciful grant that our needs be supplied with dignity.

May the All-merciful break the oppressor's yoke from our neck and lead us upright to our land.

May the All-merciful send the fullness of blessing on this household and bless this table at

which we have eaten.

Blessed are You...

This, the fourth blessing of the Grace after Meals, was added during the period of the Tannaim in the second century CE. The Talmud relates it to the period after the defeat of the Bar Kochba rebellion, at Betar. It represents a moment of thanksgiving in one of the darkest periods of Jewish history, when the Roman army gave permission to the Jewish community to bury its dead. Over time, the Grace after Meals grew with the addition of further praises and prayers

הָרַחֲמָן הוּא יִשְׁלַח לָנוּ אֶת אֵלִיָּהוּ
הַנָּבִיא זָכוּר לַטּוֹב וִיבַשֶּׂר לָנוּ
בְּשׂוֹרוֹת טוֹבוֹת יְשׁוּעוֹת וְנֶחָמוֹת:

Say whichever of the following is appropriate:

At one's parents' table say:

הָרַחֲמָן הוּא יְבָרֵךְ אֶת (אָבִי מוֹרִי)
בַּעַל הַבַּיִת הַזֶּה וְאֶת
(אִמִּי מוֹרָתִי) בַּעֲלַת הַבַּיִת הַזֶּה.
אוֹתָם וְאֶת בֵּיתָם וְאֶת זַרְעָם וְאֶת כָּל אֲשֶׁר לָהֶם.

At one's own table say:

אוֹתִי (וְאֶת אִשְׁתִּי/בַּעֲלִי וְאֶת זַרְעִי) וְאֶת כָּל אֲשֶׁר לִי

וְאֶת כָּל הַמְסֻבִּין כָּאן.
אוֹתָנוּ וְאֶת כָּל אֲשֶׁר לָנוּ כְּמוֹ שֶׁנִּתְבָּרְכוּ אֲבוֹתֵינוּ
אַבְרָהָם יִצְחָק וְיַעֲקֹב בַּכֹּל מִכֹּל כֹּל כֵּן יְבָרֵךְ אוֹתָנוּ
כֻּלָּנוּ יַחַד בִּבְרָכָה שְׁלֵמָה וְנֹאמַר אָמֵן:

בַּמָּרוֹם יְלַמְּדוּ עֲלֵיהֶם וְעָלֵינוּ זְכוּת שֶׁתְּהֵא לְמִשְׁמֶרֶת
שָׁלוֹם. וְנִשָּׂא בְרָכָה מֵאֵת יְהוָה וּצְדָקָה מֵאֱלֹהֵי יִשְׁעֵנוּ
וְנִמְצָא חֵן וְשֵׂכֶל טוֹב בְּעֵינֵי אֱלֹהִים וְאָדָם:

The following sentence is added on the Sabbath:

הָרַחֲמָן הוּא יַנְחִילֵנוּ יוֹם שֶׁכֻּלּוֹ שַׁבָּת
וּמְנוּחָה לְחַיֵּי הָעוֹלָמִים:

On both Seder nights say the following sentence:

הָרַחֲמָן הוּא יַנְחִילֵנוּ יוֹם שֶׁכֻּלּוֹ טוֹב.

On the two Seder nights some people add the following sentence:

(יוֹם שֶׁכֻּלּוֹ אָרוּךְ. יוֹם שֶׁהַצַּדִּיקִים יוֹשְׁבִים וְעַטְרוֹתֵיהֶם
בְּרָאשֵׁיהֶם וְנֶהֱנִים מִזִּיו הַשְּׁכִינָה וִיהִי חֶלְקֵנוּ עִמָּהֶם:)

May the All-merciful send to us the prophet Elijah, of blessed memory,
bearing good tidings of deliverance and comfort.

Say whichever of the following is appropriate:

At one's parents' table say:
May the All-merciful bless:
my honoured father, master of this house,
and my honoured mother, mistress of this house;
them, their household, their children,
and all that is theirs;

At one's own table say:
Me (my wife/my husband, my children)
and all that belong to me.

And all who are sitting here;
Us and all that is ours.
May He bless us together with perfect blessings,
even as our ancestors Abraham, Isaac and Jacob were blessed
with every manner of blessing, and let us say Amen.

On high may there be invoked for them and for us such grace
as shall ever be a safeguard of peace. Then shall we receive blessing from
the Eternal and righteousness from the God of our salvation, and may
we find grace and understanding in the eyes of God and of man.

The following sentence is added on the Sabbath:
May the All-merciful grant us a day that shall be
altogether Sabbath and repose in eternal life.

On both seder nights say the following sentence:
May the All-merciful grant us a day that shall be altogether good.

On the two Seder nights some people add the following sentence:
A day without end, a day on which the righteous sit, their crowns on their heads,
Bathed in the light of the Divine presence,
And may our share be with them.

הָרַחֲמָן הוּא יְזַכֵּנוּ לִימוֹת הַמָּשִׁיחַ וּלְחַיֵּי הָעוֹלָם הַבָּא. מִגְדּוֹל יְשׁוּעוֹת מַלְכּוֹ וְעֹשֶׂה חֶסֶד לִמְשִׁיחוֹ לְדָוִד וּלְזַרְעוֹ עַד עוֹלָם. עֹשֶׂה שָׁלוֹם בִּמְרוֹמָיו הוּא יַעֲשֶׂה שָׁלוֹם עָלֵינוּ וְעַל כָּל יִשְׂרָאֵל וְאִמְרוּ אָמֵן:

יְראוּ אֶת יהוה קְדשָׁיו כִּי אֵין מַחְסוֹר לִירֵאָיו. כְּפִירִים רָשׁוּ וְרָעֵבוּ וְדֹרְשֵׁי יהוה לֹא־יַחְסְרוּ כָל טוֹב. הוֹדוּ לַיהוה כִּי טוֹב כִּי לְעוֹלָם חַסְדּוֹ. פּוֹתֵחַ אֶת יָדֶךָ וּמַשְׂבִּיעַ לְכָל חַי רָצוֹן. בָּרוּךְ הַגֶּבֶר אֲשֶׁר יִבְטַח בַּיהוה וְהָיָה יהוה מִבְטַחוֹ. נַעַר הָיִיתִי גַּם זָקַנְתִּי וְלֹא רָאִיתִי צַדִּיק נֶעֱזָב וְזַרְעוֹ מְבַקֶּשׁ לָחֶם. יהוה עֹז לְעַמּוֹ יִתֵּן יהוה יְבָרֵךְ אֶת עַמּוֹ בַשָּׁלוֹם:

בָּרוּךְ אַתָּה יהוה אֱלֹהֵינוּ מֶלֶךְ הָעוֹלָם בּוֹרֵא פְּרִי הַגָּפֶן:

Drink the third cup of wine while leaning to the left.

I was young and now am old, yet I have not seen the righteous forsaken or his children begging for bread

This line, from Psalm 37:25, has often raised questions. Surely throughout history there were times when the righteous *were* forsaken? Indeed this is one of the questions that, according to the Talmud, Moses asked God: 'Why do the righteous suffer?' The English writer Edmond Blunden wrote a poem, *Report on Experience*, on this theme:

> I have been young, and now am not too old;
> And I have seen the righteous forsaken,
> His health, his honour and his quality taken.
> This is not what we were formerly told.

I once heard a beautiful explanation from R. Moses Feuerstein of Boston. The key phrase of the verse is *lo ra'iti*, standardly translated as 'I have not seen'. The verb *ra'iti*, though, occurs twice in the Book of Esther with a quite different meaning. 'How can I bear to watch (*eichachah uchal vera'iti*) the disaster which will befall my people? And how can I bear to watch the destruction of my family?' (Esther 8:6). The verb here

May the All-merciful make us worthy of seeing the days of the Messiah and life in the world to come. He is a tower of salvation to His king and shows kindness to His anointed, to David and his seed forever. May the Creator of peace in the heavens create peace for us and for all Israel, and let us say, Amen.

Venerate the Eternal, you His holy ones, for those who revere Him lack nothing.

Young lions may be in want and suffer hunger, but they who seek the Eternal shall lack no good thing. Give thanks unto the Eternal for He is good, and His mercy endures forever.

You open Your hand and satisfy every living thing.

Blessed is the man who trusts in the Eternal, and the Eternal is his stronghold.

I was young and now am old, yet I have not seen a righteous man forsaken or his children begging for bread.

The Eternal will give strength to His people; the Eternal will bless His people with peace.

Blessed are You, Eternal our God, Ruler of the universe, Creator of the fruit of the vine.

Drink the third cup of wine while leaning to the left.

---

does not mean 'to see'. It means 'to stand by and watch, to be a passive witness, a disengaged spectator'. *Ra'iti* in this sense means to see and do nothing to help. That, for Esther as for the Psalmist, is a moral impossibility. We may not 'stand idly by the blood of our neighbour'. We *are* our brother's keeper.

Translated thus, the verse states: 'I was young and now am old and I have not merely stood still and watched when the righteous was forsaken and his children forced to beg for bread.' Read this way, not only does it make sense. It also emerges from the core of Jewish sensibility. It ends the grace after meals with a moral commitment. Yes, we have eaten and are satisfied. But that has not made us indifferent to the needs of others.

The conclusion of the meal, so understood, echoes the opening of the seder service with its invitation to 'all who are needy – come and eat.' Maimonides writes about the command to rejoice on the festivals: 'And while one eats and drinks himself, it is a duty to feed the stranger, the orphan, the widow, and other poor and unfortunate people, for he who locks the doors of his courtyard and eats and drinks with his wife and family, without giving anything to eat and drink to the poor and bitter in soul – his meal is not a rejoicing in a divine commandment but a rejoicing in his own stomach… Rejoicing of this kind is a disgrace to those who indulge in it.' (*Hilkhot Yom Tov* 6:18).

Fill the fourth cup of wine and the cup of Elijah the Prophet. Open the door for Elijah. All rise.

שְׁפֹךְ חֲמָתְךָ אֶל הַגּוֹיִם אֲשֶׁר לֹא יְדָעוּךָ וְעַל מַמְלָכוֹת
אֲשֶׁר בְּשִׁמְךָ לֹא קָרָאוּ: כִּי אָכַל אֶת יַעֲקֹב וְאֶת נָוֵהוּ
הֵשַׁמּוּ: שְׁפָךְ עֲלֵיהֶם זַעְמֶךָ וַחֲרוֹן אַפְּךָ יַשִּׂיגֵם: תִּרְדֹּף
בְּאַף וְתַשְׁמִידֵם מִתַּחַת שְׁמֵי יְהוָה:

The door is closed

הַלֵּל

לֹא לָנוּ יְהוָה לֹא לָנוּ כִּי לְשִׁמְךָ תֵּן כָּבוֹד עַל חַסְדְּךָ עַל
אֲמִתֶּךָ: לָמָּה יֹאמְרוּ הַגּוֹיִם אַיֵּה נָא אֱלֹהֵיהֶם: וֵאלֹהֵינוּ
בַשָּׁמָיִם כֹּל אֲשֶׁר חָפֵץ עָשָׂה: עֲצַבֵּיהֶם כֶּסֶף וְזָהָב מַעֲשֵׂה
יְדֵי אָדָם: פֶּה לָהֶם וְלֹא יְדַבֵּרוּ עֵינַיִם לָהֶם וְלֹא יִרְאוּ:
אָזְנַיִם לָהֶם וְלֹא יִשְׁמָעוּ אַף לָהֶם וְלֹא יְרִיחוּן:
יְדֵיהֶם וְלֹא יְמִישׁוּן רַגְלֵיהֶם וְלֹא יְהַלֵּכוּ לֹא יֶהְגּוּ בִּגְרוֹנָם:
כְּמוֹהֶם יִהְיוּ עֹשֵׂיהֶם כֹּל אֲשֶׁר בֹּטֵחַ בָּהֶם:
יִשְׂרָאֵל בְּטַח בַּיהוָה עֶזְרָם וּמָגִנָּם הוּא: בֵּית אַהֲרֹן
בִּטְחוּ בַיהוָה עֶזְרָם וּמָגִנָּם הוּא: יִרְאֵי יְהוָה
בִּטְחוּ בַיהוָה עֶזְרָם וּמָגִנָּם הוּא:

Pour out Your wrath on the nations

This passage, not part of the earliest Haggadot, was added during the Middle Ages, during one of the darkest periods of anti-Jewish persecution. It began with the First Crusade (1096), in which, on their way to the Holy Land, the Crusaders stopped to massacre Jewish communities in Worms, Speyer and Mainz. It was the beginning of centuries of persecution, often in the name of religion.

One of the recurring events that made Pesach in particular a time of fear was the 'blood libel'. This originated in Norwich in 1144, and eventually spread throughout Europe. It is one of the few cases where persecution has left its mark on Jewish law. Several authorities ruled that though, preferably, the wine drunk on Pesach should be red, in communities where there is risk of a blood libel, white wine may be used instead.

What is notable about this addition to the Haggadah is its restraint. For centuries, Jews suffered a series of devastating blows – massacres, pogroms, forced conversions, inquisitions, confinement to ghettos, punitive taxation, and expulsions, culminating, in the very heart of 'enlightened' Europe, in the Holocaust. Yet these verses, two from Psalms, one from the Book of Lamentations, are almost the only trace left by this experience on the Haggadah, the night when we recall our past.

Albert Einstein once spoke of the 'almost fanatical love of justice' as one of the 'features of the Jewish

Fill the fourth cup of wine and the cup of Elijah the Prophet. Open the door for Elijah. All rise.

Pour out Your wrath on the nations that do not acknowledge You, and on the kingdoms that do not call on Your name. For they have devoured Jacob and laid waste his habitation (Psalm 79:6–7).

Pour out Your indignation upon them, and let Your fierce anger overtake them (Psalm 69:25).

Pursue them in wrath and destroy them under the heavens of the Lord (Lamentations 3:66).

The door is closed

Hallel The Praise

Not to us, O God, not to us, but to Your name give glory for Your mercy and truth.

Why should the nations say, "Where is their God?"

Our God is in heaven, all that He wants He does.

Their idols are silver and gold, the work of human hands.

They have a mouth, but cannot speak; they have eyes but cannot see.

They have ears, but cannot hear; they have a nose but cannot smell.

They have hands, but cannot feel; they have feet, but cannot walk;

they make no sound with their throats.

May those who make them be like them, all who trust in them.

Let Israel trust in God, He is their help and shield.

Let the house of Aaron trust in God, He is their help and shield.

Let the God-fearing trust in God, He is their help and shield.

---

tradition which make me thank my stars that I belong to it.' Judaism is a religion of justice. It is also a religion of love, compassion, forgiveness, generosity and peace. But from the beginning it has wrestled with the question of how to bring the Divine presence down to earth, in the structures and institutions of society. The necessary precondition is justice. Once that exists, there is room for the many other virtues that humanise our world. But without justice, something fundamental is missing. 'Pour out Your wrath' is not a call for vengeance. It is not a call to human action at all. It is, rather, a prayer for Divine justice.

At this point in the seder, as we turn from the past to the future, we reflect on the tragedy of the Jewish people in the past, the many thousands and millions of our people who were murdered, sometimes in the name of the God of love. We ask God to reveal to us, at the end of days, the meaning of all this suffering. These verses are a cry of pain coming to us from one of the dark nights of the Jewish soul, as if to say: 'Let us understand, one day if not now, the justice of Your world, O judge of all the earth.'

Pour out Your wrath on the nations

In one manuscript from Worms, 1521, there is a unique addition to the Haggadah alongside 'Pour out Your wrath'. It is a prayer of thanks for the righteous gentiles throughout history who, rather than persecuting

יהוה זְכָרָנוּ יְבָרֵךְ יְבָרֵךְ אֶת בֵּית יִשְׂרָאֵל יְבָרֵךְ אֶת
בֵּית אַהֲרֹן: יְבָרֵךְ יִרְאֵי יהוה הַקְּטַנִּים עִם הַגְּדֹלִים:
יֹסֵף יהוה עֲלֵיכֶם עֲלֵיכֶם וְעַל בְּנֵיכֶם: בְּרוּכִים אַתֶּם
לַיהוה עֹשֵׂה שָׁמַיִם וָאָרֶץ: הַשָּׁמַיִם שָׁמַיִם לַיהוה וְהָאָרֶץ
נָתַן לִבְנֵי אָדָם: לֹא הַמֵּתִים יְהַלְלוּ־יָהּ וְלֹא כָּל יֹרְדֵי
דוּמָה: וַאֲנַחְנוּ נְבָרֵךְ יָהּ מֵעַתָּה וְעַד עוֹלָם הַלְלוּיָהּ:

אָהַבְתִּי כִּי יִשְׁמַע יהוה אֶת קוֹלִי תַּחֲנוּנָי: כִּי
הִטָּה אָזְנוֹ לִי וּבְיָמַי אֶקְרָא: אֲפָפוּנִי חֶבְלֵי מָוֶת וּמְצָרֵי
שְׁאוֹל מְצָאוּנִי צָרָה וְיָגוֹן אֶמְצָא: וּבְשֵׁם יהוה אֶקְרָא אָנָּה
יהוה מַלְּטָה נַפְשִׁי: חַנּוּן יהוה וְצַדִּיק וֵאלֹהֵינוּ מְרַחֵם:
שֹׁמֵר פְּתָאִים יהוה דַּלּוֹתִי וְלִי יְהוֹשִׁיעַ: שׁוּבִי נַפְשִׁי
לִמְנוּחָיְכִי כִּי יהוה גָּמַל עָלָיְכִי: כִּי חִלַּצְתָּ נַפְשִׁי
מִמָּוֶת אֶת עֵינִי מִן דִּמְעָה אֶת רַגְלִי מִדֶּחִי: אֶתְהַלֵּךְ
לִפְנֵי יהוה בְּאַרְצוֹת הַחַיִּים: הֶאֱמַנְתִּי כִּי אֲדַבֵּר אֲנִי
עָנִיתִי מְאֹד: אֲנִי אָמַרְתִּי בְחָפְזִי כָּל הָאָדָם כֹּזֵב:

Jews, befriended them and protected them at times of danger:

> Pour out Your love on the nations who have known You,
> And on the kingdoms who call upon Your name.
> For they show loving-kindness to the seed of Jacob,
> And they defend Your people Israel from those
> Who would devour them alive.
> May they live to see the sukkah of peace spread over Your chosen ones,
> And to participate in the joy of your nations.

Pour out Your wrath on the nations

Some add, at this point, the following prayer in memory of the victims of the Holocaust and the courage of those in the Warsaw ghetto who, on the eve of Pesach 1943, rose up against the Nazis who had planned to destroy the ghetto and kill all its inhabitants on the first day of Pesach:

> On this night of the Seder we remember with reverence and love the six million of our
> people of the European exile who perished at the hands of a tyrant more wicked than the
> Pharaoh who enslaved our forefathers in Egypt. Come, he said to his minions, let us cut

God will remember us, He will bless,

He will bless the house of Israel, He will bless the house of Aaron.

He will bless those who fear God, small and great alike.

May God add to you, to you and to your children.

Blessed are you by God, maker of heaven and earth.

The heavens are the heavens of God, but the earth He has given to mankind.

The dead do not praise God, nor those who sink down in silence.

But we will bless God, now and forever:

Halleluyah – Praise God!

I love God because He heard my voice and my prayer,

Because He listened to me on the day I called.

The cords of death were around me, the agony of the grave had found me:

I was in trouble and sorrow.

I called in God's name, "O God, save my soul!"

God is kind and just; our God has pity.

God preserves the simple; I was brought low and He saved me.

Rest once again, my soul, for God has been good to you.

You have delivered my soul from death, my eyes from tears, my foot from stumbling.

I will walk before God in the world of the living.

I had faith, though I spoke – I was in such great trouble

That in panic I said, "Everything human is false."

---

them off from being a people, that the name of Israel may be remembered no more.

And they slew the blameless and pure, men and women and little ones, with poisonous gas and burned them with fire. But we abstain from dwelling on the deeds of the evil ones lest we defame the image of God in which man was created.

Now, the remnants of our people who were left in the ghettos and camps of annihilation rose up against the wicked ones for the sanctification of the Name, and slew many of them before they died. On the first day of Passover the remnants in the ghetto of Warsaw rose up against the adversary, even as in the days of Judah the Maccabee. They were lovely and pleasant in their lives, and in their death they were not divided, and they brought redemption to the name of Israel through all the world.

And from the depths of their affliction the martyrs lifted up their voices in a song of faith in the coming of the Messiah, when justice and brotherhood will reign among mankind.

All sing:
Ani ma'amin be'emunah shelemah bevi'at hamashi'ach. Ve'af al pi sheyitmahme'ah im kol zeh achakeh lo sheyavo.
I believe with perfect faith in the coming of the Messiah. And even though he tarry, still I believe.

מָה אָשִׁיב לַיהוה כָּל תַּגְמוּלוֹהִי עָלָי: כּוֹס יְשׁוּעוֹת אֶשָּׂא
וּבְשֵׁם יהוה אֶקְרָא: נְדָרַי לַיהוה אֲשַׁלֵּם נֶגְדָה נָּא
לְכָל־עַמּוֹ: יָקָר בְּעֵינֵי יהוה הַמָּוְתָה לַחֲסִידָיו: אָנָּא
יהוה כִּי אֲנִי עַבְדֶּךָ אֲנִי עַבְדְּךָ בֶּן אֲמָתֶךָ פִּתַּחְתָּ
לְמוֹסֵרָי: לְךָ אֶזְבַּח זֶבַח תּוֹדָה וּבְשֵׁם יהוה אֶקְרָא:
נְדָרַי לַיהוה אֲשַׁלֵּם נֶגְדָה נָּא לְכָל עַמּוֹ:
בְּחַצְרוֹת בֵּית יהוה בְּתוֹכֵכִי יְרוּשָׁלַיִם הַלְלוּיָהּ:

הַלְלוּ אֶת יהוה כָּל גּוֹיִם שַׁבְּחוּהוּ כָּל הָאֻמִּים:
כִּי גָבַר עָלֵינוּ חַסְדּוֹ וֶאֱמֶת יהוה לְעוֹלָם הַלְלוּיָהּ:

כִּי לְעוֹלָם חַסְדּוֹ:	הוֹדוּ לַיהוה כִּי טוֹב
כִּי לְעוֹלָם חַסְדּוֹ:	יֹאמַר נָא יִשְׂרָאֵל
כִּי לְעוֹלָם חַסְדּוֹ:	יֹאמְרוּ נָא בֵית אַהֲרֹן
כִּי לְעוֹלָם חַסְדּוֹ:	יֹאמְרוּ נָא יִרְאֵי יהוה

מִן הַמֵּצַר קָרָאתִי יָּהּ עָנָנִי בַמֶּרְחָב יָהּ: יהוה לִי לֹא אִירָא
מַה יַּעֲשֶׂה לִי אָדָם: יהוה לִי בְּעֹזְרָי וַאֲנִי אֶרְאֶה בְשֹׂנְאָי:
טוֹב לַחֲסוֹת בַּיהוה מִבְּטֹחַ בָּאָדָם:
טוֹב לַחֲסוֹת בַּיהוה מִבְּטֹחַ בִּנְדִיבִים: כָּל גּוֹיִם סְבָבוּנִי
בְּשֵׁם יהוה כִּי אֲמִילַם: סַבּוּנִי גַם סְבָבוּנִי בְּשֵׁם יהוה
כִּי אֲמִילַם: סַבּוּנִי כִדְבֹרִים דֹּעֲכוּ כְּאֵשׁ קוֹצִים בְּשֵׁם
יהוה כִּי אֲמִילַם: דָּחֹה דְחִיתַנִי לִנְפֹּל וַיהוה עֲזָרָנִי:
עָזִּי וְזִמְרָת יָהּ וַיְהִי לִי לִישׁוּעָה: קוֹל רִנָּה וִישׁוּעָה בְּאָהֳלֵי
צַדִּיקִים יְמִין יהוה עֹשָׂה חָיִל: יְמִין יהוה רוֹמֵמָה יְמִין
יהוה עֹשָׂה חָיִל: לֹא אָמוּת כִּי אֶחְיֶה וַאֲסַפֵּר מַעֲשֵׂי יָהּ:
יַסֹּר יִסְּרַנִּי יָּהּ וְלַמָּוֶת לֹא נְתָנָנִי: פִּתְחוּ לִי שַׁעֲרֵי צֶדֶק
אָבֹא בָם אוֹדֶה יָהּ: זֶה הַשַּׁעַר לַיהוה צַדִּיקִים יָבֹאוּ בוֹ:

What can I give back to God, for all His kindness to me?

I will lift a cup of hope, and call in the name of God.

I will honour my promises to God, in the presence of all His people.

Precious in God's eyes is the death of His saints.

O God, I am Your servant; I am Your servant, son of Your handmaiden;
You have undone my chains.

I will bring a thank-offering to You; I will call on the name of God.

I will pay up my promises to God, yes in the presence of all His people.

In the courts of God's temple, in the midst of Jerusalem;
Halleluyah – Praise God!

Let all the nations praise God, let all peoples glorify Him.

For His love for us is strong, and God is true forever.

Halleluyah – Praise God!

Thank God because He is good	His love is infinite.
Let Israel say it	His love is infinite.
Let the house of Aaron say it	His love is infinite.
Let those who fear God say it	His love is infinite.

In my distress I called to God. God answered me with relief.

God is with me, I will not fear. What can man do to me?

God is with me as my helper; I can overlook my enemies.

It is better to rely on God than to trust in man.

It is better to rely on God than to trust in princes.

All the nations surround me; in God's name I will cut them down.

They go around me and surround me; in God's name I will cut them down.

They surround me like bees, but they will be extinguished like a fire of thorns;
in God's name I will cut them down.

They pushed me hard to make me fall, but God helped me.

God is my strength and song, He has become my hope.

The sound of joy and hope is in the tents of the righteous;
God's right hand does mighty deeds.

God's right hand is lifted high; God's right hand does mighty deeds.

I will not die, but live, and speak of God's deeds.

You have made me suffer, O God, but do not let me die.

Open for me the gates of righteousness; let me enter and thank God.

This is God's gate, the righteous shall enter through it.

אוֹדְךָ כִּי עֲנִיתָנִי וַתְּהִי לִי לִישׁוּעָה:

אוֹדְךָ כִּי עֲנִיתָנִי וַתְּהִי לִי לִישׁוּעָה:

אֶבֶן מָאֲסוּ הַבּוֹנִים הָיְתָה לְרֹאשׁ פִּנָּה:

אֶבֶן מָאֲסוּ הַבּוֹנִים הָיְתָה לְרֹאשׁ פִּנָּה:

מֵאֵת יְהוָה הָיְתָה זֹּאת הִיא נִפְלָאת בְּעֵינֵינוּ:

מֵאֵת יְהוָה הָיְתָה זֹּאת הִיא נִפְלָאת בְּעֵינֵינוּ:

זֶה הַיּוֹם עָשָׂה יְהוָה נָגִילָה וְנִשְׂמְחָה בוֹ:

זֶה הַיּוֹם עָשָׂה יְהוָה נָגִילָה וְנִשְׂמְחָה בוֹ:

אָנָּא יְהוָה הוֹשִׁיעָה נָּא:

אָנָּא יְהוָה הוֹשִׁיעָה נָּא:

אָנָּא יְהוָה הַצְלִיחָה נָּא:

אָנָּא יְהוָה הַצְלִיחָה נָּא:

בָּרוּךְ הַבָּא בְּשֵׁם יְהוָה בֵּרַכְנוּכֶם מִבֵּית יְהוָה:

בָּרוּךְ הַבָּא בְּשֵׁם יְהוָה בֵּרַכְנוּכֶם מִבֵּית יְהוָה:

אֵל יְהוָה וַיָּאֶר לָנוּ אִסְרוּ חַג בַּעֲבֹתִים עַד קַרְנוֹת הַמִּזְבֵּחַ:

אֵל יְהוָה וַיָּאֶר לָנוּ אִסְרוּ חַג בַּעֲבֹתִים עַד קַרְנוֹת הַמִּזְבֵּחַ:

אֵלִי אַתָּה וְאוֹדֶךָּ אֱלֹהַי אֲרוֹמְמֶךָּ:

אֵלִי אַתָּה וְאוֹדֶךָּ אֱלֹהַי אֲרוֹמְמֶךָּ:

הוֹדוּ לַיהוָה כִּי טוֹב כִּי לְעוֹלָם חַסְדּוֹ:

הוֹדוּ לַיהוָה כִּי טוֹב כִּי לְעוֹלָם חַסְדּוֹ:

יְהַלְלוּךָ יְהוָה אֱלֹהֵינוּ כָּל מַעֲשֶׂיךָ

וַחֲסִידֶיךָ צַדִּיקִים עוֹשֵׂי רְצוֹנֶךָ וְכָל

עַמְּךָ בֵּית יִשְׂרָאֵל בְּרִנָּה יוֹדוּ וִיבָרְכוּ וִישַׁבְּחוּ

וִיפָאֲרוּ וִירוֹמְמוּ וְיַעֲרִיצוּ וְיַקְדִּישׁוּ וְיַמְלִיכוּ אֶת שִׁמְךָ

מַלְכֵּנוּ כִּי לְךָ טוֹב לְהוֹדוֹת וּלְשִׁמְךָ נָאֶה לְזַמֵּר

כִּי מֵעוֹלָם וְעַד עוֹלָם אַתָּה אֵל:

I will thank You, for You answered me, and You became my hope.

I will thank You, for You answered me, and You became my hope.

The stone discarded by the builders has become the main cornerstone.

The stone discarded by the builders has become the main cornerstone.

This was indeed from God: it is wondrous in our eyes.

This was indeed from God: it is wondrous in our eyes.

This is the day on which God has acted: we will be happy and rejoice in Him.

This is the day on which God has acted: we will be happy and rejoice in Him.

God, save us!   God, save us!

God, help us!   God, help us!

Welcome in God's name, we bless you from the house of God.

Welcome in God's name, we bless you from the house of God.

Mighty is God, He gives us light; bind the feast with myrtle on the horns of the Altar.

Mighty is God, He gives us light; bind the feast with myrtle on the horns of the Altar.

You are my God and I thank You; my God, to all heights I praise You.

You are my God and I thank You; my God, to all heights I praise You.

Thank God because He is good; boundless is His love.

Thank God because He is good; boundless is His love.

All Your works praise You, God our Lord,

And Your faithful ones, the righteous who do Your will,

Together with all Your people, the house of Israel,

Joyfully thank, bless, praise, glorify,

Exalt, revere, sanctify and proclaim

The sovereignty of Your name, O our king.

To You it is good to offer thanks,

And right to sing psalms to Your name,

For from eternity to eternity, You are God.

כִּי לְעוֹלָם חַסְדּוֹ:	הוֹדוּ לַיהוה כִּי טוֹב
כִּי לְעוֹלָם חַסְדּוֹ:	הוֹדוּ לֵאלֹהֵי הָאֱלֹהִים
כִּי לְעוֹלָם חַסְדּוֹ:	הוֹדוּ לַאֲדֹנֵי הָאֲדֹנִים
כִּי לְעוֹלָם חַסְדּוֹ:	לְעֹשֵׂה נִפְלָאוֹת גְּדֹלוֹת לְבַדּוֹ
כִּי לְעוֹלָם חַסְדּוֹ:	לְעֹשֵׂה הַשָּׁמַיִם בִּתְבוּנָה
כִּי לְעוֹלָם חַסְדּוֹ:	לְרוֹקַע הָאָרֶץ עַל הַמָּיִם
כִּי לְעוֹלָם חַסְדּוֹ:	לְעֹשֵׂה אוֹרִים גְּדֹלִים
כִּי לְעוֹלָם חַסְדּוֹ:	אֶת הַשֶּׁמֶשׁ לְמֶמְשֶׁלֶת בַּיּוֹם
כִּי לְעוֹלָם חַסְדּוֹ:	אֶת הַיָּרֵחַ וְכוֹכָבִים לְמֶמְשְׁלוֹת בַּלָּיְלָה
כִּי לְעוֹלָם חַסְדּוֹ:	לְמַכֵּה מִצְרַיִם בִּבְכוֹרֵיהֶם
כִּי לְעוֹלָם חַסְדּוֹ:	וַיּוֹצֵא יִשְׂרָאֵל מִתּוֹכָם
כִּי לְעוֹלָם חַסְדּוֹ:	בְּיָד חֲזָקָה וּבִזְרוֹעַ נְטוּיָה
כִּי לְעוֹלָם חַסְדּוֹ:	לְגֹזֵר יַם סוּף לִגְזָרִים
כִּי לְעוֹלָם חַסְדּוֹ:	וְהֶעֱבִיר יִשְׂרָאֵל בְּתוֹכוֹ
כִּי לְעוֹלָם חַסְדּוֹ:	וְנִעֵר פַּרְעֹה וְחֵילוֹ בְיַם סוּף
כִּי לְעוֹלָם חַסְדּוֹ:	לְמוֹלִיךְ עַמּוֹ בַּמִּדְבָּר
כִּי לְעוֹלָם חַסְדּוֹ:	לְמַכֵּה מְלָכִים גְּדֹלִים
כִּי לְעוֹלָם חַסְדּוֹ:	וַיַּהֲרֹג מְלָכִים אַדִּירִים
כִּי לְעוֹלָם חַסְדּוֹ:	לְסִיחוֹן מֶלֶךְ הָאֱמֹרִי
כִּי לְעוֹלָם חַסְדּוֹ:	וּלְעוֹג מֶלֶךְ הַבָּשָׁן
כִּי לְעוֹלָם חַסְדּוֹ:	וְנָתַן אַרְצָם לְנַחֲלָה
כִּי לְעוֹלָם חַסְדּוֹ:	נַחֲלָה לְיִשְׂרָאֵל עַבְדּוֹ
כִּי לְעוֹלָם חַסְדּוֹ:	שֶׁבְּשִׁפְלֵנוּ זָכַר לָנוּ
כִּי לְעוֹלָם חַסְדּוֹ:	וַיִּפְרְקֵנוּ מִצָּרֵינוּ
כִּי לְעוֹלָם חַסְדּוֹ:	נֹתֵן לֶחֶם לְכָל בָּשָׂר
כִּי לְעוֹלָם חַסְדּוֹ:	הוֹדוּ לְאֵל הַשָּׁמָיִם

1. Thank God for He is good	Boundless is His love.
2 Thank the God of gods	Boundless is His love.
3 Thank the Lord of lords	Boundless is His love.
4 For doing great wonders all alone	Boundless is His love.
5 For making the heavens with wisdom	Boundless is His love.
6 For spreading the land over the waters	Boundless is His love.
7 For making great lights	Boundless is His love.
8 The sun to rule by day	Boundless is His love.
9 The moon and stars to rule by night	Boundless is His love.
10 For striking Egypt through their first-born	Boundless is His love.
11 And delivering Israel from among them	Boundless is His love.
12 With a strong hand and outstretched arm	Boundless is His love.
13 For splitting the Red Sea into lanes	Boundless is His love.
14 And leading Israel through it	Boundless is His love.
15 For casting Pharaoh and his army in the Red Sea	Boundless is His love.
16 For leading His people in the desert	Boundless is His love.
17 For striking down great kings	Boundless is His love.
18 And killing mighty rulers	Boundless is His love.
19 Sichon, king of the Amorites	Boundless is His love.
20 And Og, king of the Bashon	Boundless is His love.
21 He gave us their land to keep	Boundless is His love.
22 For Israel, His servant to keep	Boundless is His love.
23 When we were low, He remembered us	Boundless is His love.
24 And saved us from our enemies	Boundless is His love.
25 He gives bread to all flesh	Boundless is His love.
26 Thank the God of heaven	Boundless is His love.

נִשְׁמַת כָּל חַי תְּבָרֵךְ אֶת שִׁמְךָ יהוה
אֱלֹהֵינוּ וְרוּחַ כָּל בָּשָׂר תְּפָאֵר וּתְרוֹמֵם
זִכְרְךָ מַלְכֵּנוּ תָּמִיד. מִן הָעוֹלָם וְעַד הָעוֹלָם אַתָּה
אֵל וּמִבַּלְעָדֶיךָ אֵין לָנוּ מֶלֶךְ גּוֹאֵל וּמוֹשִׁיעַ
פּוֹדֶה וּמַצִּיל וּמְפַרְנֵס וּמְרַחֵם. בְּכָל עֵת צָרָה
וְצוּקָה. אֵין לָנוּ מֶלֶךְ אֶלָּא אָתָּה. אֱלֹהֵי הָרִאשׁוֹנִים
וְהָאַחֲרוֹנִים אֱלוֹהַּ כָּל בְּרִיּוֹת אֲדוֹן כָּל תּוֹלָדוֹת
הַמְהֻלָּל בְּרוֹב הַתִּשְׁבָּחוֹת הַמְנַהֵג
עוֹלָמוֹ בְּחֶסֶד וּבְרִיּוֹתָיו בְּרַחֲמִים.
וַיהוה לֹא יָנוּם וְלֹא יִישָׁן הַמְּעוֹרֵר
יְשֵׁנִים וְהַמֵּקִיץ נִרְדָּמִים וְהַמֵּשִׂיחַ
אִלְּמִים וְהַמַּתִּיר אֲסוּרִים וְהַסּוֹמֵךְ
נוֹפְלִים וְהַזּוֹקֵף כְּפוּפִים לְךָ לְבַדְּךָ אֲנַחְנוּ מוֹדִים.
אִלּוּ פִינוּ מָלֵא שִׁירָה כַּיָּם וּלְשׁוֹנֵנוּ רִנָּה כַּהֲמוֹן גַּלָּיו
וְשִׂפְתוֹתֵינוּ שֶׁבַח כְּמֶרְחֲבֵי רָקִיעַ וְעֵינֵינוּ
מְאִירוֹת כַּשֶּׁמֶשׁ וְכַיָּרֵחַ וְיָדֵינוּ
פְרוּשׂוֹת כְּנִשְׁרֵי שָׁמָיִם וְרַגְלֵינוּ קַלּוֹת
כָּאַיָּלוֹת אֵין אֲנַחְנוּ מַסְפִּיקִים לְהוֹדוֹת
לְךָ יהוה אֱלֹהֵינוּ וֵאלֹהֵי אֲבוֹתֵינוּ
וּלְבָרֵךְ אֶת שְׁמֶךָ עַל אַחַת מֵאֶלֶף אֶלֶף
אַלְפֵי אֲלָפִים וְרִבֵּי רְבָבוֹת פְּעָמִים הַטּוֹבוֹת
שֶׁעָשִׂיתָ עִם אֲבוֹתֵינוּ וְעִמָּנוּ.

The soul of every living thing shall bless

Your name, O God our Lord, and the spirit of all flesh

shall always praise and glorify Your fame, O our King.

From the beginning to the end of time, You are God.

Besides You we have no King who saves and helps,

frees and rescues, who grants our needs, has mercy

and answers us in all times of trouble and pain.

We have no king, helper, and support other than You.

God, first and last, God of all creatures, Master of all history,

praised in song, who guides His world with love, and His

creatures with mercy. God does not slumber nor sleep.

He wakes the sleeping, arouses those who slumber, brings the

dead to life, heals the sick, gives sight to the blind, raises the

depressed, makes the dumb speak, and discloses the hidden.

To You alone we offer thanks.

If our mouths were filled with song like the sea, and our

tongues with jubilation like its many waves; if our lips were

filled with praise as broad as the sky, and our eyes could shine

like the sun and moon; if our hands were spread out like the

eagles of the sky, and our feet could run lightly as deer, it

would still not be enough to thank You, O God our Lord, or

to bless Your name, our King, for even one thousandth – a

millionth or a billionth – of all the good, the miracles and

wonders You have done for our fathers and ourselves.

מִמִּצְרַיִם גְּאַלְתָּנוּ יהוה אֱלֹהֵינוּ וּמִבֵּית
עֲבָדִים פְּדִיתָנוּ בְּרָעָב זַנְתָּנוּ
וּבְשָׂבָע כִּלְכַּלְתָּנוּ מֵחֶרֶב הִצַּלְתָּנוּ וּמִדֶּבֶר
מִלַּטְתָּנוּ וּמֵחֳלָיִם רָעִים וְנֶאֱמָנִים
דִּלִּיתָנוּ. עַד הֵנָּה עֲזָרוּנוּ רַחֲמֶיךָ וְלֹא עֲזָבוּנוּ
חֲסָדֶיךָ וְאַל תִּטְּשֵׁנוּ יהוה אֱלֹהֵינוּ לָנֶצַח.
עַל כֵּן אֵבָרִים שֶׁפִּלַּגְתָּ בָּנוּ וְרוּחַ וּנְשָׁמָה שֶׁנָּפַחְתָּ
בְּאַפֵּינוּ וְלָשׁוֹן אֲשֶׁר שַׂמְתָּ בְּפִינוּ הֵן הֵם
יוֹדוּ וִיבָרְכוּ וִישַׁבְּחוּ וִיפָאֲרוּ וִירוֹמְמוּ
וְיַעֲרִיצוּ וְיַקְדִּישׁוּ וְיַמְלִיכוּ אֶת שִׁמְךָ מַלְכֵּנוּ.
כִּי כָל פֶּה לְךָ יוֹדֶה וְכָל לָשׁוֹן לְךָ תִשָּׁבַע וְכָל בֶּרֶךְ
לְךָ תִכְרַע וְכָל קוֹמָה לְפָנֶיךָ תִשְׁתַּחֲוֶה.
וְכָל לְבָבוֹת יִירָאוּךָ וְכָל קֶרֶב וּכְלָיוֹת יְזַמְּרוּ
לִשְׁמֶךָ. כַּדָּבָר שֶׁכָּתוּב כָּל עַצְמֹתַי
תֹּאמַרְנָה יהוה מִי כָמוֹךָ מַצִּיל עָנִי
מֵחָזָק מִמֶּנּוּ וְעָנִי וְאֶבְיוֹן מִגֹּזְלוֹ.
מִי יִדְמֶה לָּךְ וּמִי יִשְׁוֶה לָּךְ וּמִי יַעֲרָךְ לָךְ הָאֵל
הַגָּדוֹל הַגִּבּוֹר וְהַנּוֹרָא אֵל עֶלְיוֹן
קֹנֵה שָׁמַיִם וָאָרֶץ. נְהַלֶּלְךָ וּנְשַׁבֵּחֲךָ
וּנְפָאֶרְךָ וּנְבָרֵךְ אֶת שֵׁם קָדְשֶׁךָ כָּאָמוּר
לְדָוִד בָּרְכִי נַפְשִׁי אֶת יהוה וְכָל קְרָבַי
אֶת שֵׁם קָדְשׁוֹ:

You freed us from Egypt, O God our Lord,

and rescued us from the house of slaves.

[When we were] in hunger, You fed us;

in plenty, You sustained us.

You saved us from the sword, delivered us from the

plague, and safeguarded us from many serious illnesses.

Until now Your mercy has helped us,

and Your love has not failed us.

Therefore, the limbs You gave us, the breath and soul You

breathed into our nostrils, the tongue You placed in our mouths –

all of them will constantly thank, bless, praise, glorify, and sing

out to Your name, O our King.

For every mouth shall thank You, every tongue shall offer praise,

every knee shall bow, and all who stand shall kneel before You.

Hearts will fear You, and every person's inner self shall sing praises

to Your name.

It is thus written, "All my bones shall say, 'O God, who is like

you? [You] help the poor from those stronger than him, the poor

and needy from those who would rob him'" (Psalms 35:10).

Who can be likened to You, who is equal to You, who can be

compared to You, the Great, Mighty, Awesome God, God most

high, possessor of heaven and earth!

We will laud You, praise You, and glorify You, and we will bless

Your holy Name, as it is said; [A Psalm] by David;

bless the Lord, O my soul, and all that is within me [bless]

His holy Name.

הָאֵל בְּתַעֲצֻמוֹת עֻזֶּךָ הַגָּדוֹל בִּכְבוֹד
שְׁמֶךָ הַגִּבּוֹר לָנֶצַח וְהַנּוֹרָא בְּנוֹרְאוֹתֶיךָ
הַמֶּלֶךְ הַיּוֹשֵׁב עַל כִּסֵּא רָם וְנִשָּׂא:

שׁוֹכֵן עַד מָרוֹם וְקָדוֹשׁ שְׁמוֹ.
וְכָתוּב רַנְּנוּ צַדִּיקִים בַּיהוָה לַיְשָׁרִים
נָאוָה תְהִלָּה: בְּפִי יְשָׁרִים תִּתְהַלָּל וּבְדִבְרֵי
צַדִּיקִים תִּתְבָּרַךְ וּבִלְשׁוֹן חֲסִידִים
תִּתְרוֹמָם וּבְקֶרֶב קְדוֹשִׁים תִּתְקַדָּשׁ:

וּבְמַקְהֲלוֹת רִבְבוֹת עַמְּךָ בֵּית יִשְׂרָאֵל
בְּרִנָּה יִתְפָּאֵר שִׁמְךָ מַלְכֵּנוּ בְּכָל דּוֹר וָדוֹר.
שֶׁכֵּן חוֹבַת כָּל הַיְצוּרִים לְפָנֶיךָ יְהוָה אֱלֹהֵינוּ
וֵאלֹהֵי אֲבוֹתֵינוּ לְהוֹדוֹת לְהַלֵּל לְשַׁבֵּחַ
לְפָאֵר לְרוֹמֵם לְהַדֵּר לְבָרֵךְ לְעַלֵּה וּלְקַלֵּס
עַל כָּל דִּבְרֵי שִׁירוֹת וְתִשְׁבְּחוֹת דָּוִד בֶּן
יִשַׁי עַבְדְּךָ מְשִׁיחֶךָ:

יִשְׁתַּבַּח שִׁמְךָ לָעַד מַלְכֵּנוּ הָאֵל
הַמֶּלֶךְ הַגָּדוֹל וְהַקָּדוֹשׁ בַּשָּׁמַיִם וּבָאָרֶץ כִּי
לְךָ נָאֶה יְהוָה אֱלֹהֵינוּ וֵאלֹהֵי אֲבוֹתֵינוּ
שִׁיר וּשְׁבָחָה הַלֵּל וְזִמְרָה עֹז וּמֶמְשָׁלָה
נֶצַח גְּדֻלָּה וּגְבוּרָה תְּהִלָּה וְתִפְאֶרֶת
קְדֻשָּׁה וּמַלְכוּת בְּרָכוֹת וְהוֹדָאוֹת מֵעַתָּה
וְעַד־עוֹלָם. בָּרוּךְ אַתָּה יְהוָה אֵל
מֶלֶךְ גָּדוֹל בַּתִּשְׁבָּחוֹת אֵל הַהוֹדָאוֹת אֲדוֹן
הַנִּפְלָאוֹת הַבּוֹחֵר בְּשִׁירֵי זִמְרָה מֶלֶךְ
אֵל חֵי הָעוֹלָמִים:

You are the Almighty God in the power of Your strength; the Great in the glory of Your Name; the Mighty forever, Awesome in Your awesome deeds; the king who sits upon a lofty and exalted throne.

He who dwells for Eternity, lofty and holy is His Name.
And it is written,
"Let saints rejoice in God, it is right for the just to praise Him" (Psalms 33:1).

By the mouths of the just, You allow Yourself to be exalted;
By the lips of the saints, You allow Yourself to be blessed;
By the tongues of the pious, You allow Yourself to be praised;
And among the holy, You allow Yourself to be sanctified.

In the congregations of the myriads of Your people, the house of Israel,
Your name, O our king, shall be glorified with joyful song in every generation.
For it is the duty of all creatures before You, O God our Lord and Lord of our fathers,
to thank, praise, be grateful, glorify, raise high, beautify, and sing triumphantly,
above all the songs and praise of (even) David, son of Jesse, Your anointed servant.

May Your name be praised forever, our King, the great and holy God and King
in heaven and earth. For to You, O God our Lord and Lord of our fathers, song
and praise belong – hymn and psalm, power and dominion, victory, greatness and strength,
prayer, beauty, holiness and kingship, blessing and thanks to Your great and holy name,
from now and for ever.

Blessed are you O God, Lord and King,
Great in praises, Lord of thanksgivings,
Master of wonders,
Who delights in melodious songs,
O King and ever-living God.

בָּרוּךְ אַתָּה יהוה אֱלֹהֵינוּ מֶלֶךְ
הָעוֹלָם בּוֹרֵא פְּרִי הַגָּפֶן:

Drink the fourth cup of wine while leaning to the left.

בָּרוּךְ אַתָּה יהוה אֱלֹהֵינוּ מֶלֶךְ הָעוֹלָם
עַל הַגֶּפֶן וְעַל פְּרִי הַגֶּפֶן וְעַל תְּנוּבַת
הַשָּׂדֶה וְעַל אֶרֶץ חֶמְדָּה טוֹבָה וּרְחָבָה
שֶׁרָצִיתָ וְהִנְחַלְתָּ לַאֲבוֹתֵינוּ
לֶאֱכֹל מִפִּרְיָהּ וְלִשְׂבֹּעַ מִטּוּבָהּ. רַחֶם נָא
יהוה אֱלֹהֵינוּ עַל יִשְׂרָאֵל עַמֶּךָ וְעַל
יְרוּשָׁלַיִם עִירֶךָ וְעַל צִיּוֹן מִשְׁכַּן
כְּבוֹדֶךָ וְעַל מִזְבַּחֶךָ וְעַל הֵיכָלֶךָ וּבְנֵה
יְרוּשָׁלַיִם עִיר הַקֹּדֶשׁ בִּמְהֵרָה בְיָמֵינוּ
וְהַעֲלֵנוּ לְתוֹכָהּ וְשַׂמְּחֵנוּ בְּבִנְיָנָהּ וְנֹאכַל
מִפִּרְיָהּ וְנִשְׂבַּע מִטּוּבָהּ וּנְבָרֶכְךָ עָלֶיהָ
בִּקְדֻשָּׁה וּבְטָהֳרָה
(וּרְצֵה וְהַחֲלִיצֵנוּ בְּיוֹם הַשַּׁבָּת הַזֶּה)
וְשַׂמְּחֵנוּ בְּיוֹם חַג הַמַּצּוֹת
הַזֶּה כִּי אַתָּה יהוה טוֹב וּמֵטִיב לַכֹּל
וְנוֹדֶה לְּךָ עַל הָאָרֶץ וְעַל פְּרִי הַגָּפֶן:
בָּרוּךְ אַתָּה יהוה עַל הָאָרֶץ וְעַל פְּרִי הַגָּפֶן:

Blessed are You, O Lord our God, King of the world,

Creator of the fruit of the vine.

Drink the fourth cup of wine while leaning to the left.

Blessed are You, O God our Lord, King of the world,

for the vine, for the fruit of the vine, for the crops of the field,

and the desirable, good and spacious land that You desired and granted to our fathers,

to eat its fruits and be satisfied with its goodness.

Have mercy, O God our Lord, upon us, upon Israel Your people,

and upon Mount Zion, home of Your glory.

O rebuild Jerusalem, the holy city, soon,

in our days, and bring us up to it.

(Also console us on this Sabbath day,)

and cause us to rejoice on this festival of unleavened bread.

For You are good, and You do good to all.

We will thank You, O God our Lord, for the land and for the fruit of the vine.

Blessed are You O God, for the land and for the fruit of the vine.

This is only recited on the first night

וּבְכֵן וַיְהִי בַּחֲצִי הַלַּיְלָה

אָז רוֹב נִסִּים הִפְלֵאתָ   בַּלַּיְלָה.

בְּרֹאשׁ אַשְׁמוֹרֶת זֶה   הַלַּיְלָה.

גֵּר צֶדֶק נִצַּחְתּוֹ כְּנֶחֱלַק לוֹ   לַיְלָה.

וַיְהִי בַּחֲצִי הַלַּיְלָה:

דַּנְתָּ מֶלֶךְ גְּרָר בַּחֲלוֹם   הַלַּיְלָה.

הִפְחַדְתָּ אֲרַמִּי בְּאֶמֶשׁ   לַיְלָה.

וַיָּשַׂר יִשְׂרָאֵל לְמַלְאָךְ וַיּוּכַל לוֹ   לַיְלָה.

וַיְהִי בַּחֲצִי הַלַּיְלָה:

זֶרַע בְּכוֹרֵי פַתְרוֹס מָחַצְתָּ בַּחֲצִי   הַלַּיְלָה.

חֵילָם לֹא מָצְאוּ בְּקוּמָם   בַּלַּיְלָה.

טִיסַת נְגִיד חֲרוֹשֶׁת סִלִּיתָ בְּכוֹכְבֵי   לַיְלָה.

וַיְהִי בַּחֲצִי הַלַּיְלָה:

And it was at midnight

Yannai, who wrote this hymn, was one of the earliest and most influential of Judaism's liturgical poets. Much of his work has been rediscovered in the twentieth century through findings such as the Cairo genizah. He lived during or before the sixth century CE.

Since the seder service is one of the few rituals to take place at night, Yannai enumerates other saving events that took place at night. Abraham won his battle against the four kings (Genesis 14:15). Avimelekh, king of Gerar, was told by God that by taking Sarah he was stealing Abraham's wife (Genesis 20:2–3). Laban was visited by God in a dream and told not to harm his son-in-law Jacob (Genesis 31:29). Jacob wrestled with

This is only recited on the first night

And it was at Midnight!

The many miracles
were performed by you at night;
At the beginning of watches
On this very night;
You made the righteous convert win
(When Abraham) divided his men at night;
And it was at midnight!

You judged the king of Gerar (Abimelekh)
In a dream at night;
You made the Syrian (Laban) tremble
In the deep darkness of night;
And Israel struggled with an angel
And overcame him at night;
And it was at midnight!

The first-born of Pathros (Egypt)
You smote at midnight;
They could not find their strength
When they woke up at night;
The forces of the prince of Charosheth (Sisera)
Were swept away by the stars of night;
And it was at midnight!

---

an angel (Genesis 32:25). Sisera, the Cannanite general, was defeated by Deborah and Barak (Judges 5). Sennacherib, King of Assyria, withdrew from his threatened assault on Hezekiah when a large part of his army died mysteriously at night (II Kings 19). Daniel was granted a revelation of the meaning of Nebuchadnezzar's dream, and was rescued from the lion's den (Daniel 2:19, 6:20). Belshazar, who removed the vessels from the Temple, died (Daniel 5:30). Ahasuerus, unable to sleep, had his servant read to him from the royal chronicles and remembered that Mordechai had saved his life (Esther 6:1) – the beginning of the events that led to the downfall of Haman and the deliverance we recall on Purim. These are the many echoes of *leil shimurim*, the 'night of God's protection'.

יָעַץ מְחָרֵף לְנוֹפֵף אִוּוּי הוֹבַשְׁתָּ פְגָרָיו **בַּלַּיְלָה.**

כָּרַע בֵּל וּמַצָּבוֹ בְּאִישׁוֹן **לַיְלָה.**

לְאִישׁ חֲמוּדוֹת נִגְלָה רָז חֲזוֹת **לַיְלָה.**

וַיְהִי בַּחֲצִי הַלַּיְלָה:

מִשְׁתַּכֵּר בִּכְלֵי קֹדֶשׁ נֶהֱרַג בּוֹ **בַּלַּיְלָה.**

נוֹשַׁע מִבּוֹר אֲרָיוֹת פּוֹתֵר בְּעֲתוּתֵי **לַיְלָה.**

שִׂנְאָה נָטַר אֲגָגִי וְכָתַב סְפָרִים **בַּלַּיְלָה.**

וַיְהִי בַּחֲצִי הַלַּיְלָה:

עוֹרַרְתָּ נִצְחֲךָ עָלָיו בְּנֶדֶד שְׁנַת **לַיְלָה.**

פּוּרָה תִדְרֹךְ לְשׁוֹמֵר מַה **מִלַּיְלָה.**

צָרַח כַּשּׁוֹמֵר וְשָׂח אָתָא בֹקֶר וְגַם **לַיְלָה.**

וַיְהִי בַּחֲצִי הַלַּיְלָה:

קָרֵב יוֹם אֲשֶׁר הוּא לֹא יוֹם וְלֹא **לַיְלָה.**

רָם הוֹדַע כִּי לְךָ הַיּוֹם אַף לְךָ **הַלַּיְלָה.**

שׁוֹמְרִים הַפְקֵד לְעִירְךָ כָּל הַיּוֹם וְכָל **הַלַּיְלָה.**

תָּאִיר כְּאוֹר יוֹם חֶשְׁכַּת **לַיְלָה.**

וַיְהִי בַּחֲצִי הַלַּיְלָה:

Without respect (Sennacherib) besieged Jerusalem
But You dried up his corpse at night;
Bal and its pedestal were thrown down
In the darkness of night;
To the beloved (Daniel)
You revealed mysteries in a vision at night;
And it was at midnight!

He drank from the holy vessels
And so (Belshazzar) was killed at night;
(Daniel) was saved from the lion's den
And interpreted fearsome dreams of the night;
(Haman) of Agag nurtured hate
And wrote letters at night;
And it was at midnight!

You rose and beat Haman
By not letting the king sleep at night;
You crushed the wicked
To protect us from the forces at night;
He cried out like the watchman:
Morning is coming and also…the night;
And it was at midnight!

May the day soon come
That is neither day nor night;
So that all shall know
That day is Yours, and also the night,
Set up guards for Your city
For all the day and all the night;
That bright as day may shine
The darkness of night;
And it was at midnight!

This is only recited on the second night

וּבְכֵן וַאֲמַרְתֶּם זֶבַח פֶּסַח

בְּפֶסַח.	אֹמֶץ גְּבוּרוֹתֶיךָ הִפְלֵאתָ
פֶּסַח.	בְּרֹאשׁ כָּל מוֹעֲדוֹת נִשֵּׂאתָ
פֶּסַח.	גִּלִּיתָ לְאֶזְרָחִי חֲצוֹת לֵיל
	וַאֲמַרְתֶּם זֶבַח פֶּסַח :

בְּפֶסַח.	דְּלָתָיו דָּפַקְתָּ כְּחֹם הַיּוֹם
בְּפֶסַח.	הִסְעִיד נוֹצְצִים עֻגוֹת מַצּוֹת
פֶּסַח.	וְאֶל הַבָּקָר רָץ זֵכֶר לְשׁוֹר עֵרֶךְ
	וַאֲמַרְתֶּם זֶבַח פֶּסַח :

בְּפֶסַח.	זוֹעֲמוּ סְדוֹמִים וְלוֹהֲטוּ בָּאֵשׁ
פֶּסַח.	חֻלַּץ לוֹט מֵהֶם וּמַצּוֹת אָפָה בְּקֵץ
בְּפֶסַח.	טִאטֵאתָ אַדְמַת מוֹף וְנוֹף בְּעָבְרְךָ
	וַאֲמַרְתֶּם זֶבַח פֶּסַח :

So declare the Pesach feast

This poem, read on the second night, was written by Yannai's disciple, the poet Elazar Kalir. The refrain is taken from Exodus 12:27: when your child asks you to explain the meaning of the Pesach rituals, 'you shall say, "It is a sacrifice of the Passover."'

Kalir gathers together the many events which, according to tradition, took place on Pesach. Abraham, at the 'covenant between the pieces' foresaw that his descendants would suffer exile and affliction (Genesis 15:12–21). He was visited by the angels who told him that Sarah would have a child (Genesis 18). Lot, too, was visited by the angels who rescued him from the destruction of Sodom (Genesis 19). God protected the Israelites and devastated the Egyptians during the last plague, the death of the firstborn (Exodus 12:29–32).

This is only recited on the second night

So Declare the Pesach Feast!

Mighty acts of power
Were done by You on Pesach;
To the first of all festivals
You raised the feast of Pesach;
You revealed Yourself to the Oriental
(Abraham) on the midnight of Pesach;
So declare the Pesach feast!

You knocked at Abraham's door
In the heat of the day on Pesach;
He fed the angels
Cakes of matzah on Pesach;
He ran to the cattle
Recalling the ox prepared on Pesach;
So declare the Pesach feast!

The men of Sodom angered (God)
And were destroyed by fire on Pesach;
Lot escaped from them
And baked matzot on Pesach;
You swept the land of Mof and Nof
When you passed through (Egypt) on Pesach;
So declare the Pesach feast!

Jericho was besieged and destroyed by Joshua after the Israelites had celebrated Pesach (Joshua 5–6). Gideon defeated the Midianites (Judges 6–7), and Sennacherib, the Assyrians and Babylonians all suffered setbacks at this time of the year. Esther fasted and Haman was hanged on Pesach.

Pesach was thus the time, not of one deliverance, but of many. It is characteristic of the rabbinic sense of time to combine the recollection of many events into a single day. Thus Tisha b'Av became the time when we recall the many tragedies of Jewish history. Pesach was a moment to remember many liberations. In this way time itself is woven into a text whose theme – exile, suffering, redemption, freedom, return – is written into the structure of Jewish history and becomes the master-narrative through which we understand who we are and the story of which we are a part.

יָהּ רֹאשׁ כָּל אוֹן מָחַצְתָּ בְּלֵיל שִׁמּוּר   פֶּסַח.

כַּבִּיר עַל בֵּן בְּכוֹר פָּסַחְתָּ בְּדַם   פֶּסַח.

לְבִלְתִּי תֵּת מַשְׁחִית לָבֹא בִּפְתָחַי   בְּפֶסַח.

וַאֲמַרְתֶּם זֶבַח פֶּסַח :

מִסְגֶּרֶת סֻגָּרָה בְּעִתּוֹתֵי   פֶּסַח.

נִשְׁמְדָה מִדְיָן בִּצְלִיל שְׂעוֹרֵי עֹמֶר   פֶּסַח.

שׂוֹרְפוּ מִשְׁמַנֵּי פּוּל וְלוּד בִּיקַד יְקוֹד   פֶּסַח.

וַאֲמַרְתֶּם זֶבַח פֶּסַח :

עוֹד הַיּוֹם בְּנוֹב לַעֲמוֹד עַד גָּעָה עוֹנַת   פֶּסַח.

פַּס יַד כָּתְבָה לְקַעֲקֵעַ צוּל   בְּפֶסַח.

צָפֹה הַצָּפִית עָרוֹךְ הַשֻּׁלְחָן   בְּפֶסַח.

וַאֲמַרְתֶּם זֶבַח פֶּסַח :

קָהָל כִּנְּסָה הֲדַסָּה צוֹם לְשַׁלֵּשׁ   בְּפֶסַח.

רֹאשׁ מִבֵּית רָשָׁע מָחַצְתָּ בְּעֵץ חֲמִשִּׁים   בְּפֶסַח.

שְׁתֵּי אֵלֶּה רֶגַע תָּבִיא לְעוּצִית   בְּפֶסַח.

תָּעֹז יָדְךָ וְתָרוּם יְמִינֶךָ כְּלֵיל הִתְקַדֶּשׁ חַג   פֶּסַח.

וַאֲמַרְתֶּם זֶבַח פֶּסַח :

God, You smote the first-born

On the guarded night of Pesach;

Mighty One, You passed over Israel

Your own first-born on Pesach;

You let no destruction come

Enter our doors on Pesach;

So declare the Pesach feast!

The strong walled city (Jericho)

(Fell) at the season of Pesach;

Midian was destroyed (by Gideon)

Through a dream of a barley loaf on Pesach;

The fat Pul and Lud (Sennacherib's chiefs)

Were burned in a blazing flame on Pesach.

So declare the Pesach feast!

(Sennacherib) stood and waited in Nob

For a day until the feast of Pesach;

A hand wrote (for Belshazzar)

Tattooing a shadow on the wall on Pesach;

They lit the lamps

And prepared the table on Pesach;

So declare the Pesach feast!

Hadassah (Esther) gathered a congregation

For a three day fast on Pesach;

The head of the evil house (Haman)

Was hanged on a fifty foot gallows on Pesach;

Two punishments You shall suddenly bring

On the wicked kingdom on Pesach;

Raise Your mighty hand in strength

As on the night You made holy on Pesach;

So declare the Pesach feast!

כִּי לֹא נָאֶה. כִּי לֹא יָאֶה

אַדִּיר בִּמְלוּכָה. בָּחוּר כַּהֲלָכָה. גְּדוּדָיו יֹאמְרוּ לוֹ.
לְךָ וּלְךָ. לְךָ כִּי לְךָ. לְךָ אַף לְךָ.
לְךָ יהוה הַמַּמְלָכָה. כִּי לֹא נָאֶה. כִּי לֹא יָאֶה:

דָּגוּל בִּמְלוּכָה. הָדוּר כַּהֲלָכָה. וָתִיקָיו יֹאמְרוּ לוֹ.
לְךָ וּלְךָ. לְךָ כִּי לְךָ. לְךָ אַף לְךָ.
לְךָ יהוה הַמַּמְלָכָה. כִּי לֹא נָאֶה. כִּי לֹא יָאֶה:

זַכַּאי בִּמְלוּכָה. חָסִין כַּהֲלָכָה. טַפְסְרָיו יֹאמְרוּ לוֹ.
לְךָ וּלְךָ. לְךָ כִּי לְךָ. לְךָ אַף לְךָ.
לְךָ יהוה הַמַּמְלָכָה. כִּי לֹא נָאֶה. כִּי לֹא יָאֶה:

יָחִיד בִּמְלוּכָה. כַּבִּיר כַּהֲלָכָה. לִמּוּדָיו יֹאמְרוּ לוֹ.
לְךָ וּלְךָ. לְךָ כִּי לְךָ. לְךָ אַף לְךָ.
לְךָ יהוה הַמַּמְלָכָה. כִּי לֹא נָאֶה. כִּי לֹא יָאֶה:

To You and just You

This poem which, like the others that follow, has no specific connection to Pesach, may have been composed by R. Jacob Chazan of London. It appears in his work *Etz Chayyim*, and may therefore be the one British contribution to the Haggadah. It is built around the word *Lekha*, 'To you' – as in such biblical phrases as 'To You is the day and also the night' (Psalm 74:16), 'To You are the heavens and also the earth' (Psalm 89:12), 'To You, O Lord, is the greatness and the power' (I Chronicles 19:11), 'To You is it due' (Jeremiah 10:7). According to Abrabanel, the seven-fold repetition of *Lekha* represents the seven heavens, the seven constellations and the seven days of the week. It may also be a reference to the seven occasions in the Bible where the word *Lekha* is used to state that to God alone belong strength and praise. The opening words, *Adir bimelukhah*, 'Mighty in kingship', may have suggested a link with Pesach, for it was then, with the defeat of Pharaoh, that the sovereignty of God over all human powers was first demonstrated and established as a principle of faith.

Ki Lo Na'eh

For His delight and for His right!
Mighty as a King, Supreme in everything,
His armies say to Him:

To You and just You.
To you for just You.
To You, yes just You.
To You O God the throne is due
For His delight and for His right!

Famous as a King, Brilliant in everything,
His good ones say to Him:

To You and just You.
To you for just You.
To You, yes just You.
To You O God the throne is due
For His delight and for His right!

Purest as a King, Sturdy in everything,
His servants say to Him:

To You and just You.
To you for just You.
To You, yes just You.
To You O God the throne is due
For His delight and for His right!

Alone as a King, Strongest in everything,
His wise ones say to Him:

To You and just You.
To you for just You.
To You, yes just You.
To You O God the throne is due
For His delight and for His right!

מֶלֶךְ בִּמְלוּכָה. נוֹרָא בַּהֲלָכָה. סְבִיבָיו יֹאמְרוּ לוֹ.

לְךָ וּלְךָ. לְךָ כִּי לְךָ. לְךָ אַף לְךָ.

לְךָ יהוה הַמַּמְלָכָה. כִּי לוֹ נָאֶה. כִּי לוֹ יָאֶה:

עָנָיו בִּמְלוּכָה. פּוֹדֶה בַּהֲלָכָה. צַדִּיקָיו יֹאמְרוּ לוֹ.

לְךָ וּלְךָ. לְךָ כִּי לְךָ. לְךָ אַף לְךָ.

לְךָ יהוה הַמַּמְלָכָה. כִּי לוֹ נָאֶה. כִּי לוֹ יָאֶה:

קָדוֹשׁ בִּמְלוּכָה. רַחוּם בַּהֲלָכָה. שִׁנְאַנָּיו יֹאמְרוּ לוֹ.

לְךָ וּלְךָ. לְךָ כִּי לְךָ. לְךָ אַף לְךָ.

לְךָ יהוה הַמַּמְלָכָה. כִּי לוֹ נָאֶה. כִּי לוֹ יָאֶה:

תַּקִּיף בִּמְלוּכָה. תּוֹמֵךְ בַּהֲלָכָה. תְּמִימָיו יֹאמְרוּ לוֹ.

לְךָ וּלְךָ. לְךָ כִּי לְךָ. לְךָ אַף לְךָ.

לְךָ יהוה הַמַּמְלָכָה. כִּי לוֹ נָאֶה. כִּי לוֹ יָאֶה:

Ruling as a King, Fearsome in everything,
Those around him say to Him:

To You and just You.
To you for just You.
To You, yes just You.
To You O God the throne is due
For His delight and for His right!

Humble as a King, Helping in everything,
His righteous say to Him:

To You and just You.
To you for just You.
To You, yes just You.
To You O God the throne is due
For His delight and for His right!

Holy as a King, Tender in everything
His angels say to Him:

To You and just You.
To you for just You.
To You, yes just You.
To You O God the throne is due
For His delight and for His right!

Forceful as a King, Support in everything,
His pure ones say to Him:

To You and just You.
To you for just You.
To You, yes just You.
To You O God the throne is due
For His delight and for His right!

נִרְצָה

חֲסַל סִדּוּר פֶּסַח כְּהִלְכָתוֹ.
כְּכָל מִשְׁפָּטוֹ וְחֻקָּתוֹ. כַּאֲשֶׁר
זָכִינוּ לְסַדֵּר אוֹתוֹ. כֵּן נִזְכֶּה לַעֲשׂוֹתוֹ:
זָךְ שׁוֹכֵן מְעוֹנָה. קוֹמֵם קְהַל עֲדַת מִי מָנָה.
בְּקָרוֹב נַהֵל נִטְעֵי כַנָּה. פְּדוּיִם לְצִיּוֹן בְּרִנָּה:

לְשָׁנָה הַבָּאָה בִּירוּשָׁלָיִם

סְפִירַת הָעֹמֶר

On the second night, say the following:

בָּרוּךְ אַתָּה יְיָ אֱלֹהֵינוּ מֶלֶךְ הָעוֹלָם
אֲשֶׁר קִדְּשָׁנוּ בְּמִצְוֹתָיו וְצִוָּנוּ עַל סְפִירַת הָעֹמֶר:

הַיּוֹם יוֹם אֶחָד לָעֹמֶר:

Next year in Jerusalem

As at the conclusion of the prayers on Yom Kippur, so here – at the two supreme moments of the Jewish year we pray *Leshanah ha-ba'ah bi-Yerushalayim*, 'Next year in Jerusalem'.

Nothing in the imaginative life of peoples throughout the world quite compares to the Jewish love for, and attachment to, Jerusalem. A Psalm records, in unforgettable words, the feelings of the Jewish exiles in Babylon two and a half thousand years ago: 'By the waters of Babylon we sat and wept as we remembered Zion… How can we sing the songs of the Lord in a strange land? If I forget you, O Jerusalem, may my right hand forget its skill, may my tongue cleave to the roof of my mouth if I do not remember you, if I do not consider Jerusalem my highest joy' (Psalm 137:1–6).

Wherever Jews were, they preserved the memory of Jerusalem. They prayed towards it. They spoke of it continually. At weddings they broke a glass in its memory. On Tisha B'Av they sat and mourned its destruction as if it were a recent tragedy. They longed for it with an everlasting love.

The French historian, Chateaubriand, visiting Jerusalem in the early nineteenth century, was overcome with emotion as he saw for the first time the small Jewish community there, waiting patiently for the Messiah. This people, he wrote, 'has seen Jerusalem destroyed seventeen times, yet there exists nothing in the world which can discourage it or prevent it from raising its eyes to Zion. He who beholds the Jews dispersed over the face of the earth, in keeping with the Word of God, lingers and marvels. But he will be struck with

Nirtzah Prayer of Acceptance

Chasal Siddur Pesach

Ended is the Pesach Seder as the Law commands,
Its symbols and rules done by our hands;
As we were worthy to order it here,
So may we do it next year!
Pure One who dwells in the heavens on high,
Raise up Your people, countless to the eye,
Soon may You lead those You planted strong
To freedom in Zion in glorious song!

Next year in Jerusalem!

The Counting of the Omer

On the second night, say the following:
Blessed are You, O God, King of the world, who made us holy with
his commandments and commanded us concerning the counting of the Omer.

Today is the first day of the Omer.

---

amazement, as at a miracle, who finds them still in Jerusalem and perceives even, who in law and justice are the masters of Judaea, to exist as slaves and strangers in their own land; how despite all abuses they await the king who is to deliver them.' Noting how this 'small nation' had survived while the great empires who sought its destruction had vanished, he added, 'If there is anything among the nations of the world marked with the stamp of the miraculous, this, in our opinion, is that miracle.'

It is said that Napoleon, passing a synagogue on Tisha B'Av, was struck by the sounds of lament coming from the building. 'What,' he asked one of his officers, 'are the Jews crying for?' 'For Jerusalem,' came the reply. 'How long ago did they lose Jerusalem?' 'More than seventeen hundred years ago.' Napoleon was silent for a moment and then said, 'A people that can remember Jerusalem for so long will one day have it restored to them.' So it has come to pass in our time.

Ended is the Pesach seder

This passage, concluding the seder and praying that we may celebrate it again in the future, is taken from a liturgical poem (*kerovah*) composed by R. Joseph Tov Elem in the eleventh century CE. Originally it was said in the synagogue on Shabbat haGadol, the Shabbat preceding Pesach, and it was transferred to the Haggadah in the fourteen century.

   See Essays on Passover "An Afternoon in Jerusalem" page 55

Concluding Songs

אַדִּיר הוּא

אַדִּיר הוּא יִבְנֶה בֵּיתוֹ בְּקָרוֹב בִּמְהֵרָה בִּמְהֵרָה בְּיָמֵינוּ
בְּקָרוֹב. אֵל בְּנֵה אֵל בְּנֵה. בְּנֵה בֵיתְךָ בְּקָרוֹב.

בָּחוּר הוּא. גָּדוֹל הוּא. דָּגוּל הוּא.
יִבְנֶה בֵּיתוֹ בְּקָרוֹב בִּמְהֵרָה בְּיָמֵינוּ בְּקָרוֹב.
אֵל בְּנֵה אֵל בְּנֵה. בְּנֵה בֵיתְךָ בְּקָרוֹב.

הָדוּר הוּא. וָתִיק הוּא. זַכַּאי הוּא.
יִבְנֶה בֵּיתוֹ בְּקָרוֹב בִּמְהֵרָה בְּיָמֵינוּ בְּקָרוֹב.
אֵל בְּנֵה אֵל בְּנֵה. בְּנֵה בֵיתְךָ בְּקָרוֹב.

חָסִיד הוּא. טָהוֹר הוּא. יָחִיד הוּא.
יִבְנֶה בֵּיתוֹ בְּקָרוֹב בִּמְהֵרָה בְּיָמֵינוּ בְּקָרוֹב.
אֵל בְּנֵה אֵל בְּנֵה. בְּנֵה בֵיתְךָ בְּקָרוֹב.

כַּבִּיר הוּא. לָמוּד הוּא. מֶלֶךְ הוּא.
יִבְנֶה בֵּיתוֹ בְּקָרוֹב בִּמְהֵרָה בְּיָמֵינוּ בְּקָרוֹב.
אֵל בְּנֵה אֵל בְּנֵה. בְּנֵה בֵיתְךָ בְּקָרוֹב.

נוֹרָא הוּא. סַגִּיב הוּא. עִזּוּז הוּא.
יִבְנֶה בֵּיתוֹ בְּקָרוֹב בִּמְהֵרָה בְּיָמֵינוּ בְּקָרוֹב.
אֵל בְּנֵה אֵל בְּנֵה. בְּנֵה בֵיתְךָ בְּקָרוֹב.

פּוֹדֶה הוּא. צַדִּיק הוּא. קָדוֹשׁ הוּא.
יִבְנֶה בֵּיתוֹ בְּקָרוֹב בִּמְהֵרָה בְּיָמֵינוּ בְּקָרוֹב.
אֵל בְּנֵה אֵל בְּנֵה. בְּנֵה בֵיתְךָ בְּקָרוֹב.

רַחוּם הוּא. שַׁדַּי הוּא. תַּקִּיף הוּא.
יִבְנֶה בֵּיתוֹ בְּקָרוֹב בִּמְהֵרָה בְּיָמֵינוּ בְּקָרוֹב.
אֵל בְּנֵה אֵל בְּנֵה. בְּנֵה בֵיתְךָ בְּקָרוֹב.

Concluding Songs

Adir Hu

Mighty One, Mighty One
Build Your Temple soon,
Speedily, speedily,
In our days soon,
O God build, O God build
Build Your Temple soon.

Chosen One, Greatest One, Famous One
Build Your Temple soon,
Speedily, speedily,
In our days soon,
O God build, O God build
Build Your Temple soon.

Brilliant One, Faithful One, Blameless One,
Kindest One, Purest One, Only One,
Sturdy One, Wisest One, Royal One,
Fearsome One, Highest One, Boldest One,
Saving One, Righteous One, Holy One

Build Your Temple soon,
Speedily, speedily,
In our days soon,
O God build, O God build
Build Your Temple soon.

Tender One, Almighty One, Forceful One,
Build Your Temple soon,
Speedily, speedily,
In our days soon,
O God build, O God build
Build Your Temple soon.

Mighty One, build Your Temple soon

This song, sung in medieval Avignon on all festivals, entered the Haggadah in the fourteenth century. It expresses the tradition that, though the First and Second Temples were built by human hands, and were later destroyed, the Third will be built by God Himself and will endure for ever.

אֶחָד מִי יוֹדֵעַ

אֶחָד מִי יוֹדֵעַ . אֶחָד אֲנִי יוֹדֵעַ.
אֶחָד אֱלֹהֵינוּ שֶׁבַּשָּׁמַיִם וּבָאָרֶץ:

שְׁנַיִם מִי יוֹדֵעַ. שְׁנַיִם אֲנִי יוֹדֵעַ. שְׁנֵי לֻחוֹת הַבְּרִית.
אֶחָד אֱלֹהֵינוּ שֶׁבַּשָּׁמַיִם וּבָאָרֶץ:

שְׁלֹשָׁה מִי יוֹדֵעַ. שְׁלֹשָׁה אֲנִי יוֹדֵעַ. שְׁלֹשָׁה אָבוֹת. שְׁנֵי
לֻחוֹת הַבְּרִית. אֶחָד אֱלֹהֵינוּ שֶׁבַּשָּׁמַיִם וּבָאָרֶץ:

אַרְבַּע מִי יוֹדֵעַ. אַרְבַּע אֲנִי יוֹדֵעַ. אַרְבַּע אִמָּהוֹת. שְׁלֹשָׁה
אָבוֹת. שְׁנֵי לֻחוֹת הַבְּרִית. אֶחָד אֱלֹהֵינוּ שֶׁבַּשָּׁמַיִם
וּבָאָרֶץ:

חֲמִשָּׁה מִי יוֹדֵעַ. חֲמִשָּׁה אֲנִי יוֹדֵעַ. חֲמִשָּׁה חֻמְשֵׁי תוֹרָה.
אַרְבַּע אִמָּהוֹת. שְׁלֹשָׁה אָבוֹת. שְׁנֵי לֻחוֹת הַבְּרִית.
אֶחָד אֱלֹהֵינוּ שֶׁבַּשָּׁמַיִם וּבָאָרֶץ:

Who knows One?

This song, like 'One only kid', appears for the first time in the Prague Haggadah of 1590, though there is evidence that it is was known and sung several centuries earlier. In medieval Avignon it was sung on the festival of Sukkot. In Cochin, it was sung at weddings, probably having been brought to India by Spanish or Portuguese Jewish merchants. In this, as so many other medieval additions to the Haggadah, we can trace the spread of customs from one part of the Jewish world to others – testimony to the fact that though they were dispersed at an age when international travel was rare and hazardous, Jews throughout the world maintained contact with one another and saw themselves as a global people.

'Who knows One?' is almost certainly a song that comes originally from the schoolroom, and evokes the remarkable world of Jewish education at a time when the rest of Europe was largely sunk in ignorance and illiteracy. Wherever they went, Jews built schools, often supported by communal levies, to ensure that every child had an education. In the early Middle Ages a pupil of the great Christian thinker Abelard, observed: 'A Jew, however poor, if he has ten sons, will put them all to letters, not for gain as the Christians do, but for the understanding of God's law – and not only his sons but his daughters too.'

The history of Jewish education is unique. More than a thousand years before the Common Era, in the period of the judges, we read of how Gideon spoke to a young man he met in the town of Sukkot and asked him to write down the names of the town's elders. He did so, producing a list of seventy-seven names (Judges 8:14). The episode suggests that already three thousand years ago universal literacy was normal among Jews. It did not become a feature of Europe until the late nineteenth century.

Who Knows One?

Who knows One? I know one! One is our God   In heaven and on earth!

Who knows Two? I know two! Two tablets of the Covenant,
One is our God   In heaven and on earth!

Who knows Three? I know three! Three fathers of our people,
Two tablets of the Covenant,
One is our God   In heaven and on earth!

Who knows Four? I know Four! Four mothers of our nation,
Three fathers of our people, Two tablets of the Covenant,
One is our God   In heaven and on earth!

Who knows Five? I know five! Five books of the Torah, Four mothers of our nation,
Three fathers of our people, Two tablets of the Covenant,
One is our God   In heaven and on earth!

'Who knows One?' is probably the song through which Jewish children were taught to count, and suggests that even secular instruction, such as arithmetic, was infused with religious meaning. The numbers each had their significance in the spiritual life of Judaism. A lovely description has survived from medieval Ashkenaz, where this song was composed, of how a Jewish child was brought for his first day at school:

> They write the letters of the Hebrew alphabet on a board for him; and they wash him and dress him in clean garments, and they knead him three loaves of fine wheat in honey... And they boil him three eggs and bring him apples and other kinds of fruit, and seek a worthy sage to conduct him to the school house. He covers him with a prayer shawl and brings him to the synagogue, where they feed him with the loaves of honey and the eggs and fruit; and they read him the letters. After that they cover the board with honey and tell him to lick it. Then they lead him back to his mother (*Machzor Vitri*, 508).

The ceremony graphically conveyed to the child that learning was sweet, that the entire community rejoiced in the start of his studies, and that by so doing he was entering a life that would eventually see him charged with responsibility for continuing the tradition and passing it on, in turn, to his children. No other civilisation has invested the life of learning with such simple beauty and high religious drama. When a young child was first brought to school, it was said in those times, 'It is as though they brought him to Mount Sinai.'

שִׁשָּׁה מִי יוֹדֵעַ. שִׁשָּׁה אֲנִי יוֹדֵעַ. שִׁשָּׁה סִדְרֵי מִשְׁנָה.
חֲמִשָּׁה חֻמְשֵׁי תוֹרָה. אַרְבַּע אִמָּהוֹת. שְׁלֹשָׁה אָבוֹת.
שְׁנֵי לֻחוֹת הַבְּרִית. אֶחָד אֱלֹהֵינוּ שֶׁבַּשָּׁמַיִם וּבָאָרֶץ:

שִׁבְעָה מִי יוֹדֵעַ. שִׁבְעָה אֲנִי יוֹדֵעַ. שִׁבְעָה יְמֵי שַׁבַּתָּא.
שִׁשָּׁה סִדְרֵי מִשְׁנָה. חֲמִשָּׁה חֻמְשֵׁי תוֹרָה. אַרְבַּע אִמָּהוֹת.
שְׁלֹשָׁה אָבוֹת. שְׁנֵי לֻחוֹת הַבְּרִית. אֶחָד אֱלֹהֵינוּ שֶׁבַּשָּׁמַיִם
וּבָאָרֶץ:

שְׁמוֹנָה מִי יוֹדֵעַ. שְׁמוֹנָה אֲנִי יוֹדֵעַ. שְׁמוֹנָה יְמֵי מִילָה.
שִׁבְעָה יְמֵי שַׁבַּתָּא. שִׁשָּׁה סִדְרֵי מִשְׁנָה. חֲמִשָּׁה חֻמְשֵׁי
תוֹרָה. אַרְבַּע אִמָּהוֹת. שְׁלֹשָׁה אָבוֹת. שְׁנֵי לֻחוֹת הַבְּרִית.
אֶחָד אֱלֹהֵינוּ שֶׁבַּשָּׁמַיִם וּבָאָרֶץ:

תִּשְׁעָה מִי יוֹדֵעַ. תִּשְׁעָה אֲנִי יוֹדֵעַ. תִּשְׁעָה יַרְחֵי לֵדָה.
שְׁמוֹנָה יְמֵי מִילָה. שִׁבְעָה יְמֵי שַׁבַּתָּא. שִׁשָּׁה סִדְרֵי
מִשְׁנָה. חֲמִשָּׁה חֻמְשֵׁי תוֹרָה. אַרְבַּע אִמָּהוֹת. שְׁלֹשָׁה
אָבוֹת. שְׁנֵי לֻחוֹת הַבְּרִית. אֶחָד אֱלֹהֵינוּ שֶׁבַּשָּׁמַיִם
וּבָאָרֶץ:

עֲשָׂרָה מִי יוֹדֵעַ. עֲשָׂרָה אֲנִי יוֹדֵעַ. עֲשָׂרָה דִבְּרַיָּא.
תִּשְׁעָה יַרְחֵי לֵדָה. שְׁמוֹנָה יְמֵי מִילָה. שִׁבְעָה יְמֵי שַׁבַּתָּא.
שִׁשָּׁה סִדְרֵי מִשְׁנָה. חֲמִשָּׁה חֻמְשֵׁי תוֹרָה.
אַרְבַּע אִמָּהוֹת. שְׁלֹשָׁה אָבוֹת.
שְׁנֵי לֻחוֹת הַבְּרִית. אֶחָד אֱלֹהֵינוּ שֶׁבַּשָּׁמַיִם וּבָאָרֶץ:

אַחַד עָשָׂר מִי יוֹדֵעַ. אַחַד עָשָׂר אֲנִי יוֹדֵעַ. אַחַד עָשָׂר
כּוֹכְבַיָּא. עֲשָׂרָה דִבְּרַיָּא. תִּשְׁעָה יַרְחֵי לֵדָה. שְׁמוֹנָה יְמֵי
מִילָה. שִׁבְעָה יְמֵי שַׁבַּתָּא. שִׁשָּׁה סִדְרֵי מִשְׁנָה. חֲמִשָּׁה
חֻמְשֵׁי תוֹרָה. אַרְבַּע אִמָּהוֹת. שְׁלֹשָׁה אָבוֹת. שְׁנֵי לֻחוֹת
הַבְּרִית. אֶחָד אֱלֹהֵינוּ שֶׁבַּשָּׁמַיִם וּבָאָרֶץ:

Who knows Six? I know six! Six sections of the Mishnah,
Five books of the Torah, Four mothers of our nation,
Three fathers of our people, Two tablets of the Covenant,
One is our God   In heaven and on earth!

Who knows Seven? I know seven!
Seven days for the Sabbath, Six sections of the Mishnah,
Five books of the Torah, Four mothers of our nation,
Three fathers of our people, Two tablets of the Covenant,
One is our God   In heaven and on earth!

Who knows Eight? I know eight! Eight days before the Brith
Seven days for the Sabbath, Six sections of the Mishnah,
Five books of the Torah, Four mothers of our nation,
Three fathers of our people, Two tablets of the Covenant,
One is our God   In heaven and on earth!

Who knows Nine? I know nine!
Nine months to have a child, Eight days before the Brith
Seven days for the Sabbath, Six sections of the Mishnah,
Five books of the Torah, Four mothers of our nation,
Three fathers of our people, Two tablets of the Covenant,
One is our God   In heaven and on earth!

Who knows Ten? I know ten! Ten Commandments at Mount Sinai,
Nine months to have a child, Eight days before the Brith,
Seven days for the Sabbath, Six sections of the Mishnah,
Five books of the Torah, Four mothers of our nation,
Three fathers of our people, Two tablets of the Covenant,
One is our God   In heaven and on earth!

Who knows Eleven? I know eleven!
Eleven stars in Joseph's dream, Ten Commandments at Mount Sinai,
Nine months to have a child, Eight days before the Brith
Seven days for the Sabbath, Six sections of the Mishnah,
Five books of the Torah, Four mothers of our nation,
Three fathers of our people, Two tablets of the Covenant,
One is our God   In heaven and on earth!

שְׁנֵים עָשָׂר מִי יוֹדֵעַ. שְׁנֵים עָשָׂר אֲנִי יוֹדֵעַ. שְׁנֵים עָשָׂר
שִׁבְטַיָּא. אַחַד עָשָׂר כּוֹכְבַיָּא. עֲשָׂרָה דִבְּרַיָּא. תִּשְׁעָה
יַרְחֵי לֵדָה. שְׁמוֹנָה יְמֵי מִילָה. שִׁבְעָה יְמֵי שַׁבַּתָּא.
שִׁשָּׁה סִדְרֵי מִשְׁנָה. חֲמִשָּׁה חֻמְשֵׁי תוֹרָה. אַרְבַּע אִמָּהוֹת.
שְׁלשָׁה אָבוֹת. שְׁנֵי לֻחוֹת הַבְּרִית. אֶחָד אֱלֹהֵינוּ
שֶׁבַּשָּׁמַיִם וּבָאָרֶץ:

שְׁלשָׁה עָשָׂר מִי יוֹדֵעַ. שְׁלשָׁה עָשָׂר אֲנִי יוֹדֵעַ.
שְׁלשָׁה עָשָׂר מִדַּיָּא. שְׁנֵים עָשָׂר שִׁבְטַיָּא. אַחַד עָשָׂר
כּוֹכְבַיָּא. עֲשָׂרָה דִבְּרַיָּא. תִּשְׁעָה יַרְחֵי לֵדָה. שְׁמוֹנָה יְמֵי
מִילָה. שִׁבְעָה יְמֵי שַׁבַּתָּא. שִׁשָּׁה סִדְרֵי מִשְׁנָה. חֲמִשָּׁה
חֻמְשֵׁי תוֹרָה. אַרְבַּע אִמָּהוֹת. שְׁלשָׁה אָבוֹת. שְׁנֵי לֻחוֹת
הַבְּרִית. אֶחָד אֱלֹהֵינוּ שֶׁבַּשָּׁמַיִם וּבָאָרֶץ:

חַד גַּדְיָא

חַד גַּדְיָא. חַד גַּדְיָא. דְּזַבִּין אַבָּא בִּתְרֵי זוּזֵי. חַד גַּדְיָא.
חַד גַּדְיָא:

וְאָתָא שׁוּנְרָא וְאָכְלָא לְגַדְיָא. דְּזַבִּין אַבָּא בִּתְרֵי זוּזֵי.
חַד גַּדְיָא חַד גַּדְיָא:

וְאָתָא כַלְבָּא וְנָשַׁךְ לְשׁוּנְרָא. דְּאָכְלָא לְגַדְיָא.
דְּזַבִּין אַבָּא בִּתְרֵי זוּזֵי. חַד גַּדְיָא חַד גַּדְיָא:

One only kid

That we end one of Judaism's most sacred rituals with a children's song tells us much about what sustained Judaism as a faith for longer, under more arduous circumstances, than any other heritage in the West. The Jewish love of children means that Jews look forward to the future even more than we look back to the past. Just as we began the seder with the questions of a child, so we conclude it with a nursery rhyme, reminding ourselves that what sustains a faith is not strength or power, but its ability to inspire successive generations of children to add their voices to our people's song.

The song itself, disarming in its simplicity, teaches the great truth of Jewish hope: that though many nations (symbolized by the cat, the dog, and so on) attacked Israel (the 'kid'), each in turn has vanished into oblivion. At the end of days God will vanquish the angel of death and inaugurate a world of life and peace, the two great Jewish loves.

Who knows Twelve? I know twelve! Twelve tribes of Israel,

Eleven stars in Joseph's dream, Ten Commandments at Mount Sinai,

Nine months to have a child, Eight days before the Brith,

Seven days for the Sabbath, Six sections of the Mishnah,

Five books of the Torah, Four mothers of our nation,

Three fathers of our people, Two tablets of the Covenant,

One is our God   In heaven and on earth!

Who knows Thirteen? I know thirteen!

Thirteen ways of God's mercy, Twelve tribes of Israel,

Eleven stars in Joseph's dream, Ten Commandments at Mount Sinai,

Nine months to have a child, Eight days before the Brith

Seven days for the Sabbath, Six sections of the Mishnah,

Five books of the Torah, Four mothers of our nation,

Three fathers of our people, Two tablets of the Covenant,

One is our God   In heaven and on earth!

Chad Gadya – One Little Kid

One little kid, one little kid!

That daddy bought for two zuzim, One little kid, one little kid!

Then along came a Cat, And ate the little kid,

That daddy bought for two zuzim, One little kid, one little kid!

Then along came a Dog, And bit the cat, That ate the little kid,

That daddy bought for two zuzim, One little kid, one little kid!

Perhaps, too, there is deeper symbolism. The kid eaten by the cat reminds us of the story of Joseph, sold into slavery. His brothers then slaughtered a kid, dipped Joseph's coat in its blood, and showed it to their father to persuade him that Joseph had been killed by a wild animal. Outwardly, Jacob accepted their story. However, the Torah says that 'he refused to be comforted'. Jewish law states that there is a limit to the period of mourning. Why then did Jacob say that he would *never* be comforted? A profound rabbinic commentary explains that there is a time limit to mourning only when one is sure that someone has died. Jacob, however, never gave up believing that there was a chance, however slim, that Joseph was still alive. His refusal to be comforted was a refusal to give up hope, and in the end it was justified. Joseph *was* still alive, and he and his father were eventually reunited.

Chad Gadya expresses the Jewish refusal to give up hope. Though history is full of man's inhumanity to man – dog bites cat, stick hits dog - that is not the final verse. The Haggadah ends with the death of death in eternal life, a fitting end for the story of a people dedicated to Moses' great command, 'Choose life'.

וְאָתָא חוּטְרָא וְהִכָּה לְכַלְבָּא. דְּנָשַׁךְ לְשׁוּנְרָא. דְּאָכְלָא
לְגַדְיָא. דְּזַבִּין אַבָּא בִּתְרֵי זוּזֵי. חַד גַּדְיָא חַד גַּדְיָא:

וְאָתָא נוּרָא. וְשָׂרַף לְחוּטְרָא. דְּהִכָּה לְכַלְבָּא. דְּנָשַׁךְ
לְשׁוּנְרָא. דְּאָכְלָא לְגַדְיָא. דְּזַבִּין אַבָּא בִּתְרֵי זוּזֵי.
חַד גַּדְיָא חַד גַּדְיָא:

וְאָתָא מַיָּא וְכָבָה לְנוּרָא דְּשָׂרַף לְחוּטְרָא. דְּהִכָּה לְכַלְבָּא.
דְּנָשַׁךְ לְשׁוּנְרָא. דְּאָכְלָא לְגַדְיָא. דְּזַבִּין אַבָּא בִּתְרֵי זוּזֵי.
חַד גַּדְיָא חַד גַּדְיָא:

וְאָתָא תוֹרָא וְשָׁתָה לְמַיָּא. דְּכָבָה לְנוּרָא. דְּשָׂרַף
לְחוּטְרָא. דְּהִכָּה לְכַלְבָּא. דְּנָשַׁךְ לְשׁוּנְרָא. דְּאָכְלָא
לְגַדְיָא. דְּזַבִּין אַבָּא בִּתְרֵי זוּזֵי. חַד גַּדְיָא חַד גַּדְיָא:

וְאָתָא הַשּׁוֹחֵט וְשָׁחַט לְתוֹרָא. דְּשָׁתָה לְמַיָּא. דְּכָבָה
לְנוּרָא. דְּשָׂרַף לְחוּטְרָא. דְּהִכָּה לְכַלְבָּא.
דְּנָשַׁךְ לְשׁוּנְרָא.דְּאָכְלָא לְגַדְיָא.
דְּזַבִּין אַבָּא בִּתְרֵי זוּזֵי. חַד גַּדְיָא חַד גַּדְיָא:

וְאָתָא מַלְאַךְ הַמָּוֶת וְשָׁחַט לְשׁוֹחֵט. דְּשָׁחַט לְתוֹרָא.
דְּשָׁתָה לְמַיָּא. דְּכָבָה לְנוּרָא. דְּשָׂרַף לְחוּטְרָא. דְּהִכָּה
לְכַלְבָּא. דְּנָשַׁךְ לְשׁוּנְרָא. דְּאָכְלָא לְגַדְיָא. דְּזַבִּין אַבָּא
בִּתְרֵי זוּזֵי. חַד גַּדְיָא חַד גַּדְיָא:

וְאָתָא הַקָּדוֹשׁ בָּרוּךְ הוּא וְשָׁחַט לְמַלְאַךְ הַמָּוֶת. דְּשָׁחַט
לְשׁוֹחֵט. דְּשָׁחַט לְתוֹרָא. דְּשָׁתָה לְמַיָּא. דְּכָבָה לְנוּרָא.
דְּשָׂרַף לְחוּטְרָא. דְּהִכָּה לְכַלְבָּא. דְּנָשַׁךְ לְשׁוּנְרָא. דְּאָכְלָא
לְגַדְיָא. דְּזַבִּין אַבָּא בִּתְרֵי זוּזֵי. חַד גַּדְיָא חַד גַּדְיָא:

Then along came a Stick, And beat the dog,
That bit the cat, That ate the little kid,
That daddy bought for two zuzim, One little kid, one little kid!

Then along came a Fire, And burned the stick
That beat the dog, That bit the cat, That ate the little kid,
That daddy brought for two zuzim, One little kid, one little kid!

Then along came some Water, And put out the fire
That burned the stick, That beat the dog,
That bit the cat, That ate the little kid,
That daddy bought for two zuzim, One little kid, one little kid!

Then along came an Ox, That drank the water
That put out the fire, That burned the stick
That beat the dog, That bit the cat, That ate the little kid,
That daddy bought for two zuzim, One little kid, one little kid!

Then along came a Butcher, Who killed the ox
That drank the water, That put out the fire
That burned the stick, That beat the dog,
That bit the cat, That ate the little kid,
That daddy brought for two zuzim, One little kid, one little kid!

Then along came the Angel of Death, And killed the butcher
Who killed the ox, That drank the water
That put out the fire, That burned the stick
That beat the dog, That bit the cat, That ate the little kid,
That daddy bought for two zuzim, One little kid, one little kid!

Then along came the Holy One Blessed be He, And smote the Angel of Death
Who killed the butcher, Who killed the ox
That drank the water, That put out the fire
That burned the stick, That beat the dog,
That bit the cat, That ate the little kid
That daddy bought for two zuzim, One little kid, one little kid!